PARENTS AND TEACHERS

Helping Children Learn to Read and Write

PARENTS AND TEACHERS

Helping Children Learn to Read and Write

Edited by

Timothy V. Rasinski

Kent State University

Harcourt Brace College Publishers

Fort Worth   Philadelphia   San Diego   New York   Orlando   Austin   San Antonio
Toronto   Montreal   London   Sydney   Tokyo

Vice President, Publisher	Ted Buchholz
Executive Editor	Christopher P. Klein
Acquisitions Editor	Jo-Anne Weaver
Assistant Editor	Pam Hatley
Senior Project Editor	Charles J. Dierker
Production Manager	Thomas Urquhart IV
Art Director	Diana Jean Parks, Sue Hart

Cover photography by Donna Buie

ISBN: 0-15-501315-7
Library of Congress Catalog Card Number: 94-75766

Address for Editorial Correspondence: Harcourt Brace College Publishers, 301 Commerce Street, Suite 3700, Fort Worth, TX 76102.

Address for Orders: Harcourt Brace & Company, 6277 Sea Harbor Drive, Orlando, FL 32887-6777, 1-800-782-4479, or 1-800-433-0001 (in Florida).

Printed in the United States of America

4 5 6 7 8 9 0 1 2 3   039   9 8 7 6 5 4 3 2 1

To my children,
Michael, Emily, Mary, and Jennifer,
whose patience and encouragement
helped this father learn what parenting
is all about.

PREFACE

One of the remedies that we hear from time to time for the ills facing American education in general, and literacy education in particular, is greater parental involvement in children's learning. Yet despite such calls, educators haven't made a great deal of progress in getting parents more involved. Sure, there are model programs across the country that are successful in connecting home, school, and learning. But, for the most part, these programs are the exception and not the rule.

Current research seems to suggest that despite the acknowledgment that parents can make a tremendous difference in their children's learning, most teachers do little in the way of systematic, consistent, and substantive parent involvement. Many of the involvement programs that schools offer parents are one-time affairs with activities that are often simplistic, that lack authenticity, and that cause parents and children to lose interest quickly. This is truly unfortunate because the research also tells us that parent involvement really does work. When parents are involved, children's learning improves.

Reading and writing, in particular, have been shown to be areas in which parents can make a profound impact. This book aims to help teachers and parents realize the potential they have, when they work together, for improving children's literacy development. It was developed with several purposes in mind. First, this book offers teachers sound information that they can communicate to parents about a wide range of topics on literacy education. Teachers can use the information in this book as the basis for parental workshops on home literacy development. Teachers could also share appropriate information in this book in informal discussions with parents at conference time or by copying particular chapters from the book and sending them to parents. Additionally, teachers can use this book to involve parents in their classrooms as volunteer tutors in reading and writing. Parents, of course, will be able to use the information directly to guide them in helping their children learn to read and write.

The articles in this book have been written by experienced educators and outstanding scholars in the area of parent involvement in literacy education. The ideas presented here are based on sound research, theory, and actual practice. In many ways they represent the state of the art in terms of how parents and teachers can work together to nurture children's literacy development.

Our intent was to make the chapters easily accessible to laypersons as well as education professionals. The chapters are brief and readable, yet filled with information that will help parents and teachers improve children's ability in and enjoyment of reading and writing. Chapters 1 through 15 focus on improving literacy learning at home. By sharing the information in these chapters with parents, teachers can initiate home programs that complement the literacy instruction they provide in their classrooms. Chapters 16 through 24 deal more specifically with connections between home and school. These chapters will help parents understand the roles they can play in school to promote their children's literacy development and assist teachers in doing the same.

We have a long way to go in developing the kinds of partnerships between parents and teachers that take full advantage of the talents each brings to children's literacy learning. I sincerely hope that this book can help break down some of the barriers that separate parents and teachers and move us closer to literacy education that is the shared responsibility of home and school.

TABLE OF CONTENTS

PARENTS AND TEACHERS

Helping Children Learn to Read and Write

Introduction

Teacher-Parent Partnerships

Timothy V. Rasinski

T im Rasinski is a professor of Curriculum & Instruction at Kent State University. A parent of four children and a former elementary school teacher, he is interested in how parents and teachers can work together to nurture children's literacy development.

C athy and Jim Howe are parents of first and fifth grade girls. Both are doing exceptionally well in school. In fact, both children learned to read before entering first grade. The girls love to read. When I asked the Howes what they thought made the difference in their children's growth in and love of reading they told me that they themselves played a key role, that they began reading to their children from early in their lives, and continue to read to their children nearly every day. Both Cathy and Jim love to read themselves and they make it a point to read with their children at home and talk about what they are reading with their youngsters. The Howes note that books, magazines, paper, markers, pencils, and pens are readily available in their home and that they often play with their children in activities and games that involve reading and writing. In short, the Howes acknowledge that reading and writing are important parts of their own lives and they have tried to make reading and writing an integral part of their family life. As a result, literacy has become a natural and important part of their children's lives, both in and out of school.

One of the most common pieces of advice that parents of school-age children hear today is "read to your child." This message is so prevalent that it has almost become a cliché. Nevertheless, this advice represents a much deeper understanding about the importance of parents and families in children's literacy development. Researchers who have studied how children learn to read and write unanimously endorse the notion that parent involvement is crucial to children's growth in literacy.

Several research studies have investigated the roles that parents play in their children's achievement in school and, in particular, reading. The clear conclusion of these studies is that when parents are involved good things happen. Children's academic achievement invariably improves, and parents and teachers more readily accept and acknowledge the important role that the other plays in the lives of children.

From the point of view of teachers, parental involvement in reading has enormous positive potential. Teachers find that when parents are involved in nurturing literacy in their children, the literacy teaching that occurs in school is reinforced at home. Children receive extra practice in learning critical skills and competencies in reading, children's reading achievement and attitude toward reading improves, and parents develop a greater appreciation of the roles of schools and teachers.

From the point of view of parents, parental involvement in reading has equally great potential. When parents are asked and encouraged to become involved with their children in reading, they find that they interact with their children more often in meaningful and satisfying ways, they develop a greater understanding of the roles written and oral language play in their children's lives and the roles that schools play in helping children become literate, and they make significant contributions to the development of their children as competent and knowledgeable readers and writers.

And, from the children's point of view, the outcomes of parental involvement in literacy learning are, perhaps, greatest of all. When parents become involved in their children's literacy development, children see that reading and writing extend naturally beyond the boundaries of the school. Reading isn't just for school. The opportunities to work with their parents help children view their parents as sources of help and encouragement, and develop stronger bonds of love and affection with their parents. And, of course, through their work with their parents, children realize that they become better readers and writers and are more willing to read and write outside of school.

Despite such awesome potential, the sad fact remains that most programs aimed at involving parents in the reading and writing development of their children fail. Although such programs often begin with the best of intentions, most programs aimed at involving parents rarely move beyond the beginning stages of implementation. A variety of reasons can be cited for this unfulfilled promise.

Most Parent Involvement Programs Fail

Nearly all parent involvement programs are initiated by the school. Yet, many programs fail because they lack the commitment and coordination on the part of the school that are required to maintain such programs. Often, parental involvement programs are mandated by school administrators or government programs such as Chapter 1. While the intent of such mandates is certainly praiseworthy, unless the persons charged with carrying out the mandate share the commitment with those making the mandate, the program may be doomed to failure even before it begins. Teachers are overloaded with required activities. Requiring them further to develop and implement a parental involvement program without sufficient support, guidance, or rationale will likely result in halfhearted efforts. Unless the teachers carrying out the program are committed to parental involvement and feel part of the decision-making process, parental involvement programs mandated by others may be implemented, but without the enthusiasm, coordination, and follow-through required to make them work over a long period of time.

Just as programs may fail when teachers do not feel part of the decision-making process, they may also fail when parents, themselves, are not included in the process, as well. Parents need to understand that the input they provide goes beyond mere tokenism. Parental involvement programs work best when both parents and teachers can feel a sense of ownership and pride in the program.

Parental programs often fail because of the types of activities parents are asked to engage in with their children. One of the biggest obstacles to successful programs is the lack of consistency in the program. Activities may change so drastically from one week to the next that parents have little sense of what they are supposed to do over time and they never get a chance to feel competent in any one particular activity. As a result parents never feel a sense of ownership or control over the program and can easily choose to bow out.

Other activities parents may be asked to engage in may not involve real reading or writing, or may simply not be enjoyable and satisfying for parents and children. Parents may question the value and enjoyment potential of doing worksheets or reading drills with their children. Again, in these cases, parents and their children may opt out of such activities.

Making Parental Involvement in Literacy Work

Parental involvement can work. Many model programs exist across the country that demonstrate the power and potential of combining teachers and parents in helping children achieve their potential in reading and writing. Several criteria or principles can aid in the development of parental involvement programs that work.

Real reading and writing. We know that children who read and write well do a lot of reading and writing. Real reading and writing, and not worksheets or flashcards, will result in the maximum amount of reading and writing growth.

Enjoyable, efficient, and easy. Parents and children need to find the activities they are asked to engage in enjoyable and satisfying as well as easy to implement and efficient in the amount of time required to implement. This will ensure continued involvement. Programs and activities may be so complex that parents lack the expertise or time to carry them out satisfactorily.

Consistency and commitment. The activities that are part of a parental involvement program should follow a logical and consistent progression. Wide variations in activities should be minimized. Programs should be designed for the long term and not as a series of one-shot activities that do little more than satisfy some requirement.

Ownership. Parental involvement programs should be designed to involve teachers and parents in the ownership of the program from planning to implementation. When people feel that a program is their own, they are more committed to seeing it through and making it a success.

Communication, training, and follow up. Provisions should be made to train parents in the activities they are asked to engage in. Moreover, frequent communication between school and home should ensure that teachers are aware of progress made in the program and that parents' concerns and questions can be addressed quickly and completely.

Connection between home and school. Above all, parent involvement programs work when teachers and parents view the programs as true partnerships between school and home. A mutual sense of respect and trust must be nurtured from the earliest stages of each program's development.

Working Together, Parents and Teachers Can Revolutionize Literacy Learning

It is easy to become discouraged by reports of studies that many children are failing to learn to read and write at levels needed for today's rapidly changing society. Recent reports tell us that nearly half of all adult Americans have severely limited literacy skills and that over 40 percent of all fourth graders in the United States have reading levels that are considered "below basic" and that only 4 percent are considered "advanced." Equally distressing are research studies that look at actual reading behavior of children and find that, on average, fifth grade students spend less than five minutes per day reading books.

As painful as those reports and studies may be, they do point out what must be done by parents and teachers, working together, to improve this situation. Students' success in learning to read is, to a large extent, dependent upon the amount of reading they do both in and out of school. So many elementary students spend too little time reading at home—13 percent of fourth graders say they never or hardly ever read for fun. Would not increasing students' reading outside of school be an appropriate goal for parents and teachers to tackle? If the minutes most students read at home can be measured in the single digits, think of how easy it could be, with active and coordinated parent and teacher involvement, to double or even triple this amount.

This is the type of goal that is worth achieving and is achievable. All parents want their children to be successful readers and writers. And most parents are willing to help their children learn to read and write. Many parents, however, are not aware of what they can do to help their children. They need the help and guidance from teachers who are in the best position to provide it. It is that connection between home and school, between knowledgeable teachers and willing parents, that can make all the difference in children's literacy learning.

part one

Literacy
Learning
at Home

Chapter 1

Seven Steps to Creating a Literate Home Environment

Mary Steele Mastain

Mary Mastain has been a reading specialist and has taught every elementary grade in her teaching career. She has written and self-published a book for parents of preschoolers and kindergartners on reading, *A Parent's Guide to Reading* (1992), and she writes a biweekly column on teaching children in the *Orangevale* (California) *News*. Her brochure "Rock and Read" has been distributed to hospitals and schools in the Sacramento area and has been translated into Spanish, Russian, and Vietnamese. She has four adult children and four grandchildren.

When I became a reading specialist, I found almost immediately that some kindergartners were eager to learn what I had to teach them; others had no interest and were unable to sit still, listen to a story. They had no desire to even look at a book. Then, after a few months of puzzlement, I attended a conference on reading and found the answer when I picked up a pin at one of the booths that had printed on it, "Parents Are Teachers Too." "That's it," I said. "Parents are the ones who motivate their children from birth to listen, talk, write, and read!" Parents who take the time to talk with their children and read books to them give their children a rich foundation that will affect how they do in school.

Parenting is the most important job there is, but it is not an easy one. Being a good parent does not come with giving birth to a child; it is a skill that is learned, and takes a great deal of love, time, and energy.

As a parent of four children now grown with children of their own, I know how much I needed to learn, and to keep learning throughout their childhood, and into adulthood. A scholar once said, "Once you're pregnant, you're always pregnant," and I believe it is true because I am still parenting, and still learning the best ways to be a caring parent—and a grandparent! However, parenting today is quite different from when my children grew up in the 1950s and 1960s. There is a new pattern of parenting today with its own challenges and problems.

Today's Families

Today, the family unit is often made up of a single parent. A large number of school-age children live with only one parent; live with a parent and a stepparent; or live in two homes with parents who are separated or divorced. It is difficult to be a single parent, and success in rearing educationally motivated children requires new kinds of parenting skills.

Another trend in parenting today is the mobility of families. Over 65 percent of children from preschool through sixth grade will move at least twice during their school years. When families are uprooted a heavier burden is placed upon parents to make their children's home as loving and consistent as possible when everything else is new and strange.

Today, there are more families with both parents working outside the home than ever before, and the number is increasing. No longer do all children come home from school to a parent who is waiting for them. With both parents working, there needs to be a new extended family responsibility, which includes grandparents, aunts, uncles and baby-sitters. Day care is an essential part of many family's network.

Another feature of today's families is the ever-increasing presence of television. Except for sleeping, TV watching takes up more hours than any other activity in the home, including talking, reading, and eating. A recent Nielson Survey indicates that the average American adult watches 7.5 hours of television a day. Jim Trelease, author of *The Read-Aloud Handbook,* states that by the time a child begins kindergarten, he or she has logged 5,000 hours of television watching—enough time to get a college degree!

Teachers are aware that parenting is more difficult today. Teachers also realize that their classes are only as strong as the support and time given by parents at home.

Only 10–12 percent of a child's school year is spent in school. The remaining time is spent at home or in the community.

Parents set the tone for their children's basic understanding of the importance of education and learning. Children learn from their parents to value education, and respect achievement and learning. Children who come to school from happy and literate home environments are those who are a joy to teach and who are blessed with that inner desire to learn. Success in reading and school are guaranteed.

Because the success teachers have in teaching their students depends so heavily on the home environment, today's teachers must take on the added responsibility of helping parents learn how to make their home a loving place to learn. It is important for parents to realize that the learning environment should be established for their child at birth.

Teachers can help parents make certain they are doing the best to prepare their child to be successful in school. Here are seven simple steps for parents to create a literate home environment:

Nancy Larrick, author of *Encourage Your Child to Read,* says that many parents spend an average of only 16.5 minutes per week talking with their children. Meanwhile, the children in these homes spend an average of 24 hours each week watching television. Talking is imperative to learning.

Step I: Talk with Your Child

1. Make sure your child understands what you're talking about by asking him or her questions about your conversation.

2. Talk at the dinner table together every day about the day's events. Each member takes a turn.

3. Take advantage of time in the car to chat with your child. Sing together as well as talk.

4. Try taking a 15-minute walk each day with your child to share special conversations.

5. Talk about your life and your parents' as well. Give your child the gift of your family's heritage by telling personal stories of the past when you were a child, or a grandchild.

6. Talk about the future, what you hope to do, what your family can do, what dreams your child may wish to share.

7. If you travel, be sure to call your child on the telephone while you're gone. Be regular about it so your child will expect the call and look forward to chatting with you.

Children who have parents who listen to them develop into good language users with rich vocabularies, which, in turn, leads to excited readers.

Step II: Listen to Your Child

1. When your child wants to tell you something, stop what you're doing, and really listen. Comment about the topic. Be encouraging.

2. Repeat what your child has told you, and comment or elaborate on what was said.

3. Ask about things that interest her—the best part of school, her friend's party, a favorite book, a game or program.

4. Suggest your child call grandma or a cousin on the telephone to share something important that has happened.

5. Be sure to include your child in conversations you may be having with others. Make certain he has a chance to converse too.

6. Encourage your child to share school experiences. Ask your child to tell you a favorite story, sing you a song, or recite a poem just memorized.

Step III: Read Aloud to and With Your Child Every Day

THIS IS THE MOST IMPORTANT STEP TOWARD HAVING A TRULY LITERATE HOME. Reading to your child should begin at birth, and continue into high school. There is no better way to help your youngster learn about and solve problems she encounters in life than while reading for pleasure with a parent.

1. The Lap Method: Dr. James Moffitt, a professor at California State University, San Francisco, suggests that parents put their young children on their laps while reading a book because it provides an aura of love that surrounds the book, and makes reading a joy. As the child grows older, sitting closely together establishes that same caring feeling while reading together.

2. There are three important factors that motivate a child to want to read:

   Most important: The person who has been away all day from home takes the time to read to the child every day.

   Second: The nurturing person at home reads to the child every day, as often as possible.

   Third: The child has a place (shelf, box, drawer) to keep books— borrowed or owned. No one else's books can be put there.

3. Go to the public library with your child every week (or ask grandpa to take his grandchild). This is extremely important because your child can pick out books that are of interest to him.

4. Buy books as gifts for every possible occasion, and ask relatives and friends to do the same. A book with your child's name written inside is a proud possession.

5. If you travel a lot, read a story on tape for your child to enjoy hearing at bedtime when you are not there.

6. Be sure your child has a reading light beside her bed, and a large, firm pillow for reading in bed. Give your child permission to read an extra 15 minutes or more before bedtime. Let your child decide when she is sleepy and turn off her own light.

7. Make certain that a wide variety of printed material—books, magazines, newspapers, comics—is available for all to read in your home. Filled bookshelves make any room a potential reader's paradise. Besides these general printed materials, here is a list of books that every home with children should have:

- An illustrated Mother Goose book

- A child's songbook with music

- A modern book of poetry for children

- An illustrated folk tale collection

- Children's and adult's dictionaries

- A child's atlas, and one for adults as well

- A set of encyclopedias

Everyone needs praise. Let your child know how proud you are of his accomplishments in reading and writing. Use comments like: "Keep up the good work," "Wow, great job," "Thank you for working so hard," "Beautiful!," "Let's put a star on that paper," "Thank you for bringing this paper home," "You're special."

Step IV:
Praise Your
Child

Model for your child your own love of reading for pleasure by doing it often. Share your enthusiasm for reading . . . it's catching.

Step V:
Be a Reader
Yourself

1. Check out books for yourself when you take your child to the library.

2. Have a family time to read silently together each night. (This is called "Sustained Silent Reading" at school.) Everyone chooses a book or magazine, and finds a comfortable place to read. There is no talking, just quiet, pleasant reading for 15 to 30 minutes. Take time afterwards to share what everyone has read for pleasure.

3. Tell your youngster about books you liked as a child. Give some of your favorites as special gifts.

4. Talk about books you have enjoyed with other adults, and share each other's books.

5. Shut the television off, and choose to read for fun instead. Your child will notice and copy you.

Becoming literate means learning to write as well as read. Provide a place for your child to write—a desk, or a corner of the kitchen table. Have pencils with erasers and pens (crayons and magic markers for younger children) and plenty of ruled and unruled paper available. Older children should have their own notebook or spiral-bound journal in which to write.

Step VI:
Write with
Your Child
Everyday

Parents help their children become literate by talking with them about their reading and writing.

1. Set aside a time each day when the family writes together, just like reading together. Each family member writes whatever he or she wants. Parents show that writing is important to them, and find the time beneficial for letters needing to be written, grocery or chore lists, or plans for the next project. Younger children have the time to scribble or write favorite words, or copy a page from a book. Older children have the time to jot down ideas, concerns, or develop a story, poem, or essay about whatever is of interest.

2. Preschoolers: After your child has written something, or drawn a picture, say, "Tell me about your picture" (rather than "What is it?"). Write on her paper exactly what she tells you. This is called dictation in school. Then read back what you have written, and suggest your child read those dictated words when sharing the scribble or picture with grandma or others.

3. School children: Your older child needs plenty of praise for what he has written. Comment about the writing in a positive, caring way. Often, writing skills develop slowly, but when there is encouragement and time set aside to enjoy writing, progress will come. With that progress, your

child will develop a personal satisfaction that will stay with him for a
lifetime.

4. Treat your child's writing with care and respect. Display what has
   been written and drawn on the refrigerator door or bulletin board.
   Put those creations in an album or a frame to be shared when company comes.

5. Give your child as many opportunities as you can to write shopping lists,
   stories, messages, thank-you letters, and notes and postcards to friends
   and relatives.

Writing leads naturally to reading. They reinforce each other. By encouraging your
child to write, you are helping strengthen the normal and satisfying connection of
writing to reading, and reading to writing.

---

*Step VII:
Limit
Television
Watching*

Be in control of that TV set. Television is here to stay, and there are good, educational programs that are beneficial for children. There is a big problem, however, because too much time is wasted watching television, robbing our children of precious
time to read, converse, write, imagine, and think! A syndrome is developing from
excessive TV watching that I call "shallow thinking." With the viewing of so many
simplified situation comedies, students often quit when they have a problem, or are
given an assignment that requires deep thought and research. The sitcom tells them
that problems are solved in a half-hour—no need to dig in with hard work and per-
severance.

1. Television is an integral part of every home, but it must not be the center
   of home life. Don't say, "Watch television," do say, "Watch programs."
   Let your child choose one or two a day, and then shut the set off. Limit
   watching to an hour a day and give equal time to reading and writing.

2. Stress the similarities of reading and television. Both are relaxing and
   enjoyable activities; they provide distraction from daily activities and
   problems, and they stimulate new interests.

3. Monitor what your child watches and try to be there to answer any
   questions or concerns. Let your child know how you feel about what
   she selects. Express disgust with too much violence, aggression, and
   unfairness. Praise your child when a good quality program is chosen.
   Make your opinion known. Watch good programs with your child and
   talk about them. Help your child connect TV programs with books of a
   similar topic or genre.

4. Do not let your child have a television set in his or her bedroom. It is
   unmonitored and can easily be viewed to excess.

Here is a checklist for parents to observe how they are doing in their sometimes over-
whelming and always important role as parents. I suggest they tack it on the cabinet
by the kitchen sink, or tape it to the refrigerator door to look over occasionally.

A Parent's Checklist
To Encourage My Child to Listen, Speak, Write, and Read

I take time to talk with my child every day—every chance I get.

I take time to listen to my child, and answer all his or her countless questions.

I sing and recite nursery songs and rhymes to my young child, and favorite songs & poems with my older child.

I read something for myself (newspaper, magazine, book) every day. Every day I model for my child that I get pleasure and information from reading.

I have a library card (the best of all credit cards), and I will get one for my child as soon as she or he can write.

I take my child to the library weekly (or as often as possible). We both select books to read by ourselves and together at home.

Together we look at books and magazines, each of us sharing our interests and questions.

I ask my child to tell me a story, or describe something he or she has done or seen.

I often write down what my child tells me and read back the "story" exactly as it was dictated to me.

I take my child on excursions (walks, car rides, shopping trips, visits to the park, farm, firehouse, and zoo), and we talk about them before, during, and after.

We play games together—word, listening and reasoning games, as well as ball, hopscotch, and so on.

My child has his or her own bookshelf (or a box or a drawer) for all his or her books, including those borrowed from the library.

My child watches carefully selected television programs, and I limit TV viewing so that there is equal time for reading and writing.

We talk about TV programs, and often pursue the interest stimulated with reading and writing.

I praise my child's efforts and accomplishments so that she or he will have self-confidence and zest for new learning experiences.

I encourage my child to do things as independently as possible.

I am on the lookout for signs of problems in hearing, seeing, and speaking.

I TAKE TIME TO READ ALOUD TO MY CHILD EACH DAY AS OFTEN AS MY CHILD WILL LISTEN TO ME, OR ASKS ME TO READ. I ENCOURAGE ALL MEMBERS OF MY FAMILY TO DO THE SAME.

Teachers are confronted with children of wider and more diversified backgrounds these days, and some children come to school with fear, anger, and poor health. Unfortunately, these are the signs of the times, and they make teaching more difficult than ever before. The challenge is multiplied because children must learn more in school than ever before to compete in this high-tech world.

Parents who create a caring and literate home environment can make the difference for the citizens of tomorrow, by helping them be successful and motivated students of today.

Chapter 2

About Play, Literacy, and Growing Up

Kathy Roskos

K athy Roskos is an associate professor at John Carroll University in University Heights, Ohio. One of her research interests is how children's literacy and language learning are fostered through play.

I'd like to tell you a story about my son and me. It's about some problems we had with reading and writing and how we handled them together.

Just so you know, before my son went to school we had a lot of fun reading and writing together. I suppose you would call it "just playing," because he couldn't read and write for real. That is to say, he was only pretending he could read and write.

Nonetheless, he read a lot of books then, like *Goodnight Moon* by Margaret Wise Brown and *Are You My Mother?* by P. D. Eastman; he read Dr. Seuss and, of course, *Winnie-the-Pooh* by A. A. Milne. And he was quite a writer, too—lists to Santa Claus, letters to Grandma, love notes to me, warnings on secret stuff, and the like. He enjoyed "getting lost in a book," trying out every sort of writing instrument, joining book clubs, playing school, and snuggling up close to me as we buried ourselves in books—he in his and me in mine. Maybe it was the challenge, maybe a fascination with the new, maybe the fun. I don't know for sure, but he did love reading and writing. Yes, he did.

Then he went to school. And as I watched that towheaded little boy grow out of second grade and into the third, I noticed his interest in literacy began to fade. By the time he was heading into fifth grade, it definitely had dimmed to a flicker. Reading and writing just weren't fun any more. In their place were headphones and tapes, TV shows, computer games, telephone conversations, and long spells of doing nothing as he stretched and reached for independence. No books. No personal writing. No reading books together.

I thought to myself, "Should his desire for independence be at the expense of reading and writing? Should it come between he and I enjoying these activities together?"

No way! But how could I rekindle the interest in literacy that my son had once so joyfully expressed and we had so warmly shared?

Easier said than done, I soon found out, to attract a budding adolescent to the literacy flame. He just wasn't willing to "reach out and touch" text. "No way!" he said. And so it went, back and forth—I trying any gimmick to incite interest (I even kept a reading chart on the refrigerator once) and he successfully resisting each and every one.

It was then that I learned: When the going gets tough, the tough start . . . playing. Playing? Did I say playing? Indeed, playing! And let me tell you why.

It all began when I started to wonder what may have sparked so much of my son's interest in literacy before the age of five. My wondering led me to Margaret Meek's wonderful book, *Learning to Read* (1982). And there it was. "For very young beginners," she writes, "reading is a kind of play, something you do because you like it . . . If reading looks like play to a child, it will be taken seriously" (p. 35).

So that was it! When playful, reading (and probably writing, too) is attractive, desirable, and occasionally downright exciting. Margaret Meek made me realize, right then, that "just playing" with reading and writing may still be quite important to do, even if you are well beyond five years old. Playfulness evokes enjoyment. And enjoyment is the very feeling that beckons an individual to the world of print, again and again.

Learning to read should be play—for parents as well as for children.

But how? A good question (and an important one) that led me to the interesting work of a man with a very long name, Mihaly Csikszentmihalyi (you don't have to say it, just read it). He has for some years been studying the nature of enjoyment, trying to find out what makes the doing of something its own reward—like climbing tall mountains, painstakingly building ships in small bottles, reading big volumes, and writing long stories (1990).

So far, he has noted four things that distinguish enjoyable times from the humdrum moments of our lives. One of these is *intense involvement*. When we really enjoy something, we seem to become one with what we do, like the dancer who cannot be separated from the dance, the singer from the song or the reader from the story.

Another is the presence of *challenge*. Whatever it is you enjoy doing is not too easy. But it's not too hard, either. It's just right, having sufficient difficulty to incite your interest and maintain your involvement.

Playing "catch" is a good example. My son and I have always liked to play catch, tossing the ball back and forth for quite a long time. What keeps us at this is that every now and then we "challenge" one another with difficult "throws." These are spaced just so, keeping us alert and "on guard." It's the delicious and unpredictable challenge of the throw which delights us as we strive to catch each one tossed our way successfully. That's what we enjoy and that's why we keep doing it.

Activities we enjoy also have a way of letting us know how well we are doing. That is, there are *"point outs" of progress.* Let me give you another quick example. Once my son and I built a computer desk, the written directions for which were truly a reading challenge. But what kept our interest and made it enjoyable were the clear indications along the way that the structure was actually beginning to look like a desk. In other words, we had concrete evidence of progress or "point outs" that things were going well.

And a fourth feature of enjoyment is having *a sense of control* of a situation—sort of a feeling of being "in charge." To be in charge, you first have to believe in yourself. Then you can concentrate on doing whatever it is you are doing, not on what you cannot do.

This circumstance is similar to something Dag Hammarskjöld, the former Secretary to the UN, once confided about himself. He wrote: "Really nothing was easier than to step from one rope ladder to the other—over the chasm. But, you failed because the thought occurred to you that you might . . . fall" (1964, p. 116). When things are enjoyable to do, you do not worry about falling (or failing). You concentrate on succeeding and you do!

Combine these features (intense involvement, meaningful challenge, progress "point outs," and a sense of control) and you've got pure enjoyment! And there's also something else you've got—motivation coming from the inside of you: You do something because you wish to do it (even if it's really hard to do).

Relating all this back to my son and his lagging interest in literacy, it seemed clear that what I needed to do was to make reading and writing more playful. If my son was to possess that "wish" to read and write, then reading and writing had to be enjoyable for him to do. And where better to start modeling this than with myself—good ol' mom.

So, quite deliberately, I began to put "play" back into reading and writing. I started to demonstrate how much "fun" literacy can be. Since this is rather important stuff if you're a parent in my situation, let me share some playful literacy pursuits I tried. Actually, they worked surprisingly well.

1. Jokes! I started with jokes, the likes of Gary Larson's *The Far Side* (1984) and those in the *Reader's Digest.* I put them on the refrigerator door and inevitably he read them (sometimes—I confess—only after I had read them aloud). And we laughed together.

Eventually we began to talk about what makes a joke a joke—a discussion, by the way, which involves a lot of hard thinking. Soon, he was reciprocating, putting jokes of his choice on the refrigerator door and explaining to me why they were funny. Back and forth, we enjoyed this activity, got to know one another better, and even tried to figure out a few of those political cartoons!

2. The Stump Mom Game. This game was simple, but not so easy. (Remember, challenge is important in enjoyment.) It consisted of asking each other questions about something we both had read, a strategy known as ReQuest (*Re*ciprocal *Quest*ioning) to reading teachers.

For example, we would each read a short passage from his social studies homework. First, he would ask me a question about it (and try to stump me, which he usually did). Then I would ask him one about the same passage (and try to stump him, which I rarely did at first). On we'd go to the next paragraph or section in the same manner.

We would do this only for a short while—a kind of "warm up" to the homework. But it worked fabulously! He seized the challenge to stump mom and to demonstrate his own mental prowess. Of course, he also had to read very carefully. We got a lot of homework done this way and I relearned all the state capitals.

3. Playing Doogie Howser. If you have ever watched this television program, you already have some clue as to what this activity is about.

Using the family computer, we each wrote in our journals almost every night (on separate disks, of course). There were no writing rules for these journals, but one computer rule: No reading each other's disks unless invited to do so.

Well, I started first and said he could read certain entries of mine and leave a comment if he liked. And he did. Soon, he invited me to read certain entries of his and to comment. And I did. Needless to say, it was easy to lose yourself in these entries—to read and write with *intense involvement.*

Playing Doogie was a smashing success and probably would have worked even if we didn't have a computer. Paper and pencil would have done just fine. At any rate, all this personal writing stimulated his interest in reading biographies, I think, while I gained some interesting new vocabulary meaningful only to the adolescent mind.

4. Literacy-Related Collections. What's this? It's collecting anything that is related to reading and writing, but no, it doesn't need to be books.

Actually I borrowed this idea from a friend who collects literacy-related posters. As for my son and me, we started gathering two kinds of literacy objects: pens and picture postcards of people reading. This turned out to be a most enjoyable activity. Actually it has become a quest (there's that challenge again)—like finding that rare baseball card, climbing the highest mountain or swimming the English Channel.

The activity definitely has progress "point outs," since we love to display the many pens and postcards in our collection. It is also an activity cluttered with literacy opportunities. If you buy a pen, you have to write with it some time. And the postcards can be sorted, categorized, labelled—and used (if you buy a duplicate).

Then, too, all this collecting of a specific item makes you smarter about it. My son, for example, became (and still is) quite an expert on pens (brandnames, quality, special features, locations, etc.). He even wrote a *Community Guidebook to Pens and More Pens.* All this interest in pens had an interesting side effect. He began to design his own letterhead to use these pens on, which (as you have undoubtedly guessed), sparked a good deal of letter writing. Now Grandma was receiving letters again. No, not so much for the purposes of communication, but more so to show-off the latest letterhead design.

Moreover, he started paying attention to reading activity beyond that depicted on postcards—people reading books and magazines in drug stores, in record shops, and while riding on all modes of transportation. He concluded that reading is a pretty popular and useful thing to do—an observation of no small consequence.

5. Reading Side by Side. Once we got into some of the above activities (which, by the way, didn't happen overnight), we had made some headway in reviving his interest in literacy. I knew it for sure when one evening, late, he came into the living room, flopped down next to me on the sofa, and without a word opened a book. We read, then, together—he in his and me in mine. And still do.

My son is nearly 15 now. No, he's not an avid reader nor a prolific writer. This is not a "miracle cure" story. But he likes to read and does. He likes to write a lot (that may be close to a miracle), especially lists, letters, informational stuff and his personal thoughts (in a computer journal). He still collects pens and designs letterhead stationery. In short, he chooses to read and write to fit his needs, finding both enjoyable to do. But, after all, isn't that what literacy is all about—fitting it into your life in ways that are personally satisfying?

So, that's the story of my son and me. It's a story about play, literacy, and growing up. It's just an ordinary story, but it has an extraordinary message for us parents. Play always belongs in literacy. It is not just something children do before they "really" read and write. If they are to enjoy and use reading and writing as expressive tools, playing with them is something they must do throughout their lifetime. As good parents, we need to remind our children of this sometimes. And sometimes we even need to show them how to have fun with reading and writing. That's our responsibility and our joy!

References and Other Readings on the Topic

Csikzentmihalyi, Mihaly (1990). Literacy and intrinsic motivation. *Daedelus, 119,* 2, 115–140.

Hammarskjöld, Dag (1964). *Markings* (L. Sjöberg & W. H. Auden, Trans.). NY: Alfred A. Knopf.

Meek, Margaret (1982). *Learning to read.* London: The Bodley Head, Ltd.

Children's Books

Brown, Margaret (1947). *Goodnight moon.* NY: Harper & Row.

Eastman, P.D. (1960). *Are you my mother?* NY: Random House.

Milne, A.A. (1926). *Winnie-the-Pooh.* NY: E. P. Dutton & Co.

Larson, G. (1984). *The far side gallery 3.* NY: Andrews & McMeel.

Chapter 3

Storytelling Connections: Ways to Catch Children's Imaginations and Excite Them about Learning

Olga Nelson

Olga Nelson has been a children's librarian in both school and public libraries in New York, Texas, and Ohio. As a professional storyteller, her audiences included preschoolers through adults. Sharing the importance of storytelling in her lives has always been a topic near and dear to her heart and beliefs about learning. She teaches literacy education and storytelling at Eastern Michigan University and storytelling workshops at Kent State University in the summer.

I will never forget the first time I actually became aware of the power of story-telling. The senior Girl Scout troop I belonged to was camping out in a rather primitive area. I was about thirteen or fourteen at the time. The day had been somewhat overcast with showers interspersed. Late evening found about ten of us sitting on cots gathered closely together in a large wall tent, grateful for someplace to get away from the dampness and the puddles outside. In the distance, rumblings of an approaching storm could be heard, but we were quite content. As darkness descended on our campsite, a friend began to tell a chilling story set in a small college town somewhere in the midwest. We became steeped in her story as she wove her tale. I remember having to lean in closer to hear her even though she was right beside me because she had lowered her voice to a whisper. I was hanging on to her every word; my eyes were transfixed on her face. You could have heard a pin drop in the tent, everything was that still. We were spellbound. As she came to that part in her story where all good "gotcha" stories get you, she cried out and lunged at us with precision timing. Bingo! She had caught us in the web she had been weaving all along. We gasped and fell back like dominoes, then scrambled to get away from her. For you see, our storyteller had delivered her tale so well that we had become suspended in it for awhile. In our mind's eye we saw her as the person in the story relating the events from her own experience.

I still marvel when I think about that experience so long ago. I was amazed at the teller's command of words, with just the right pace, mood, volume, and timing. Her eye contact and quiet voice held us rapt in her story. It was at that moment I knew that I wanted to be a storyteller. It is that power to transcend the moment, to transport the listener to another place and time, that I found so awe inspiring.

Not all stories need to be scary to get that effect. When I share folk and fairy tales or other stories with children, invariably they share how they felt or tell me similar stories from their own experiences. I love hearing these stories. One cannot listen to stories without becoming caught up in them emotionally in some way, sometimes to laughter, joy, other times to fears and tears. Storytellers ignite our own imaginations, and transport us to another plane. Thus, the storytelling loop continues and is constantly evolving with each listener. Audiences not only listen to the story, but create it from their own perspective along with the teller.

Storytelling is a wonderful way to spark children's imaginations and excite them about learning. It is a natural bridge to nurture their interest in writing and reading their own stories. This chapter provides some ways parents (and teachers) can take part in helping children make connections between stories and books using storytelling as the vehicle.

Parents who help children use language by listening, telling, reading, and writing their own stories are already creating a language- and story-rich environment. Storytelling is a way to generate an excitement about stories. It promotes children's understanding and enjoyment of stories by making them part of the process when they listen to stories.

Storytelling experiences are stepping stones to reading, writing, and comprehending a variety of written materials in and outside of school. There are many ways parents can assist their children in this process. Children are natural storytellers; they simply need opportunities and invitations to tell and write their own stories. Several strategies for helping parents get started telling stories, interpreting stories, creating original stories with their own children, establishing routines, and understanding the patterns in stories will be covered.

One of the easiest and most enjoyable ways to motivate children to love and partake in the art of storytelling starts with telling family experience stories that I like to call "Elbow Stories." These are stories or vignettes about events that have occurred over time in the family, sometimes even before the parents themselves were born. As a little girl I remember hearing my relatives tell Elbow Stories about themselves and other family members. I never tired of hearing those stories, no matter how many times I heard them. It seemed this storytelling ritual invariably took place after we had eaten a meal together and elbows were propped up on the table. No one was ever in too much of a hurry to move away from the table. The stories not only served to construct a family history for me, but also helped create roots, connections to a past and to other family members. I always felt welcome, although I mostly listened at that time. It felt wonderful to be a part of my family. Today, those same stories still go around the table, patio, or family room whenever we meet for family reunions in the summer and during the holidays. My mother has become the family historian and storyteller at these occasions. Life has become busier for most of us and we have moved away from each other, but the bonds and the unity of the family exist through our Elbow Stories. And through such stories, my cousins, who never had the opportunity to meet my three uncles—Mike, Louie, and Bill—or their Grandpa George, have a very good notion of who they were as real, living, and breathing people with their own personalities. Like my relatives before me, I see myself taking my turn as transmitter of the family history stories, assuring that the cycle will be carried on by my cousins and their children after me.

With family life becoming busier all the time, it is getting more difficult to meet around the table to share these stories. One way to preserve family heritage and help children make connections with their past is to share these stories on car trips, whether on vacation or going shopping. Telling these stories sets the tone for the family get-togethers, invites intimacy, creates bonds, and defines certain characters and events in the family through rich description. Invariably, children will want to know more about certain people. This is a wonderful time to bring out the family photo album and continue those connections between the past and the present.

Getting Started: Experience Stories

Experience stories are natural vehicles that can be used in school settings. Nancy Taylor, a fourth grade teacher and storyteller in Columbus, Ohio, uses family histories like my Elbow Stories to urge her students to go home and collect family stories by interviewing parents and other relatives, transcribe and share these stories with others. The project begins with Nancy modeling storytelling techniques by telling her own experience stories, sharing her own family album, and exploring experience stories in existing children's literature with her students. Some of the books Nancy has used to help her students have a better grasp of experience stories include *When I Was Young in the Mountains* and *The Relatives Came* by Cynthia Rylant, *Freddy*

Family History Stories and the Curriculum

My Grandfather by Nola Langner, *Nathan's Hanukhah Bargain* by Jacqueline D. Greene, and Miska Miles's *Annie and the Old One.* This extensive project spans seven weeks and culminates with students publishing family histories and telling their stories to classmates and other classes in the school. History can be exciting, fun, and personal when starting with family experience stories.

Identifying and Changing Patterns in Stories	Another easy and pleasant way to help children identify certain patterns and motifs or recurrent themes in stories is for parents to tell the folk and fairy tales that they know. This can be done in a playful manner. If some details are forgotten, children are very forgiving. They will even help parents fill in the blanks or create their own details. Many anthologies and single editions of folk and fairy tales can be obtained in the children's room of local public libraries to give parents a starting point.

After parents feel comfortable with telling stories in their own words, they might play some games with those familiar stories by changing certain events, characters, details, problems, solutions, and/or points of view. This activity extends children's creativity and encourages children to apply their knowledge about how stories are constructed in order to create new versions and variants of the original story. (A version is the same story with the same characters but with some differences in episodes, language, actions, or outcomes. A variant is similar to an already existing story in theme, pattern, or plot, but is an entirely different story with distinctive characters.)

There are several books available that can help parents and children get started creating their own versions and variants. *The True Story of the 3 Little Pigs* by Jon Scieszka is a hilarious book that gives the wolf's point of view of what "really happened." Children and adults both love this book. *Prince Cinders,* by Babette Cole is a variant of the Cinderella story. Children will instantly be reminded of Cinderella and be tickled by the amusing twist in the characters, events, and outcome. *Mufaro's Beautiful Daughters,* by John Steptoe, and *The Talking Eggs,* by Robert San Souci, may also remind children of Cinderella because of the contrast in the sisters' personalities. There will be no mistaking that *Ruby* by Michael Emberly is a variant of Little Red Riding Hood because of the obvious plot, similar problems, and characters' conversations. This story, however, is set in a totally different environment. Children will thoroughly enjoy the upbeat flavor of the language and the engaging characters, especially Ruby herself. *Flossie and the Fox* by Patricia McKissick would be wonderful to use in conjunction with *Ruby.* Rather than telling children what this story is about, just read the story and then wait for children to tell you what story it reminds them of. The answer should come quite readily once children become familiar with folk and fairy tales.

In comparing these stories, parents may ask children to describe the similarities and differences they see between characters and other aspects of the stories. Invite children to make up their own versions or variants of Little Red Riding Hood, Cinderella, The Three Little Pigs, or any other familiar story. The function of these stories is to help children and parents develop a sense of story by playing with the various parts of the stories.

Finally, parents and children might want to make up different endings or "Just Suppose . . ." stories. In these stories parents, together with their child or a group of children, make up continuations to stories or change the endings. The results are usually quite interesting and amusing. The more people involved, the merrier the story will become. A good book to start parents and children thinking about these different versions is Jon Scieszka's *The Frog Prince Continued*. In this book, the author shares his version of what happened to the princess and the frog after those famous words: "And they lived happily ever after."

An experienced professional storytelling friend of mine likes to take his two children on imaginary journeys with him. He has ingeniously developed a game that he plays with them everyday. In the morning, he asks his children to name a character, a place, and two things. Then, during the day, he develops an original story employing all the information they have given him. By bedtime, the children can hardly wait for the story to unfold. He established a positive ritual with them that makes going to bed a pleasurable and anticipated event. Children learn to love stories and look forward to the intimacy and enjoyment the storytelling situation provides. In addition, they gain a larger knowledge about how stories are constructed in a most natural and beguiling way, that is, by observing and experiencing their father's stories and storytelling style. Inviting children to become co-creators in thinking up unusual details for the purpose of stumping their parents establishes a different kind of rapport with children. Of course, the next step in this process is to turn the tables and give the children a few details in the morning and have them create their own original stories to tell parents or caregivers at the end of the day. This is a wonderful way to bring closure to each day, and continuity with the next. Rituals such as these end the day on a positive note.

With continued practice, stories and storytelling will become easier because tellers and listeners will become more experienced in the numerous possibilities for making up stories. Children will begin to take more and more risks in playing with various components of all stories: characters, plot, problems, events, solutions, and outcomes.

Creating Original Stories for Fun and Intrigue

As discussed here, storytelling is a means for children to share in their own family, community, cultural values, and heritage. Storytelling, by its very social nature, engages children in a special intimacy that television and other media cannot come close to duplicating. There is a positive, intimate interaction between the teller and the listener. When the storytelling event is over, much can be built upon that interaction. Exploring stories, sharing interpretations and feelings with children through active imaginative play, and constructing original stories, such as versions and variants, truly sets children free to experience a sense of awe and wonder. The sooner children begin to be involved in these kinds of interactions with stories, the more experienced and prepared they will be for reading, writing, telling, and sharing their own stories and the stories they encounter in children's trade books at home and in school.

Storytelling: Connection to Learning, Reading, and Writing

Children's Books

Cole, B. (1988). *Prince Cinders.* New York: Putnam.

Emberly, M. (1990). *Ruby.* Boston: Little Brown and Co.

Greene, J.D. (1986). *Nathan's Hanukhah bargain.* Rockville, MD: Ken Ben Copies.

Langner, N. (1979). *Freddy my grandfather.* New York: Four Winds Press.

McKissack, P. (1986). *Flossie and the fox.* New York: Dial.

Miles, M. (1971). *Annie and the old one.* Boston: Little Brown and Co.

Rylant, C. (1985). *The relatives came.* New York: Bradbury Press.

———. (1982). *When I was young in the mountains.* New York: Dutton.

San Souci, R.D. (1989). *The talking eggs.* New York: Scholastic, Inc.

Scieszka, J. (1989). *The true story of the 3 little pigs.* New York: Viking.

———. (1991). *The Frog Prince continued.* New York: Viking.

Steptoe, J. (1987). *Mufaro's beautiful daughters.* New York: Lothrop.

Storytelling Resources for Parents

Allison, C. (1987). *I'll tell you a story, I'll sing you a song.* New York: Delacorte.

> Includes many helpful hints for parents on how to use and remember the stories, verses, and songs of childhood.

Barton, B. (1986). *Tell me another: Storytelling and reading aloud at home, at school and in the community.* Markham, Ontario, Canada: Pembroke Pub. Ltd.

> This book contains good advice on story selection, presentation, and making the story your own.

Maguire, J. (1985). *Creative storytelling: Choosing, inventing, and sharing tales for children.* Cambridge, MA: Yellow Moon Press.

> This helpful tool for beginning and advanced tellers provides strategies for making a story your own. The essence and value of storytelling in our lives rings clear and true.

NAPPS: National Association for the Preservation and Perpetuation of Storytelling, P.O. Box 309, Jonesborough, Tenn. 37659.

> Write to this national organization for information about storytelling books, cassettes, publications, and local and state storytellers, organizations, and events. Membership fee.

Nelson, O. (1989). Storytelling: Language experience for meaning-making. *The Reading Teacher, 42,* 386–390.

> Provides an example of how storytelling can be used to encourage children to tell and write their own stories.

Nelson, P. (1992). *Magic minutes: Quick read-alouds for every day.* Englewood, CO: Libraries Unlimited.

> One hundred eighty humorous, touching, and whimsical stories that, at one page long, are perfect for parents to read aloud at bedtime and learn to tell easily and quickly in their own words.

Pellowski, A. (1987). *The family storytelling handbook.* New York: Macmillian.

> This book provides unusual and easy-to-tell stories from around the world that can enrich family traditions.

Smith, C. A. (1990). *From wonder to wisdom: Using stories to help children grow.* New York: Penguin Books.

> This specialist in human development explains how childhood stories and fairy tales can help children learn timeless lessons about life.

Yolen, J. (1981). *Touch magic: Fantasy, faerie, and folklore in literature of childhood.* New York: Philomel Books.

> Yolen provides rationale for why it is important for children to have a variety of stories told and read to them firsthand. A must for parents.

Chapter 4

Children Never Outgrow "Read Me Another . . ."

Karla Hawkins Wendelin

An associate professor of Curriculum & Instruction at the University of Nebraska, Karla Wendelin teaches courses in elementary school literacy education and children's literature. She has conducted numerous workshops for parents and teachers in both school and community settings on literacy learning and books for children.

"R ead me another story!"
   "That was a good one! Now read *this* one!"
   "Just one more story, please . . . ."

These are the requests of children for whom hearing stories read aloud is part of their daily lives. Jim Trelease, author of *The Read-Aloud Handbook,* calls reading aloud an "advertisement." Indeed it is. It is an advertisement for books and for the reading itself. Children who have books read to them learn about the power of reading, and the adults who do the reading are their role models as readers. Little else associated with reading development can accomplish so much with such relative ease.

Values of Reading Aloud

Reading aloud to children contributes to children's growth in reading for themselves and in their interest in reading. The values of reading aloud span the years of childhood from infancy through the elementary grades.

Language Development

The language in books differs from spoken language. Sentence structures and patterns of words in books tend to be more complex than the less formal language children often hear spoken around them or on television. Book language also contains vivid, colorful descriptions, such as "wee, small cottage deep in the forest," and rhythmic repetitions, such as "not by the hair of my chinny chin chin," that children often incorporate into their pretend play after they have heard stories. Books provide a wider range of language formats than is typically available through oral language in the environment. Nonfiction books that describe the life cycle of a butterfly or tell what animals do in winter utilize a writing style that is different from a book of poetry or a folktale or a fictional story of a boy who has lost his dog. For their own language growth, children need exposure to a variety of language patterns, and books are the most readily available material for providing such variety.

Vocabulary Development

Reading aloud adds new words to children's vocabularies. Research studies show that children learn the meanings of unfamiliar words incidentally by hearing them read within the context of stories. Studies have also shown that literature exposes children to significantly greater numbers of new words than their typical school reading books. It is difficult for children—or adults—to *read* a word they have never heard before. Pronouncing it correctly, through a variety of decoding strategies, is possible, but the word meaning is not usually present. Hearing words within a context created by the situation in a story allows children to attach meaning to unknown words and to apply those meanings to other experiences.

Enhancing Comprehension

Throughout their elementary school years, most children can comprehend, by listening, material that is written at a higher difficulty level than what they can read. Because their listening comprehension exceeds their reading comprehension, reading aloud to children enables children to acquire information on topics that might not be available to them until much later. This information builds backgrounds of experiences for children that they will eventually use when they read. Research supports the importance of extensive knowledge in reading comprehension.

*When parents show interest in books and reading, children's interest
will soon follow.*

Listening to stories assists comprehension in other ways. Children become familiar with basic story patterns. They learn that stories have a beginning, a middle,
and an end. They learn that stories have characters and that story events revolve
around these characters. They learn that stories have a time and place setting and that
stories quite often have a "message." In short, they acquire a knowledge of different
story structures and components of literature, all of which will assist them with reading comprehension.

Influence on Writing

As children become acquainted with characters, plots, interesting words and phrases,
and different kinds of literature, this knowledge begins to spill over into their writing.

Just as adult writers do, children borrow elements from books they know to use in their own stories. Books are an important source of ideas and inspiration for children. Picture-book author Mem Fox has stated that the reason some children have nothing to write about except the currently popular TV cartoon character or the violent actions of a movie hero/villain is that their "literary storehouses" are empty. Reading to children from a variety of literature can help fill those storehouses.

Development of Book Handling Skills and Print Concepts

The values of reading aloud discussed thus far apply to readers of all ages. However, for infants, toddlers, and preschool children, the values have an even broader scope. Reading to very young children introduces them to how to handle a book. They learn how to hold a book right side up, the difference between the front cover and the back cover, and how to turn the pages. In the process, they begin to learn the proper care for a book. After more experience with books, they begin to learn that the print and the illustrations serve different functions. They learn that the story is largely contained in the little black "squiggles" and that the pictures are good for pointing out or looking for things mentioned in the story. It is at this point that young children who have heard a favorite story repeatedly can pick up the book and "read" it perfectly with all the appropriate voice inflections and aside comments of the adult who has read it to them. This activity should not be dismissed lightly as "memorizing" instead of "real reading." It is an important progression toward reading that is a direct outgrowth of reading aloud to children. As their experience with books matures, they learn that we read the left-hand page before the right-hand page and that we read a line of print left to right across the page. Eventually, children become curious about those little black squiggles and ask to have letters identified, and the questions of "What's that say?" indicate a real interest in wanting to know words. Adults may have a tendency to overlook this type of learning. Yet learning book-related concepts is a critical step in children's development of literacy.

Enjoyment

Reading aloud has its emotional and social rewards too. For an infant and toddler, the enjoyment comes from the warmth and security of being held while hearing a story. For an older child, the undivided attention from an adult and the interchange of laughter and talk contribute to the pleasure of the activity. Quite possibly the greatest value of all is the positive attitude and interest in reading that is generated from sharing a book. The adult who values the reading of a book to a child enough to spend time doing it sends a message to children about the importance of reading. Hearing good books often sends children to reading good books. Reading to children when they are young may very well set the stage for a lifelong habit of reading.

Effective Read-Aloud Sessions

Adults often become discouraged when read-aloud sessions do not turn out to be quite as they had envisioned them. When the major players—adults and children—are in place, consideration needs to be given to appropriate book choice and timing of the activity.

Choosing the Right Book

With thousands of new children's books published each year, choosing good read-alouds can seem an insurmountable task. The following suggestions may help parents and teachers in the selection process:

1. Trust in old personal favorites, but be aware that it takes time to "grow into" some of the "classics." Children still enjoy Margaret Wise Brown's *Goodnight Moon, Make Way for Ducklings* by Robert McCloskey, and *The Tale of Peter Rabbit* by Beatrix Potter. Some experience with literature is needed, however, before children are ready to hear *The Wind in the Willows, Black Beauty,* or *Tom Sawyer.*

2. Look for quality in both the story and the artwork, but don't necessarily assume that all award-winning books are great read-alouds. Picture books often serve as children's introduction to art, and the illustrations in current picture books represent some of the world's best artists. These books require time for children to examine the pictures and talk about them. Picture books should not be overlooked for older readers either, whose primary reading material is "chapter books." The artwork and themes in many picture books, such as those by Chris Van Allsburg and Paul Goble, are at a level of sophistication that is appropriate for older children. A great read-aloud book usually moves quickly into the action of the story, has a good pace with memorable, descriptive characters, and utilizes vivid language and snappy dialogue.

3. Read from a variety of types and formats of literature. Much of our literature sharing with infants is done orally instead of with books. Nursery rhymes, such as "Patty Cake" and "This Little Piggie Went to Market," and songs, such as "Hush Little Baby," can be introduced later to children in printed versions. Board books are ideal for very young readers because small fingers can scratch at the pictures, turn the reinforced pages, and even chew on them with little harm done. Preschool children are curious about everything around them. Concept books that deal with letters, numbers, colors, size and spatial relationships, and help children label their world, allow for considerable adult-child interaction about the pictures. A wealth of fiction—contemporary and historical, fantasy and realistic—is available to children in picture-book and novel form. Children appreciate poetry as well, and poetry is meant to be read aloud. Young people of all ages seem to enjoy the light verse of Shel Silverstein and Jack Prelutsky. Poets such as John Ciardi, Eve Merriam, and Arnold Adoff have published extensive collections of poetry for children. Nonfiction books should never be avoided. These books are available on a large variety of topics and are often illustrated with high quality photographs. Though these books are not usually read cover to cover in read-aloud sessions, the read-talk-read format with interspersed questions and comments by both the adult and the child provide a valuable book-sharing opportunity.

4. Seek recommendations of good read-aloud books from experts. Adults should ask their children's teachers for book titles and names of authors that the children enjoy. The librarian in the children's section of the public library and the school librarian are also knowledgeable sources. At the end of this chapter is a brief list of children's books that are good read-alouds and some recommended books for adults on the topic of reading to children.

5. As the adult reader, choose books that *you* enjoy as well. It is quite common for children to request a much-loved book to be read over and over. If it is a book that the adult does not like, the plea "Read it again" implies a chore. A great read-aloud is as pleasurable the five hundredth time as it is the first!

Choosing the Right Time

Time is important to the success of reading aloud. Most children respond favorably to a predictable read-aloud time. For many families, this is bedtime. However, spontaneous requests for reading a book should not be ignored.

Family reading means involving the whole family.

The amount of time children will spend listening to a story depends upon maturity, personality, and their mood at the moment. Parents should not force a story on a child when interest is not there. Another time and another story might be more appropriate. Read-aloud time should be pleasant and comfortable, not a time for correcting behavior. Withholding a story should never be used as punishment. Adults are often frustrated by trying to read a story to more than one child at a time. Although time constraints may dictate "one-story-fits-all," such books are difficult to find. Picture books work better than novels in these situations. If, for example, the five year old and the eight year old are interested in the story, but the two year old continually comes and goes, there is no need to be discouraged. It is likely that the two-year-old is actually listening to more than what is apparent. Some one-on-one time with an adult or older sibling using a book more appropriate for a toddler may help in such a situation.

Reading aloud can become a shared responsibility. Involving all family members is both beneficial and desirable. No two people read with the same voice inflections, and different reader inflections will provide multiple models of expressive reading for children. Children need to hear male voices and female voices, old voices and young voices. A family reading time that starts out at just ten minutes an evening often increases in length and in importance in the family routine.

Reading aloud should begin in infancy and continue indefinitely. Adults often stop reading to their children once they begin to read independently. The values of reading aloud—the bond between reader and listener, the challenge of a new book, the worth of reading as a recreational activity—are not limited to prereaders. They last a lifetime. Perhaps the most convincing testimonials for reading aloud lie in the memories of adults who have a few favorite books as "old friends" and the lingering voice of some special person who read to them.

Recommended Read-Alouds

Adults may add many more titles to this list as they locate their own personal favorites and those of the children with whom they share good books. Titles are coded (PB) for picture book and (N) for novel.

Aardema, Verna. (1975). *Why mosquitoes buzz in people's ears.* Illus. by Leo & Diane Dillon. New York: Dial. (PB)

Allard, Harry. (1985). *Miss Nelson has a field day.* Illus. by James Marshall. Boston: Houghton Mifflin. (PB)

Blume, Judy. (1972). *Tales of a fourth grade nothing.* New York: Dutton. (N)

Brittain, Bill. (1983). *The wish-giver.* New York: Harper & Row. (N)

Byars, Betsy. (1986). *The not-just-anybody family.* New York: Delacorte. (N)

Carle, Eric. (1969). *The very hungry caterpillar.* New York: Philomel. (PB)

Cleary, Beverly. (1981). *Ramona Quimby, age 8.* New York: Morrow. (N)

de Paola, Tomie. (1975). *Strega Nona.* Englewood Cliffs, NJ: Prentice-Hall. (PB)

Fox, Mem. (1987). *Hattie and the fox.* Illus. by Patricia Mullins. Scarsdale, NY: Bradbury. (PB)

Gardiner, John. (1980). *Stone fox.* New York: Harper & Row. (N)

Guarino, Deborah. (1989). *Is your mama a llama?* Illus. by Steven Kellogg. New York: Scholastic. (PB)

Howe, James & Deborah Howe. (1979). *Bunnicula.* New York: Atheneum. (N)

Konigsburg, E. L. (1967). *From the mixed-up files of Mrs. Basil E. Frankweiler.* New York: Atheneum. (N)

Lowry, Lois. (1989). *Number the stars.* Boston: Houghton Mifflin. (N)

MacLachlan, Patricia. (1985). *Sarah, plain and tall.* New York: Harper & Row. (N)

Marshall, James. (1988). *Goldilocks and the three bears.* New York: Dial. (PB)

Martin, Bill, Jr. & John Archambault. (1989). *Chicka chicka boom boom.* Illus. by Lois Ehlert. New York: Simon & Schuster. (PB)

McKissack, Patricia. (1986). *Flossie and the fox.* Illus. by Rachel Isadora. New York: Dial. (PB)

Paterson, Katherine. (1977). *Bridge to Terabithia.* New York: Crowell. (N)

Paulsen, Gary. (1987). *Hatchet.* Scarsdale, NY: Bradbury. (N)

Polacco, Patricia. (1988). *Rechenka's eggs.* New York: Philomel. (PB)

Robinson, Barbara. (1972). *The best Christmas pageant ever.* New York: Harper & Row. (N)

Ruckman, Ivy. (1984). *Night of the twisters.* New York: Crowell. (N)

Sendak, Maurice. (1963). *Where the wild things are.* New York: Harper & Row. (PB)

Speare, Elizabeth George. (1983). *The sign of the beaver.* Boston: Houghton Mifflin. (N)

Taylor, Mildred. (1976). *Roll of thunder, hear my cry.* New York: Dial. (N)

Van Allsburg, Chris. (1985). *The polar express.* Boston: Houghton Mifflin. (PB)

Viorst, Judith. (1972). *Alexander and the terrible, horrible, no good, very bad day.* Illus. by Ray Cruz. New York: Atheneum. (PB)

Waber, Bernard. (1972). *Ira sleeps over.* Boston: Houghton Mifflin. (PB)

Wood, Audrey. (1984). *The napping house.* Illus. by Don Wood. New York: Harcourt. (PB)

For Further Reading

The following books contain advice for adults on selecting books and sharing them with children, as well as lengthy lists of recommended books for children of all ages. These books are available at most public libraries and at bookstores.

Hearne, Betsy. (1990). *Choosing books for children* (revised edition). New York: Delacorte, (also Dell paperback).

Kimmell, Mary Margaret & Elizabeth Segel. (1988). *For reading out loud: A guide to sharing books with children* (revised edition). New York: Delacorte, (also Dell paperback).

Larrick, Nancy. (1982). *A parent's guide to children's reading* (5th edition). New York: Bantam paperback.

Trelease, Jim. (1989). *The new read-aloud handbook.* New York: Viking Penguin.

Chapter 5

It's Not Just What You Do but How You Do It That Counts

David F. Lancy

D avid Lancy is a professor of Anthropology at Utah State University, Logan, Utah. His research interests include parental influences on children's reading development.

A paradox provoked my initial interest in studying parent-child interaction during storybook reading. Both of my daughters learned to read quite early—shortly after beginning formal instruction in school. When we moved to Arizona in 1980, my wife needed to take two classes in reading pedagogy in order to activate her elementary teaching certificate. "Looking over her shoulder," I was amazed at the complex technology she had to master in order to be considered prepared to assist primary grade children to become readers.

I was confronted with two visions of learning to read—it was either very complex and chancy or quite simple and a near certainty.

Naturally, I thought immediately of the home–reading connection. My daughters were read to daily from infancy. But I was surprised to find very little research that explored this topic and, even today, there is almost no research that studies the long-term impact of home storybook reading on children's acquisition of print literacy.

With colleagues Kelly Draper and Christi Bergin, I videotaped 32 parent-child pairs as they read to each other and then analyzed the tapes for recurrent patterns. The 32 children ranged in age from five to seven and in reading ability from early, fluent readers to late, nonfluent readers.

Our tapes clearly show some children who are eager to read, who use a variety of strategies in reading and who are rapidly becoming proficient. They also show children who are struggling to read. hesitating over every word, and who rely exclusively on a decoding or "sounding out" strategy. And, of course, we see children who are somewhere along this continuum. Similarly, we see parents who read expressively, who try to engage the child's attention in the story, and who are effective coaches as their children attempt to read. We also see parents who are, alas, far less effective. These data allow me to consider not only the positive—what to do when reading with children, but the negative as well—what *not* to do, in creating successful and enjoyable read-aloud experiences for parents and children.

The Reading Environment

Parents of school-age children are bombarded with injunctions to read to their children. Too often this can be interpreted as a kind of "homework." As Roskos points out, learning to read and sustaining an interest in reading necessitates the creation of a playful atmosphere. This means *don't force* reading on your child.

In our research, the good readers all had parents who treated storybook reading as an occasion to have fun. Poor readers' parents treated joint storybook reading as an opportunity to practice skills, to "teach reading."

We also found, when we visited the homes of good readers, that there were lots of picture books—usually 50 or more. These weren't all Caldecott Medal winners—there were lots of Golden Books in evidence, but good readers and their parents tended to *shun*—at home and in our research setting—books specifically designed to teach reading in the highly structured, "Dick and Jane" manner. There were fewer than ten picture books in the homes of poor readers. Many of these lacked a story per se and were aimed at teaching the alphabet and letter sounds.

Parents of good readers reported that they read to their children regularly. Most had a set time for this and storybook reading was done in a manner that excluded other distractions like television.

Clearly, if a parent does not enjoy reading to his or her child or is "not in the mood"—and we saw considerable evidence of this—the read-aloud sessions will not accomplish anything. On the contrary, we felt strongly that some parents were reinforcing the poor readers' negative attitudes about reading. Not surprisingly, several of these parents told us they had a hard time learning to read themselves and didn't feel confident as readers. On the other hand, several of the parents who most enjoyed reading with children were not themselves avid readers.

Our advice to parents who, for whatever reason, are unable or unwilling to read with their children is to find a substitute—a sibling, grandparent, neighbor. My own experience with several volunteer programs suggests that there are lots of people in families and communities who love reading stories with kids.

How can parents make the read-aloud experience an enjoyable and learning one? First, they need to develop an occasion for reading with their children. This may be negotiated with an older child, or made part of the regular home routine—brush teeth after dinner, lights out at 8 P.M.

Next, negotiate choosing what book or books to read. It is good to allow the child some say in the manner but preschoolers do need to be "pushed" to go beyond the old faithfuls, to explore new concepts and vocabulary.

Interaction During Storybook Reading

Grandparents and other family members can make reading special.

When you read, *don't* read in a monotone. Okay, so you're not Burl Ives or Levar Burton, but children's books do lend themselves to exaggerated tone, use of accents, gestures, and so forth. Ham it up.

Do *not* read the book through cover-to-cover without stopping. Parents of good readers draw the child's attention to the identities of the author and illustrators, the title of the book and relate aspects of the story to the child's life, to favorite TV characters/shows, to other books read and so on. Savor the book and the experience with your child. Parents of poor readers tend to discourage their children from commenting on the book and ignore their questions.

Pause to ask the child to expand on what is happening in the text or to predict what will occur next. Discuss the pictures and text with the child. Call attention to punctuation marks, letters, and proper names. Gradually make the child aware of the way the text works. But *don't* let these question-and-answer exchanges become tedious exercises, either.

Emerging into Literacy

The admittedly scanty research literature suggests that there are notable differences in what parents of good readers focus their attention on as their child grows. With children who aren't yet talking, the mother primarily labels the pictures. Somewhat later, she asks "What is that funny looking person" and supplies the answer herself, "Why, that's a clown," thereby modeling for the child a routine which will be used frequently when the child can talk. By two years of age, the child should be initiating about 50 percent of the comments during the parent's reading. Labeling gives way to a full reading of the story associated with commentary by the parent and questioning of the child designed to elaborate on the text or to use the pictures to assist in making sense of the text.

Children's comments and responses to questions are always acknowledged. Further, some parents seem to find a way to provide corrective feedback without being negative.

Children who are read to often may engage in "pretend reading" alone, with dolls and/or siblings or with a parent. Even though the child "reads" a familiar book she is bound to be "inaccurate." Rather than correct the child's "errors," parents should praise the efforts and model correct reading.

Pretend reading allows children to gradually build images of themselves as readers. In turn, the child who starts formal reading instruction thinking of herself as a reader will treat errors/mistakes/misunderstandings as temporary setbacks. On the other hand, the child who begins formal reading instruction with no sense of what being a reader means, may treat these same issues as proof that he "can't learn to read" or "will never be a good reader." As parents, *don't* act in a manner that discourages your children from "flapping their wings" as new readers.

Coaching the Beginning Reader

Unfortunately, parents often cease reading regularly with their children just before kindergarten or first grade, which is arguably the critical period in children's literacy development. Now, when children are struggling with the mechanics of reading in a competitive and potentially hostile environment, they more than ever need the sheltering and helping effect of a parent/coach. They need to be reminded daily of how much fun books can be and how "easy" it is to read.

Coaching the beginning reader is not that different from reading with a pre-schooler. Unfortunately, some parents see reading storybooks to children and learning to read as fundamentally different activities. One parent read to her child with great enthusiasm, there was a great deal of discussion, and the pair were having fun. But, when it was the child's turn to read, the mother shifted gears. She made the child "sound it out." Picture and story were ignored. She even covered an illustration at one point so her daughter couldn't "cheat." Needless to say, reading for this child was a painful chore.

The parents of good readers help their children select a familiar book and/or one with familiar vocabulary. They help them maintain fluency by supplying the word when the child hesitates or by offering a meaningful clue of some sort. Parents of poor readers tend to have their children struggle longer over a word and when they do offer help it is most often the exhortation "just sound it out." Children are taught phonetic/decoding strategies in school. Parents working one-on-one are in a much better position than teachers to help children over the rough spots in reading so that they can develop their identity as readers. The parent will be amply rewarded by the exclamation, "I read the WHOLE book all by MYSELF!"

We have found that parents who read regularly with their primary grade children develop a clear sense of their children's reading vocabulary. Hence, when a child comes to a word he doesn't know, a short pause is followed by the parent supplying the word. When he comes to a familiar word, there is a longer pause, giving the child time to decode the word or retrieve it from memory. This is the essence of what educators call scaffolding. The parent provides just enough assistance so that the child doesn't grow weary and/or feels the task is insurmountable, but not so much assistance that the child never has to stretch to learn new words or to try the various decoding strategies. Even after the child is reading well, the parent has a responsibility to shape the child's out-of-school experience so that books and a time and place to read them are always available. In Chapter 2, for example, Kathy Roskos discusses special strategies to use with a fifth grader.

In several research studies—my own and others—we have found parents who see it as the school's responsibility to teach children to read. There may have been a time when we believed that schools were capable of accomplishing this task unaided, but we don't believe it anymore. At best, the school can take a kindergartner who's not been read to regularly and turn him into a skilled "word caller"—someone who can "read" almost anything but who understands little of what he reads and enjoys even less. Successful literacy learning requires more than dedicated teachers in the schools. It needs the active involvement of parents creating that literacy scaffold at home that makes reading a successful and enjoyable experience. To paraphrase Smokey the Bear, "Only you can prevent illiteracy."

Lancy, David. (Ed.) (1994.) *Children's emergent literacy: From research to practice*. New York: Praeger.

For Further Reading

Chapter 6

Hundreds of Books, Thousands of Books. . . . Finding Good Books for Eager Readers

Barbara Peterson

Barbara Peterson has been reading children's books since her childhood and began reading to her children and grandchildren when they were infants. She has been a children's librarian, Reading Recovery teacher, and university teacher of children's literature. She was editor of *The WEB* for two years, and is the author of "Selecting Books for Beginning Readers," which appears in DeFord, Lyons & Pinnell, *Bridges to Literacy: Learning from Reading Recovery* (Heinemann, 1991)

I f I were to begin by telling you that this chapter is about books—hundreds of books, thousands of books, millions, of books—your memory might be jogged to recall a story you heard somewhere, a long time ago. Perhaps, when you were a child, someone read Wanda Gag's *Millions of Cats* to you. If so, I can easily imagine a smile on your face as you start to whisper "hundreds of cats, thousands of cats, millions and billions and trillions of cats" and picture in your mind the parade of black and white cats that followed the old man home.

Good stories endure. Though first published more than 60 years ago, *Millions of Cats* continues to be popular among the children, parents, and teachers who use my neighborhood library. Perhaps you did not have books at home when you were young, but you did have stories. Maybe they were stories from the Bible or favorite folktales told aloud before bedtime, and maybe, too, you heard stories about actual events from your family history. Many scholars believe that storytelling and story sharing are important ways for human beings to communicate and preserve their culture.

Explore Your Library

Parents and teachers can build and extend children's interest in stories by introducing them to many of the wonderful and exciting books now published especially for young readers. The best place to find these books is the children's or youth services area of your public library or school library media center. I suggest that you read this chapter at the library. Why? I hope that your curiosity will send you to the shelves to pick up some of the books I mention.

I hope, too, that you will make the librarian a partner in your quest to learn more about bringing books and children together. Librarians are avid readers who love to talk about books, and if you let them know, they can help find books that will touch your special interests. Many librarians also prepare book lists on popular topics and will usually order specific books requested by patrons. Just ask!

Books for Every Reader

What kinds of books can you find at the library? Most libraries have separate sections for picture books, easy readers, and fiction. Books in each group are usually arranged in alphabetical order by the author's last name. *Picture books* are stories told through a combination of pictures and words, and usually appeal to children in preschool and the primary grades. Some picture books, such as David Wiesner's *Tuesday,* have no words, so the story is told entirely through pictures. In contrast, other books, such as Patricia Polacco's *Thunder Cake,* have long, well developed written texts that share the stage with the illustrations.

While picture books appeal to children in preschool and the primary grades, the texts in many are quite complex and difficult for many children to read on their own until they reach second and third grades. Newly independent readers, however, are eager to have "grown-up" looking books they can read by themselves. Many libraries have sections for easy reader books for this audience. Some books have special publisher designations, such as the HarperCollins *I Can Read Series.* Books in the *easy reader* section are illustrated, usually written in short chapters, and printed in large type with wide spaces between lines and along the margins.

Eventually, children like to try "chapter" books without pictures and large print. Longer chapter books are shelved together under the heading of fiction, and are written for children who can read longer stretches of text with little assistance or instruction. Most books in the *fiction* section appeal to students from about third grade on, although some make splendid "read alouds" for younger children. *Charlotte's Web* by E. B. White is a good example of a book that second graders will love when someone reads it aloud to them, even though many of them will not be able to read it on their own before third grade.

Folklore, poetry, and informational books for readers of all ages are placed side-by-side in most libraries. *Folklore* includes picture book versions of well-known folktales like Cinderella as well as less familiar variants of the Cinderella tale, like *The Egyptian Cinderella, Princess Furball,* and *Yeh Shen,* and unillustrated collections of folktales (if you are looking for traditional tales with strong female characters, check out *Clever Gretchen and Other Forgotten Folktales*). In *poetry* sections, you will find favorites for younger children like Tomie de Paola's *Mother Goose,* works by a single poet like Eve Merriam's *Blackberry Ink,* and collections of poems by several poets organized around a theme. such as *On the Farm* by Lee Bennett Hopkins. Informational books deal with topics of interest to young readers and are presented in a factual manner. Take time to browse through the poetry, folklore, and informational shelves because they are filled with wonderful treasures.

How to Choose a Good Book

The best place to begin is in picture books and folktales in picture book format, because it is easy to sample the works of many authors and illustrators in a short period of time. Ask children, friends, and colleagues to recommend some of their favorites or select from the bibliography at the end of this chapter. Borrow a few from the library and spend a couple of hours looking through them. Read the blurbs on the jacket flaps that summarize the stories and tell something about the author and illustrator. Flip through the pages to get a sense of how the story unfolds. Look at the book cover and the title page. What hints do they give about the story to come? Look at the endpapers. Do they help to frame the book as a whole by repeating an element of color and design from the interior pages?

Read the narrative silently first, then read it out loud to feel the flow and rhythm of the language. Look closely at the illustrations, noticing how the artist has used color, texture, space, and design to create a visual narrative. Have the author and artist told a good story? Do the pictures hold your attention and compel you to look more closely? Are there memorable words or phrases in the text? Was it a "page-turner," one that kept you involved and eager to go on to the next page to see what happened next? Can you imagine reading it again and again, discovering something new each time? Are you eager to read it aloud to your child or class? If you answer "yes," the book is probably a "good" book.

The same criteria also provide a good starting point for evaluating other kinds of books. In addition, there are special points to consider for different kinds of books. When looking for easy readers, select books with imaginative and entertaining stories. Nothing is more discouraging to a new reader than to have to plod through lifeless texts. If you, as a parent or teacher, think a book is boring, chances are so will your child or student. I am a great fan of Cynthia Rylant's "Henry and Mudge" books for new readers, and I enjoy reading them every bit as much as I do novels for older readers.

It is more challenging to evaluate informational or nonfiction books because most writers and readers of these books for children are not specialists in the subjects they are reading and writing about. Nevertheless, there are many talented writers who carefully research their topics and verify facts with experts in the field. As adults, we can help make sure that our children receive current and authentic information by comparing several books on the same subject, and by teaching them how to become careful, critical readers. The content of an information book, including the written text, photographs, maps, and diagrams should be clearly organized and presented. Is the book pleasing to look through? Is the language of the text interesting enough to hold the attention of a single reader or a group of listeners?

It is also helpful to get to know writers and illustrators who consistently produce high quality material (ask your librarian for recommendations). Two respected writers who have written and illustrated informational books on a wide range of subjects are Aliki (*Digging Up Dinosaurs, A Medieval Feast*) and Gail Gibbons (*How Houses Are Built, The Milk Makers*). Check jacket flaps to determine the author's qualifications. For example, Ron Hirschi, author of *Loon Lake* and many other books about nature, is a biologist. You can also look for acknowledgements inside the book that indicate special assistance from experts. For example, Joanna Cole and Bruce Degen thank the technical services staff of the American Waterworks Association for their help in preparing *The Magic School Bus at the Waterworks,* one of four "Magic School Bus" books they have developed to introduce young readers to complex topics.

A Picture Book Sampler

I do not have enough space to write about all of the books you and your children would love to get to know, so I will whet your appetite by telling you about some of my favorite picture books. In picture books you can meet spunky characters like the heroine of *Amazing Grace* (Mary Hoffman and Caroline Binch), a girl who loves stories and theater. She wants to be Peter Pan in her school play, even though her friends insist she cannot because she is a girl and black. Nevertheless, she auditions and wins the part. The play is a big success, and Grace finds out she can do anything she sets her mind on.

Picture books are filled with all sorts of other interesting characters like the eponymous heros and heroines of *Titch* (Pat Hutchins), *Chrysanthemum* (Kevin Henkes), *Strega Nona* (Tomie de Paola), and *John Patrick Norman McHennessy: The Boy Who Was Always Late* (John Burningham). Letters of the alphabet are the featured characters in *Chicka Chicka Boom Boom* (Bill Martin and John Archambault). Bring them into your home and school, and watch children rush to read.

Hold your breath to see what happens in *Flossie and the Fox* (Patricia McKissack and Rachel Isadora). Go on adventures in *Where the Wild Things Are* (Maurice Sendak) and join in the fun with *We're Going on a Bear Hunt* (Michael Rosen and Helen Oxenbury). Sing along and laugh with *Five Little Monkeys Jumping on the*

Bed (Eileen Christelow) and *I Know an Old Lady Who Swallowed a Fly* (Glen Rounds). Travel to the Pacific Ocean in *Stringbean's Trip to the Shining Sea* (Vera Williams and Jennifer Williams), and visit Egypt in *The Day of Ahmed's Secret* (Florence Parry Heide, Judith Heide Gilliland, and Ted Lewin). Cuddle up with family time stories like *Bigmama's* (Donald Crews) and *Aunt Flossie's Hats (And Crab Cakes Later)* (Elizabeth Fitzgerald Howard and James Ransome). Think about serious matters like homelessness in *Fly Away Home* (Eve Bunting and Ronald Himler).

Take time to look closely at the illustrations in picture books and notice the unique and imaginative ways artists tell stories. Enter the rooftop world of *Tar Beach* through Faith Ringgold's painted quilt. Turn Ann Jonas' *Round Trip* upside down and read a second story back to front. Touch the raised webs in Eric Carle's *The Very Busy Spider.* Puzzle through four stories at once in David Macaulay's *Black and White.* Try to put your hands around the three-dimensional–looking characters in Chris Van Allsburg's *Jumanji.* Admire the bold colors in Lois Ehlert's books, the photography of Tana Hoban and Bruce Macmillan, and the collages of Ezra Jack Keats and Leo Lionni.

Introducing Books to Children

Parents and teachers play a key role in helping children become lifelong readers. When children are provided with many many books and encouraged to read and explore them at their own pace, they will become highly competent readers and thinkers. One of the most powerful ways to hook children on books is by *reading aloud* to them at least once a day. Taking time to read aloud tells children that we, as adults, value reading. Reading aloud stretches their knowledge because they hear language and stories they might not yet be able to read on their own. Reading aloud prepares young children to become independent readers, and introduces older readers to a wide range of books they might not pick up on their own. Read-aloud time can be that special, cozy, relaxing break from hectic home and school schedules.

Set aside a *special time and place* for reading aloud. At home, bedtime is a popular time for family reading. In many families, sharing favorite stories by reading aloud continues long after children are capable of reading anything themselves. I used to read to my children while they washed the dishes, and we took turns reading to each other during long drives on family vacations! At school, a section of carpet enclosed by bookshelves filled with books can be very inviting. Consider having students gather in this area first thing in the morning and read quietly until school starts. After completing attendance and other morning business, everyone will be ready for a good story.

Read many kinds of books. At first you will want to stick with some favorites, but as read-aloud time becomes routine, bring in a bit of poetry *every* day and share some nonfiction as well. Most second, third, and fourth grade children like to read books about other children their own age, and readily jump into books by Beverly Cleary, Patricia Reilly Giff, and Johanna Hurwitz. Encourage children to read favorite authors, *but* stretch their interests by reading about "real" children who have done something unusual. Read *Dinosaur Dig* and introduce them to Max and Meribah, the children of writer Kathryn Lasky and photographer Christopher Knight, as they all search for dinosaur bones in Montana. Or take them back a couple of centuries to learn about children who were *Chimney Sweeps* (James Cross Giblin).

If reading aloud to your child or class is new to you, simply begin with a book you enjoyed and are eager to share. As time goes on, you may wish to focus on several books by one author or illustrator or link books of a similar theme. At home, parents can easily jump in and read an unfamiliar book. However, a classroom session will be more successful if teachers have practiced reading the book aloud several times so the language flows easily and they can anticipate possible directions for discussion.

Traditional storytellers begin with a phrase such as "Once upon a time," and first grade teacher Connie Compton signals the start of read-aloud time with "I have a great story for you today." You may want to think of your own way to invite children to listen. Parents and teachers develop their own styles of reading aloud, but it is always important to encourage children to participate.

Hold the book for all to see, and introduce the book by mentioning the title, author, and illustrator. Say a little bit about the story, but be careful not to give away surprise endings. Call attention to the cover illustration and title page inside the book. Generate enthusiasm for the book by inviting students to comment on what they notice or find interesting. As you read the words, take time to pause for reactions such as laughter to something funny or "uh-ohs" to something scary. Encourage them to chime in on memorable refrains like "I'll huff and I'll puff and I'll blow your house down."

After the reading, talk about the book. Try to ask questions that will encourage discussion and give children free rein to respond to the events of the story, the actions of the characters, and the illustrations. Guide them to make connections to other familiar stories by grouping similar books together. If you have just finished "Goldilocks and the Three Bears," read "The Three Billy Goats Gruff," "The Three Little Pigs," and other tales about characters that come in threes. If your children can't get enough of the comical *Rosie's Walk* (Pat Hutchins), introduce *Hattie and the Fox* (Mem Fox), *Across the Stream* (Mirra Ginsburg), and other books about a hungry fox that just can't quite catch the tasty chicken. If you liked the bright, eye-catching colors in *Feathers for Lunch,* go on a Lois Ehlert reading spree. Let your imagination carry you away!

Learning to Read with Literature

In this country we believe children should learn how to read when they are in the first grade. For parents, first grade is a scary time because learning how to read seems like such a mysterious process, and we worry about what will happen if our children have difficulty. The truth of the matter is, however, that children learn a great deal about reading long before they ever go to school, especially if they have been read to regularly.

This week, my two and a half-year-old grandson Dominic came to visit and we spent one afternoon reading books he had picked out from my collection. As we read, he looked closely at the pictures but seemed not to notice the print. After reading Jan Brett's version of *Goldilocks and the Three Bears,* I pulled out Brinton Turkle's *Deep in the Forest,* a wordless version of the same story with a slight twist—a little bear visits the empty home of a human family. I told Dominic that this book had no words, but we could talk about the story in the pictures. Much to my surprise, when I opened to the title page, he pointed to the publisher's name and emphatically informed me that those were words!

When my own children were three and four, they spontaneously began to "read along" with me when we came to refrains and other repeated language patterns in familiar books. I had made no attempt to teach them to read, and they could not identify individual words in print other than their own names. Their memory for text, however, served them well once they went to school, because they learned to connect the language they recited to the print on the page.

Parents and teachers of preschool, kindergarten, and first-grade children can help them develop naturally as readers by providing them with many, many books with *predictable* language patterns they can repeat easily. Be sure to read your children's favorites again and again because they will naturally start to memorize and repeat chunks of language, and this memorization will help them when they are ready to pay attention to the words in print. Two irresistable gems that encourage children to join in on repeated phrases are *The Chick and the Duckling* (Mirra Ginsburg and Jose Aruego) and *Just like Daddy* (Frank Asch). Folktales like *The Gingerbread Boy* (Paul Galdone) provide longer stretches of repeated text. There are many different ways for books to be predictable. Look for books with refrains and other repeated language patterns, familiar rhymes and songs, and commonly used sequences like the days of the week.

Too Easy or Too Hard?

Once children learn to read stories like these, parents and teachers often wonder how to figure out if other books are too easy or too hard. From my own experience, I think that adults worry too much about readability levels and as a result we often limit our children to books that are too easy for them. Interest is a much better guide to what we should make available and readers will rise to the task of gathering information they find important. Most publishers provide some indication of a book's audience, either by age or grade level or readability level, which can be very helpful while you are learning more about books. The more you read and notice what appeals to children, however, the less you will need to rely on those guides.

To help you out, though, I will talk about some books that can be arranged approximately in order of difficulty. I have already mentioned easy readers, which are similar to the kinds of stories found at the primer (beginning) and first and second reader levels (first grade) of instructional reading series. Start with some of the well loved series, such as Else Holmelund Minarik's *Little Bear* and others in the series, Arnold Lobel's *Frog and Toad Are Friends* and other books in that series, and Cynthia Rylant's *Henry and Mudge and The Bedtime Thumps* and other Henry and Mudge favorites.

Other books newly independent readers find appealing are funny stories and books about children like themselves. Many of these books are heavily illustrated but have longer texts than most picture books and the previously mentioned easy readers. "Nate the Great," boy detective, is a hit with second graders in his many adventures by Marjorie Weinman Sharmat. Second graders also love the comical

Amelia Bedelia books by Peggy Parish because they quickly pick up on the double meanings in the language that lead Amelia Bedelia to interpret instructions in her own unique way. Who else but Amelia Bedelia would sprinkle a box of dusting powder over the furniture after reading instructions to "dust the furniture?"

Other illustrated storybooks for readers looking for something a little more challenging than the easy readers include James Howe's *Pinky and Rex and the Spelling Bee* and other books in the series, and *Harold and Chester in Hot Fudge* and other stories about the Monroe family. Barbara Porte has written a number of books about a typical boy, Harry, and episodes from his daily life, including *Harry's Dog* and *Harry's Visit.* Each is filled with colorful illustrations, but the stories appeal to school-age children who want to read about kids like themselves.

Readers will soon be able to tackle "real" chapter books that have more print than pictures. Look for books in which each chapter is a mini-story containing a complete episode. A few favorites in this category are Ann Cameron's collections of *The Stories Julian Tells,* Johanna Hurwitz's books, *Aldo Applesauce* and *Russell and Elisa,* and Patricia Reilly Giff's *The Beast in Ms. Rooney's Room* (and other Polk Street School books).

Next, look for longer chapter books like Beverly Cleary's Ramona books, Johanna Hurwitz' *Class Clown,* Michael Bond's Paddington Bear books, and Astrid Lindgren's Pippi Longstocking books. A number of writers, well-known for their books for older children, have written chapter books within the reach of second and most third grade readers (for suggestions, check the bibliography at the end of this article). Children who can read these books are also ready for Jean Fritz's entertaining, but carefully researched biographies of Benjamin Franklin (*What's the Big Idea, Ben Franklin?*), Christopher Columbus (*Where Do You Think You're Going, Christopher Columbus?*), and other historical figures.

Making Books Part of the Curriculum

I have already talked about the importance of reading aloud every day to children of all ages. It is also essential to provide time and space for children to read by themselves every day at school and at home. In addition, there are many other ways to incorporate literature into the curriculum as you learn more about children's literature. Begin by thinking about ways other than asking questions to encourage children to respond to stories they like, either as individuals or in groups. Possibilities include many forms of writings, drama, and art. Students can make story maps, comparison charts of different versions of folktales, and construct their own museums of artifacts from stories. They can write about something that deeply moves them, or they can collect favorite poems and display them with their own illustrations. To help you get started, I will describe some ways several different teachers have used literature in their classrooms.

1. Create a personalized class version of *Mary Wore Her Red Dress* (Merle Peek), by asking each student to tell about what he or she is wearing. The teacher could take notes on chart paper and later rewrite each sentence in a big book. Students can illustrate their own page. The book can then be used for large or small group reading.

2. Capitalize on a unique situation. When a second grade teacher was on medical leave for several weeks, the substitute introduced the class to Harry Allard and James Marshall's *Miss Nelson Is Missing* and *Miss Nelson Is Back.* They thought the books were quite funny and realized they could use their imaginations to write their own variation called *Ms. Thomas Is Missing.* When Ms. Thomas returned, she was very amused by the book written about her and delighted by their progress as readers, writers, and illustrators.

3. Use a book as a springboard for trying out roles through drama. A second grade teacher read *Dr. DeSoto,* William Steig's book about a mouse dentist who must decide if it would be safe to treat a fox with a toothache. Instead of finishing the story, she stopped before the mouse decided, and asked some students to take the roles of each character and dramatize how the story might unfold. There was no script and no rehearsal; rather, the students spontaneously took on the language and mannerisms of their characters. Afterwards, the teacher reread the story from start to finish.

4. Sometimes a story inspires a class to learn more about a subject. A third grade teacher had been reading aloud Farley Mowat's *Owls in the Family,* the humorous adventure of Wol and Weeps, two owls from Saskatchewan. The students had many questions about owls, their habits and habitats, so the teacher asked the school librarian to recommend some other books. One was *An Owl in the House,* a factual account by naturalist Bernd Heinrich of how he found and cared for a stranded great horned owlet. The librarian also recommended *If the Owl Calls Again,* a collection of owl poems selected by Myra Cohn Livingston. One thing led to another, and soon an entire unit of study evolved from the reading of one book.

Learning More, Keeping Up

Once you have discovered a few new books, you will probably want to learn more! Fortunately, you are in good company because many other people who love children's literature and teaching are writing about their experiences in books and journals. Ask your librarian to find out what is available for you to borrow. Parents might want to take a look at Jim Trelease's *The Read-Aloud Handbook,* Betsy Hearne's *Choosing Books for Children,* Nancy Larrick's *A Parent's Guide to Children's Reading,* and Denny Taylor and Dorothy Strickland's *Family Storybook Reading.*

For teachers, I recommend *Children's Literature in the Classroom: Weaving Charlotte's Web* (edited by Janet Hickman and Bernice Cullinan), a collection of articles by many of Charlotte Huck's students. Two other helpful books are Nancy Larrick's *Let's Do a Poem* and *Talking About Books* (edited by Kathy Gnagey Short and Kathryn Mitchell Pierce). I also suggest taking a look at three journals that focus on connecting children and literature in the classroom. *The WEB* (Wonderfully Exciting Books)* features book reviews and a thematic web of classroom-based ideas for linking literature and the curriculum. *Book Links* features annotated bibliographies on related topics and interviews with writers and illustrators. *The New Advocate* features book reviews and articles about literature and classrooms. No matter which path you take, you have begun to discover, in the words of poet Lee Bennett Hopkins, "Good Books, Good Times!"

References and Other Readings on the Topic

Books

Aliki. (1988). *Digging up dinosaurs.* New York: HarperCollins.

Aliki. (1983). *A medieval feast.* New York: Crowell.

Allard, Harry. (1977). *Miss Nelson is missing.* Illus. by James Marshall. Boston: Houghton Mifflin.

Allard, Harry. (1982). *Miss Nelson is back.* Illus. by James Marshall. Boston: Houghton Mifflin.

Asch, Frank. (1981). *Just like Daddy.* Englewood Cliffs, NJ: Prentice-Hall.

Bond, Michael. (1973). *Paddington Bear.* New York: Random.

Brett, Jan. (1987). *Goldilocks and the three bears.* New York: Dodd, Mead.

Brown, Marcia. (1957). *The three billy goats gruff.* San Diego: Harcourt Brace Jovanovich.

Brown, Marcia. (1954). *Cinderella.* New York: Scribner's.

Bunting, Eve. (1991). *Fly away home.* Illus. by Ronald Himler. New York: Clarion.

Burningham, John. (1987). *John Patrick Norman McHennessy: The boy who was always late.* New York: Crown.

Cameron, Ann. (1989). *The stories Julian tells.* New York: Knopf. (See other books about Julian.)

Carle, Eric. (1984). *The very busy spider.* New York: Putnam.

Christelow, Eileen. (1989). *Five little monkeys jumping on the bed.* New York: Clarion.

Cleary, Beverly. (1981). *Ramona Quimby, age 8.* Morrow. (See other books about Ramona.)

Climo, Shirley. (1989). *The Egyptian Cinderella.* Illus. by Ruth Heller. New York: Crowell.

Cole, Joanna. (1986). *The magic school bus at the waterworks.* Illus. by Bruce Degen. New York: Scholastic.

Crews, Donald. (1991). *Bigmama's.* New York: Greenwillow.

de Paola, Tomie. (1985). *Tomie DePaola's Mother Goose.* New York: Putnam.

de Paola, Tomie. (1975). *Strega Nona.* Englewood Cliffs, NJ: Prentice-Hall.

Ehlert, Lois. (1990). *Feathers for lunch.* San Diego: Harcourt Brace Jovanovich.

Fox, Mem. (1987). *Hattie and the fox.* Illus. by Patricia Mullins. New York: Bradbury.

Fritz, Jean. (1976). *What's the big idea, Ben Franklin?* Illus. by Margot Tomes. New York: Coward.

Fritz, Jean. (1980). *Where do you think you're going, Christopher Columbus?* Illus. by Margot Tomes. New York: Putnam.

Gag, Wanda. (1928). *Millions of cats.* New York: Coward.

Galdone, Paul. (1975). *The gingerbread boy.* New York: Clarion.

Gibbons, Gail. (1985). *The milk makers.* New York: Macmillan.

Gibbons, Gail. (1990). *How a house is built.* New York: Holiday House.

Giblin, James Cross. (1982). *Chimney sweeps.* Illus. by Margot Tomes. New York: HarperCollins.

Giff, Patricia. (1984). *The beast in Ms. Rooney's room.* New York: Dell Yearling. (See also other books about the kids at Polk Street School).

Ginsburg, Mirra. (1982). *Across the stream.* Illus. by Nancy Tafuri. New York: Greenwillow.

Ginsburg, Mirra. (1972). *The chick and the duckling.* Illus. by Jose and Ariane Aruego. New York: Macmillan.

Hearne, Betsy. (1990). *Choosing books for children.* New York: Delacorte.

Heide, Florence Parry and Judith Heide Gilliland. (1990). *The day of Ahmed's secret.* Illus. by Ted Lewin. Lothrop, Lee & Shepard.

Heinrich, Bernd. (1990). *An owl in the house.* Adapted by Alice Calaprice. Boston: Little Brown.

Henkes, Kevin. (1991). *Chrysanthemum.* New York: Greenwillow.

Hickman, Janet and Bernice Cullinan, eds. (1989). *Children's literature in the classroom: Weaving Charlotte's web.* Norwood: MA: Christopher Gordon.

Hirschi, Ron. (1991). *Loon lake.* Photographs by Daniel Cox. New York: Cobblehill Books.

Hoffman, Mary. (1991). *Amazing Grace.* Illus. by Caroline Binch. New York: Dial.

Hopkins, Lee Bennett, selector. (1991). *On the farm.* Illus. by Laurel Molk. Boston: Little Brown.

Hopkins, Lee Bennett, selector. (1990). *Good books, good times!* New York: HarperCollins.

Howard, Elizabeth Fitzgerald. (1991). *Aunt Flossie's hats (and crab cakes later).* Illus. by James Ransome. New York: Clarion.

Howe, James. (1991). *Pinky and Rex and the spelling bee.* Illus. by Melissa Sweet. New York: Atheneum. (See other books about Pinky and Rex.)

Howe, James. (1990). *Harold and Chester in hot fudge.* Illus. by Leslie Morrill. New York: Morrow. (See other books about the Monroe family.)

Huck, Charlotte. (1989). *Princess Furball.* Illus. by Anita Lobel. New York: Greenwillow.

Hurwitz, Johanna. (1979). *Aldo Applesauce.* New York: Morrow.

Hurwitz, Johanna. (1987). *Class clown.* New York: Morrow.

Hurwitz, Johanna. (1987). *Russell and Elisa.* New York: Morrow.

Hutchins, Pat. (1971). *Titch.* New York: Macmillan.

Hutchins, Pat. (1968). *Rosie's walk.* New York: Macmillan.

Jonas, Ann. (1983). *Round trip.* New York: Greenwillow.

Larrick, Nancy. (1991). *Let's do a poem! Introducing Poetry to Children.* New York: Delacorte.

Larrick, Nancy. (1982). *A parent's guide to children's reading.* 5th ed. New York: Bantam.

Lasky, Kathryn. (1990). *Dinosaur dig.* Photographs by Christopher Knight. New York: Morrow.

Lindgren, Astrid. (1950). *Pippi Longstocking.* New York: Viking Penguin.

Livingston, Myra Cohn, selector. (1990). *If the owl calls again: A collection of owl poems.* Woodcuts by Antonio Frasconi. New York: McElderry Books.

Lobel, Arnold. (1970). *Frog and Toad are friends.* New York: HarperCollins. (See other books about Frog and Toad.)

Louie, Ai-Ling, reteller. (1982). *Yeh Shen: A Cinderella story from China.* Illus. by Ed Young. New York: Philomel.

Lurie, Alison, reteller. (1980). *Clever Gretchen and other forgotten folktales.* Illus. by Margot Tomes. New York: Crowell.

Macaulay, David. (1990). *Black and white.* Boston: Houghton Mifflin.

Martin, Bill, Jr. and John Archambault. (1989). *Chicka chicka boom boom.* Illus. by Lois Ehlert. New York: Simon and Schuster.

McKissack, Patricia. (1986). *Flossie and the fox.* Illus. by Rachel Isadora. New York: Dial.

Merriam, Eve. (1985). *Blackberry ink.* Illus. by Hans Wilhelm. New York: Morrow.

Minarik, Else Holmelund. (1957). *Little bear.* Illus. by Maurice Sendak. New York: HarperCollins. (See other books about Little Bear.)

Mowat, Farley. (1961). *Owls in the family.* Boston: Little Brown.

Parish, Peggy. (1963). *Amelia Bedelia.* Illus. by Fritz Siebel. HarperCollins. (See other books about Amelia Bedelia.)

Peek, Merle. (1985). *Mary wore her red dress.* New York: Clarion.

Polacco, Patricia. (1990). *Thunder cake.* New York: Philomel.

Porte, Barbara. (1984). *Harry's dog.* New York: Greenwillow. (See other books about Harry.)

Porte, Barbara. (1983). *Harry's visit.* New York: Greenwillow.

Ringgold, Faith. (1991). *Tar beach.* New York: Crown.

Rosen, Michael. (1987). *We're going on a bear hunt.* Illus. by Helen Oxenbury. New York: McElderry Books.

Rounds, Glen. (1990). *I know an old lady who swallowed a fly.* New York: Holiday House.

Rylant, Cynthia. (1991). *Henry and Mudge and the bedtime thumps.* Illus. by Sucie Stevenson. New York: Bradbury. (See other books about Henry and Mudge.)

Sendak, Maurice. (1963). *Where the wild things are.* New York: HarperCollins.

Sharmat, Marjorie Weinman. (1972). *Nate the great.* Illus. by Marc Simont. New York: Coward. (See other books about Nate the Great.)

Short, Kathy Gnagey and Kathryn Mitchell Pierce, eds. (1990). *Talking about books: Creating literate communities.* Portsmouth, NH: Heinemann.

Steig, William. (1982). *Dr. DeSoto.* New York: Farrar, Straus and Giroux.

Taylor, Denny and Dorothy S. Strickland. (1986). *Family storybook reading.* Portsmouth, NH: Heinemann.

Trelease, Jim. (1989). *The read-aloud handbook.* 2nd ed. New York: Penguin.

Turkle, Brinton. (1976). *Deep in the forest.* New York: Dutton.

Van Allsburg, Chris. (1981). *Jumanji.* Boston: Houghton Mifflin.

Wiesner, David. (1991). *Tuesday.* New York: Clarion.

White, E. B. (1952). *Charlotte's web.* New York: HarperCollins.

Williams, Vera and Jennifer Williams. (1988). *Stringbean's trip to the shining sea.* New York: Greenwillow.

Zemach, Margot. (1988). *The three little pigs.* New York: Farrar, Straus and Giroux.

Journals

Book Links (6 issues per year). American Library Association. 50 E. Huron St., Chicago, IL 60611. (1-800-545-2433). ISSN 1055-4742.

The New Advocate (4 issues per year). Christopher-Gordon Publishers, 480 Washington Street, Norwood, MA 02602. ISSN 0895-1381.

The WEB (Wonderfully Exciting Books) (3 issues per year; back issues available for purchase). The Ohio State University, 200 Ramseyer Hall, 29 W. Woodruff, Columbus, OH 43210.

Additional Resources

The following chapter books are suggested for third grade students for independent reading and class read-alouds. They also serve as an introduction to authors who usually write for older children.

Babbitt, Natalie. (1970). *Knee-knock rise.* New York: Farrar, Straus and Giroux.

Brooks, Bruce. (1991). *Everywhere.* New York: HarperCollins.

Byars, Betsy. (1991). *The seven treasure hunts.* New York: HarperCollins.

Cameron, Ann. (1988). *The most beautiful place in the world.* New York: Knopf.

Conrad, Pam. (1988). *Staying nine.* New York: HarperCollins.

Fleischman, Sid. (1986). *The whipping boy.* New York: Greenwillow.

Gardiner, John Reynolds. (1980). *Stone fox.* New York: HarperCollins.

Greenfield, Eloise. (1974). *Sister.* New York: HarperCollins.

Hamilton, Virginia. (1967). *Zeely.* New York: Macmillan.

Hunter, Mollie. (1988). *The mermaid summer.* New York: HarperCollins.

King-Smith, Dick. (1983). *Babe the gallant pig.* New York: Crown.

Little, Jean. (1985). *Lost and found.* New York: Viking Kestrel.

MacLachlan, Patricia. (1985). *Sarah, plain and tall.* New York: HarperCollins.

Smith, Janice Lee. (1990). *The turkeys' side of it: Adam Joshua's Thanksgiving.* New York: HarperCollins.

Stolz, Mary. (1991). *Go fish.* Illus. by Pat Cummings. New York: HarperCollins.

Stolz, Mary. (1991). *King Emmett the Second.* New York: Greenwillow.

Taylor, Mildred. (1990). *Mississippi bridge.* New York: Dial.

Tolan, Stephen S. (1991). *Marcy Hooper and the greatest treasure in the world.* New York: Morrow.

Walsh, Jill Paton. (1982). *The green book.* New York: Farrar, Straus and Giroux.

Walter, Mildred Pitts. (1986). *Justin and the best biscuits in the world.* New York: Lothrop, Lee & Shepard.

Chapter 7

Linking Children to the Past through Historical Fiction

Susan S. Lehr

S usan Lehr teaches and conducts research in the Department of Education at Skidmore College, Saratoga Springs, New York. Her doctoral research at Ohio State focused on children's understanding of theme in stories.

Hannah stepped out the door of her grandmother's Manhattan apartment and found herself in the middle of a Polish village in 1942. Hannah is a child of the modern era and she is a bored and unwilling participant at her family's Passover meal. When she opens the door to invite Elijah in, she leaves the familiar and travels back in time and experiences her family's Jewish history firsthand. *The Devil's Arithmetic* by Jane Yolen is an excellent example of the well written historical fiction available for children. Historical fiction is one genre that children will not typically read unless an interest is fostered by parents and teachers. Yet, reading historical fiction to and with children can make the past available and relevant.

Authors have become rather innovative in pulling children into historical fiction. Like Yolen, they understand their readers and are not afraid to experiment with fresh ways of enticing children into stories of the past. Thoughtful teachers and parents who challenge learners with well written literature provide ample time to read and discuss ideas in books. Additionally, children can explore and analyze plot, theme, character, setting, and other literary elements through meaningful projects and writing about books from a variety of perspectives.

In this chapter I will explore what well written historical fiction is by providing current examples. I will also explain how parents, teachers, and children can create challenging responses to this rich literature by creating jackdaws.

What Is Historical Fiction?

Children typically explore history through a tightly defined social studies curriculum. History is a part of that curriculum which also includes geography, anthropology, sociology, and political science. What textbooks offer is a concise, detached view of the world; what they frequently lack is passion and understanding.

Historical fiction can take children into the mind of a young child moving west in 1868. Literature can show how her mother stirred the cornmeal mush over an open fire, how the dust tasted as the wagon rolled over the plains, the excitement of watching a dugout being carved from sod, the feel of watching thousands of crickets eat an entire crop of wheat in minutes. Why would a family leave the comfort and safety of Boston to move west? Historical fiction puts children directly in touch with the past. Rather then merely *telling,* well written historical fiction *shows.*

Authors who have lived through an era write convincing stories. From the past, Laura Ingalls Wilder's "Little House" Series rings true because the author was there and experienced the westward expansion firsthand. Authors also take children on journeys into the not so distant past and reveal history which is still occurring. *Journey to Jo'Burg* by Beverly Naidoo and *Paperbird* by Maretha Maartens provide a glimpse of life in South Africa under the system of apartheid in the 1970s and 1980s by people who lived under that system. Through the eyes of children we experience living in a hut with no electricity or water. We visit Mma in Johannesburg, spend the night in Soweto, watch the police arrest a man without a pass. Minfong Ho writes convincingly of Thailand and Cambodia and the power of friendship even amidst the chaos of a refugee camp in *The Clay Marble* because she was there. We get her firsthand view of the terror and confusion of warring factions and the flight of a family from Cambodia to Thailand. Allan Baillies's *Little Brother* is a superb book for comparing with *The Clay Marble.* Vithy's escape from a forced labor camp in Cambodia and flight to Thailand is a gripping tale of an 11 year old's experience during Pol Pot's regime and is based on a true story. Both stories take us to Cambodia and we experience firsthand what life is like for people who have been denied peace and freedom.

What makes these books work effectively with children are their strong sense of narrative or story and their historical accuracy. The story comes first; historical fact is an integrated backdrop and never overwhelms the story. Books that preach or parade facts are not usually effective pieces of literature. Mollie Hunter, Scotland's foremost children's author, says that an author should know a historical period so intimately that he or she could reach into a person's pocket and tell you what would be found. The stories she writes of ancient Scotland are based on years of research and make ancient times come to life for children because they are about children facing problems and dilemmas in a different era.

A newer book, *Stepping on the Cracks* by Mary Downing Hahn, incorporates tough social issues with a picture of life in 1945 in a small U.S. town. "Step on a crack, break Hitler's back" is a chant two girls sing as they skip down the street. The pain of losing a brother during the war parallels the story of an army deserter. The girls also face familiar problems dealing with the sixth grade bully and discovering he is an abused child. Tough issues. Tough decisions. Children recently faced similar issues as they watched parents go off to war in the Gulf. Hahn's tone is stark but hopeful. She gives glimpses of harshness but never overwhelms, because she remembers who her readers are and offers a hopeful kind of truth.

Historical fiction that shows the universality of childhood creates bridges between the children of yesterday and today. Children see that the characters and settings are different but the themes are common. One can also experience diversity firsthand and develop respect for other cultures. Leading children to well written historical fiction is the first step in the process. Beginning to recognize names of children's authors who write effectively and engagingly will make for functional trips to libraries and bookstores. (See the bibliography for a list of authors and titles by topic.)

Responding to Literature

Responding to well written books is a critical second step. Research indicates strongly that comprehension is directly affected by a reader's background knowledge. Reading widely and deeply, as children's language scholar James Britton suggests, will improve your child's ability to comprehend written materials, because what a child brings to the act of reading is as important as the actual reading event. Reading quality historical fiction will expand a child's knowledge about the world. For example, Jan Judson has written about the experiences of a young Blackfoot Indian girl living in 1837 in *Sweetgrass*. Through her eyes we live through a raid, a smallpox epidemic, and experience the harshness of winter as food becomes scarce. Hudson doesn't tell about life in the village, she takes us into the tipi and we see what Sweetgrass sees.

One of the easiest ways of responding to books is through oral discussion. Talking about the ideas in a book helps focus the child on the meaning in the book. Listening to how a child feels about a particular character's actions, about an event in the story, about the sequence of events, and about the book's themes strengthens the child's understanding of the book as well as the historical era in which it was written. Oral response is an essential part of developing critical thinking skills. How does one begin?

Open-ended questions should invite children to explore the book's meaning. Being right or being wrong should not be the focus of any conversation. Children will become risk takers only if they feel safe in offering their views, their construction of meaning. If a child has a view that differs widely from your own, be accepting. Don't feel that deviation from what you consider obvious needs correction. It's okay if children aren't always right. It takes a while to sort through historical information. As adults, we've had extended exposure to the scope of history and over the years have built up considerable knowledge about history. Your children are just beginning.

Critical thinkers develop by becoming risk takers, by exploring meaning, by setting forth tentative ideas. Open-ended questions encourage this. "Why do you think . . . ?" "What could the main character have done when . . . ?" "What surprised you about the ending?" You may ask your child to find a conversation in the book to support his or her idea.

Discussion is a critical part of understanding a book. This is your child's opportunity to explore new ideas, to consider other perspectives and it is an important step before developing written responses or creating projects based on historical events. Discussing the book is a necessary prelude leading to other types of response to literature. In the following section I will explore how children might respond to books by making jackdaws.

What Is a Jackdaw?

A jackdaw is a bird from New Zealand similar to the American grackle. This bird is a collector of bright colorful objects. Susan Hepler defines a classroom *jackdaw* as a collection of artifacts gathered or made which explore a historical period. After children read and discuss historical fiction, they might want to respond to the book through jackdaws. Jackdaws encourage children to research the historical time frame of a book and to consider characters' actions and motives. They also encourage children to become immersed in the "culture" of an era.

Creating a jackdaw for a book allows children to combine writing, art, and research. Samples of items that children might create include journal entries written by characters as important events of the book occur. In writing a journal entry, children can consider the character's viewpoint, thereby indicating whether they are able to assume and understand a character's perspective. Children might write newspaper reports of events in the book, thus taking a reporter's stance toward the story while focusing on summarizing events in a lively manner. It might be helpful to read several articles from your newspapers so that children can see how journalists write. You might talk about important things to include in an article. Children might choose to write letters to other characters in the book. What might they say? What effect did a particular historical event have on a character's decision about something? What happened to a character after the book ended? Based on real historical research and an understanding of the book's characters, what might plausibly happen in the time period after the book? This action entails an understanding of the book, its characters, the historical framework, and a creative component that allows children to consider the world of "what ifs." Children can accomplish this through letters or sequels. Again, the emphasis is on risk taking—an invitation to create, not a focus on right or wrong.

In jackdaws, children may also research and collect historical information about the book's era. Children may be encouraged to draw maps, chart journeys, create time lines of important events, sketch clothing, create authentic menus, include pictures of famous people, draw buildings, create a glossary of special terms unique to the book, sketch tools or other implements. Some children have created charts comparing the time period of the book to the present. How are their own lives different from those of the book's characters? Have women's roles changed? Children's? What toys or games did characters play? What was their music like? What art came out of the period? Children can conduct and tape interviews with characters. The possibilities are endless.

Children can also be encouraged to respond to a book through art. Hanging mobiles which describe and show characters, special items, or important events are attractive. Dioramas made from shoeboxes can authentically recreate in miniature a scene, a room, a town, or a critical event in the story. Giant murals can be vehicles for exploring a sequence of events through art and writing. Murals can also show scenes from daily life. Children reading novels about medieval times have sketched

Shared reading can involve many books and materials for a variety of purposes.

lifesize knights complete with armor and weapons, stained-glass windows from tissue and village scenes showing crofts in medieval times.

Children can be encouraged to prepare foods which have significance for a particular culture depicted in a story. For example, hardtack was eaten by soldiers during the Civil War, as described in *Zoar Blue* by Janet Hickman. What exactly is hardtack? A recipe in the *Little House Cookbook* revealed that flour and salt are the two main ingredients. I made hardtack as part of a jackdaw on *Zoar Blue*. Before baking I had to punch holes into the dough to release air, a basic preservation technique. Eleven years later my hardtack is still preserved and edible.

As a culminating project children can design containers to house their projects. I've seen children create covered wagons from a box, wires, and cloth; log cabins from twigs or lincoln logs; suitcases painted from cardboard boxes, and boxes adorned with maps and flags. What the containers have in common is that they reflect the book and its era. When everything is completed, encourage children to share their jackdaws at school.

Conclusion

By creating jackdaws two important goals of literary learning are achieved: choice and ownership. Children have the freedom to choose what they will explore and how they will respond. Children are invested in the reading. The jackdaws are their own and that makes learning meaningful. My work with children in a fourth grade classroom has reinforced the importance of encouraging children to make their own choices. It is easy for me as a parent or teacher to be too directive, too preoccupies with what I think is important. Children learn by making decisions and acting on them.

Central to this approach to literature and literacy is the freedom to be right. Children immersed in literature and meaningful response are active learners. They are engaged in the learning process and are intrinsically motivated. Children sharing jackdaws are fascinating to observe because there is pride in their creation and accomplishment. The difference between being a passive learner and one who chooses how to respond is the difference between being spoon-fed and becoming a lifelong reader and learner.

Bibliography of Historical Fiction

U.S. History—Colonial Period to Early 1800s

Avi. (1984). *The fighting ground*. Philadelphia: Lippincott.

———. (1990). *The true confessions of Charlotte Doyle*. New York: Orchard.

Blos, J. (1979). *A gathering of days: A New England girl's journal, 1830–32*. New York: Scribner's.

Carrick, C. (1985). *Stay away from Simon*. New York: Clarion.

———. (1988). *The elephant in the dark*. New York: Clarion.

Clapp, P. (1977). *Constance: A story of early Plymouth*. New York: Lothrop.

———. (1982). *Witches' children*. New York: Lothrop.

Collier, J. and C. (1974). *My brother Sam is dead*. New York: Four Winds.

———. (1978). *The bloody country*. New York: Four Winds.

———. (1978). *The winter hero.* New York: Four Winds.

Fleishman, P. (1990). *Saturnalia.* New York: Harper & Row.

Forbes, E. (1946). *Johnny Tremain.* Boston: Houghton Mifflin.

Fritz, J. (1960). *Brady.* New York: Coward McCann.

———. (1967). *Early thunder.* New York: Coward McCann.

———. (1989). *The great little Madison.* New York: Putnam's.

Speare, E. (1957). *Calico captive.* Boston: Houghton Mifflin.

———. (1983). *Sign of the beaver.* Boston: Houghton Mifflin.

———. (1958). *Witch of Blackbird Pond.* Boston: Houghton Mifflin.

U.S. History—Western Expansion

Blos, J. (1985). *Brothers of the heart: A story of old northwest 1837–1838.* New York: Scribner's.

Conrad, P. (1985). *Prairie songs.* New York: Harper & Row.

DeFelice, C. (1990). *Weasel.* New York: Macmillan.

Fleishman, P. (1991). *The borning room.* New York: HarperCollins.

Gipson, F. (1956). *Old Yeller.* New York: Harper.

Lampman, E. (1977). *Bargain bride.* New York: Atheneum.

Lasky, K. (1983). *Beyond the divide.* New York: Macmillan.

McClung, R. (1990). *Hugh Glass, mountain man.* New York: Morrow.

Moeri, L. (1981). *Save Queen of Sheba.* New York: Dutton.

Patterson, K. (1991). *Lyddie.* New York: Dutton.

Native Americans

Crompton, A. (1980). *The ice trail.* New York: Methuen.

Dorros, M. (1992). *Morning girl.* Westport, CT: Hyperion.

Fritz, J. (1983). *The double life of Pocahontas.* New York: Putnam.

Hickman, J. (1974). *The valley of the shadow.* New York: Macmillan.

Highwater, J. (1984). *Legend days.* New York: Harper & Row.

———. (1977). *Anpao: An American Indian odyssey.* Philadelphia: Lippincott.

Hill, K. (1990). *Toughboy and sister.* New York: McElderry.

Hobbs, W. (1989). *Bearstone.* New York: Atheneum.

Hudson, J. (1990). *Dawn rider.* New York: Philomel.

———. (1989). *Sweetgrass.* New York: Philomel.

James, J.A. (1990) *Sing for a gentle rain.* New York: Atheneum.

Keehn, S. (1991). *I am Regina.* New York: Philomel.

Kroeber, T. (1964). *Ishi, last of his tribe.* New York: Parnassus.

Levin, B. (1990). *Brother Moose.* New York: Greenwillow.

Markle, S. (1992). *The fledglings.* New York: Bantam.

O'Dell, S. (1960). *Island of the blue dolphins.* Boston: Houghton Mifflin.

———. (1970). *Sing down the moon.* Boston: Houghton Mifflin.

———. (1987). *Streams to the river, river to the sea.* New York: Fawcett.

Richter, C. (1953). *The light in the forest.* New York: Knopf.

African-American History

Armstrong, W. (1969). *Sounder.* Harper & Row.

Berry, J. (1992). *Ajeemch and his son.* New York: HarperCollins.

Collier, J. and C. (1981). *Jump ship to freedom.* New York: Delacorte.

———. (1983). *War comes to Willie Freeman.* New York: Delacorte.

———. (1984). *Who is Carrie?* New York: Delacorte.

Fox, P. (1973). *The slave dancer.* Scarsdale, NY: Bradbury.

Hamilton, V. (1988). *Anthony Burns: The defeat and triumph of a fugitive slave.* New York: Knopf.

———. (1990). *Cousins.* New York: Philomel.

———. (1983). *Willie Bea and the time the martians landed.* New York: Greenwillow.

Hurmence, B. (1982). *A girl called boy.* New York: Clarion.

O'Dell, S. (1989). *My name is not Angelica.* Boston: Houghton Mifflin.

Seabrooke, B. (1992). *The bridges of summer.* Freeport, ME: Cobblehill Dutton.

Sebestyan, O. (1979). *Words by heart.* Boston: Atlantic, Little, Brown.

Taylor, M. (1981). *Let the circle be unbroken.* New York: Dial.

———. (1990). *Mississippi bridge.* New York: Dial.

———. (1976). *Roll of thunder, hear my cry.* New York: Dial.

———. (1987). *The friendship.* New York: Dial.

———. (1987). *The gold cadillac.* New York: Dial.

———. (1975). *The song of the trees.* New York: Dial.

———. (1990). *The Road to Memphis.* New York: Dial.

Canadian History

Anderson, M. (1980). *The journey of the shadow bairns.* New York: Knopf.

Bond, N. (1988). *Another shore.* New York: McElderry.

Lunn, J. (1986). *Shadow on Hawthorne Bay.* New York: Scribner's.

———. (1981). *The root cellar.* New York: Scribner's.

Speare, E. (1957). *Calico captive.* Boston: Houghton Mifflin.

U.S. History—Civil War and After

Brink, C. (1936). *Caddie Woodlawn.* New York: Macmillan.

Clapp, P. (1986). *The tamarack tree: A novel of the siege of Vicksburg.* New York: Lothrop.

Fisher, D.C. (1972). *Understood Betsy.* New York: Holt.

Hesse, K. (1992). *Letters from Rifka.* New York: Holt.

Hickman, J. (1978). *Zoar Blue.* New York: Macmillan.

Houston, G. (1990). *Littlejim.* New York: Philomel.

Howard, E. (1990). *Sister.* New York: Atheneum.

Hunt, I. (1964). *Across five Aprils.* Chicago: Follett.

———. (1966). *Up a road slowly.* Chicago: Follett.

Keith, H. (1957). *Rifles for Watie.* New York: Crowell.

Lunn, J. (1981). *The root cellar.* New York: Scribner's.

Mayerson, E. (1990). *The cat who escaped from steerage.* New York: Scribner's.

Reeder, C. (1989). *Shades of gray.* New York: Macmillan.

Wilder, L.I. (1932). *Little house in the big woods.* New York: Harper.

Yep, L. (1977). *Dragonwings.* New York: Harper & Row.

U.S. History—Depression Era and After

Avi. (1992). *Who was that masked man, anyway?* New York: Orchard.

Cleary, B. (1988). *A girl from Yamhill.* New York: Morrow.

Cleaver, V. and B. (1969). *Where the lillies bloom.* Philadelphia: Lippincott.

Hahn, M. D. (1991). *Stepping on the cracks.* New York: Clarion.

Hickman, J. (1976). *The stones.* New York: Macmillan.

———. (1981). *The thunder pup.* New York: Macmillan.

Hunt, I. (1970). *No promises in the wind.* Chicago: Follett.

Lenski, L. (1988). *Strawberry girl.* New York: Harper & Row; Philadelphia: Lippincott, 1945.

Rawl, W. (1961). *Where the red fern grows.* New York: Doubleday.

Uchida, T. (1971). *Journey to Topaz.* New York: Scribner's.

White, R. (1988). *Sweet Holler Creek.* New York: Farrar, Straus, Giroux.

———. (1992). *Weeping willow.* New York: Farrar, Straus, Giroux.

European History

Conlon-McKenna, M. (1990). *Under the hawthorn tree.* New York: Holiday House.

de Angeli, M. (1949). *The door in the wall.* New York: Doubleday.

Haugaard, E. (1978). *Cromwell's boy.* Boston: Houghton Mifflin.

Hunter, M. (1969). *The ghosts of Glencoe.* New York: Funk and Wagnalls.

———. (1974). *The stronghold.* New York: Harper & Row.

———. (1981). *You never knew her as I did!* New York: Harper & Row.

Kelly, E. (1966). *The trumpeter of Krakow.* (rev. ed.) New York: Macmillan (1928).

Konigsburg, E.L. (1973). *A proud taste for Scarlet and Miniver.* New York: Atheneum.

Lunn, J. (1987). *Shadow in Hawthorn Bay.* New York: Scribner's.

Skurzynski, G. (1979). *What happened in Hamelin.* New York: Four Winds.

Sutcliff, R. (1954). *Eagle of the ninth.* New York: Walck.

———. (1959). *The lantern bearers.* New York: Walck.

European History—World War Two Era and After

Frank, A. (1967). *Anne Frank: The diary of a young girl.* New York: Doubleday.

Hautzig, E. (1968). *The endless steppe: Growing up in Siberia.* New York: Cromwell.

Kerr, J. (1972). *When Hitler stole pink rabbit.* New York: Coward McCann.

Lowry, L. (1989). *Number the stars.* Boston: Houghton Mifflin.

McSwigan, M. (1942). *Snow treasure.* New York: Dutton.

Orgel, D. (1978). *The devil in Vienna.* New York: Dial.

Reiss, J. (1976). *The journey back.* New York: Cromwell.

———. (1972). *The upstairs room.* New York: Cromwell.

Richter, H. (1970). *Friedrich.* New York: Holt.

Sender, R. (1986). *The cage.* New York: Macmillan.

Siegel, A. (1981). *Upon the head of the goat: A childhood in Hungary, 1939–1944.* New York: Farrar, Straus.

Asian and Australian History.

Baillie, A. (1992). *Little brother.* New York: Viking.

Chang, M. and R. (1990). *In the eye of war.* New York: McElderry.

Choi, S.N. (1991). *Year of impossible goodbyes.* Boston: Houghton Mifflin.

Fritz, J. (1982). *Homesick: My own story.* New York: Putnam's.

Ho, M. (1991). *The clay marble.* New York: Farrar, Straus, Giroux.

———. (1990). *Rice without rain.* New York: Farrar, Straus, Giroux.

Paterson, K. (1974). *Of nightingales that weep.* New York: Avon.

———. (1983). *Rebels of the heavenly kingdom.* New York: Lodestar.

———. (1973). *The sign of the chrysanthemum.* New York: Avon.

———. (1975). *The master puppeteer.* New York: Avon.

Vander Els, B. (1985). *The bomber's moon.* New York: Farrar, Straus.

Ward, G. (1991). *Wandering girl.* New York: Holt.

Whelan, G. (1992). *Goodbye, Vietnam.* New York: Knopf.

Middle East and African History Twentieth Century

Cambell, E. (1992). *The year of the leopard song.* New York: Harcourt Brace Jovanovich.

Case, D. (1991). *Love David.* New York: Lodestar.

Dickinson, P. (1992). *AK.* New York: Delacorte.

Gordon, S. (1987). *Waiting for the rain.* New York: Orchard.

Jones, T. (1979). *Go well, stay well.* New York: Harper & Row.

Laird, E. (1992). *Kiss the dust.* New York: Dutton.

Levitin, S. (1987). *The return.* New York: Atheneum.

Maartens, M. (1991). *Paperbird.* New York: Clarion.

Naidoo, B. (1990). *Chain of fire.* Boston: Lippincott.

———. (1985). *Journey to Jo'burg.* Philadelphia: Lippincott.

Rochman, H. (1988). *Somehow tenderness survives.* New York: Harper & Row.

Sachs, M. (1992). *Themba.* New York: Lodestar.

Staples, S.F. (1989). *Shabanu.* New York: Knopf.

Chapter 8

Paired Reading:
A Positive Approach
to Parent–Child
Reading Time

Louisa Kozey

L ouisa Kozey is on the Education faculty at the University of Regina in Regina, Saskatchewan, Canada. She is a past chairperson of the Parents and Reading Committee of the International Reading Association.

D oes your child tend to read with little or no expression—word-by-word rather than in meaningful phrases and sentences? Does he typically struggle with reading and want to do something else after a short time? Or does she want to read materials that are more difficult than she can handle on her own? These are fairly common behaviors for beginning readers and others who have not yet learned to read well. Like many parents, you may have the time and motivation, but do not know how to encourage and help your child with reading.

Paired Reading is one way of helping the beginning reader experience the joys of fluent reading right from the start, even when the reading materials are somewhat difficult. The procedure is a positive one that guides parents in providing support in predictable and motivating ways. It enables the child to read for the story rather than just recognizing words. Reading with continuity, expression, and understanding, and doing so in a tension-free environment are emphasized. Paired Reading requires the parent and child to contract to reading on a regular basis, thereby ensuring much practice in reading. Typically, with more practice, there will be greater satisfaction in reading and more growth in reading ability.

What is Paired Reading?

Paired Reading is a procedure for a parent or another more advanced reader to help the novice reader practice reading. This approach to reading together incorporates several kinds of support for the child. It includes modeling of fluent reading by the parent, helping with difficult words, talking about ideas in the passage, and praising the child's ideas and accomplishments during reading. All of these features of Paired Reading are designed to encourage the child to read and to enjoy reading.

Paired Reading helps to build not only a lifelong love of books and reading, but also stronger bonds between parent and child. In short, Paired Reading can make reading time spent with your child more enjoyable and more productive for both of you.

How does one go about doing Paired Reading? Using a book chosen by the child and deliberately matching the child's pace, the parent reads along with the child. At first, the parent and child read aloud together with the parent following the pace of the child. When the child has difficulty in reading what's on the page—misses an important word, says another word in place of what's on the page, or hesitates for about five seconds—the parent simply says the correct word. Then the child says the word correctly, and the parent and child continue reading aloud together. Prompts given in this low key manner are expected by the child and hopefully are accepted as help, not as criticism. Because there is little interruption of the reading and no fuss about what the child doesn't know, the child can maintain focus on making sense of what's being read.

In the next stage, if the child wants to read aloud alone she signals the parent to read along silently. A tap on the page or a nudge works well. Just as in reading aloud in unison in the first stage, whenever help is needed, the parent calmly says the word, the child reads the word correctly, and then the parent once again reads aloud with the child. When the child wants to read alone again, he signals the parent to be quiet, and the parent immediately becomes a silent reader following the print, ready to help whenever help is needed.

Discussion of the book is important in all stages of the reading session. Parents should encourage discussion just before reading, at intervals during reading of the book, and after reading. Prereading discussion might include:

- why the child has chosen the book;
- what the child expects to happen in the story based on the cover, title, and pictures.

Discussion during the reading may concern:

- what the child thinks about events or characters (likes, dislikes, humor, etc.);
- similar experiences the child has had, heard about, or read about;
- general predictions of what will happen next.

After reading, discussion may include responses to the story like one or more of the following:

- likes, dislikes (or appreciation or doubts) and questions about events, characters, the ending, the illustrations, the author, etc.;
- speculation about what would have happened if some event or character had been changed;
- similarities or differences in comparing the story to others read or one's own experiences;
- other books on the topic or by the same author that might be read (if this one was particularly enjoyed).

Discussion can usually be encouraged by accepting and praising the child's ideas often—letting the child know through gentle hugs and your comments that his or her likes and ideas are being heard and are interesting and worthwhile.

Paired Reading sessions should be scheduled as a regular commitment, usually five or six days a week, 10–15 minutes a day. Figure 8.1, a summary of the steps of the Paired Reading procedure, can be used for quick reference the first few times you use the approach.

Paired Reading has been used successfully with readers of many ages in a number of countries. Though started in Britain as a technique for parents and teachers to help children having considerable difficulty in learning to read, it's been used with entire classes of young readers, and with adult literacy learners as well as children. Sometimes students who are better readers, either in the same class or from a higher grade, have served as the helpers in Paired Reading projects.

There is substantial evidence that the Paired Reading technique contributes to positive reading attitudes and increased reading ability. After studying its use with over two thousand children, Keith Topping and Marjorie Whiteley (1990) have reported success with Paired Reading school projects for classes at various grade levels, most often with parents as reading partners. Most of those taking part in the

History and Success of Paired Reading

Figure 8.1
PAIRED READING PROCEDURE

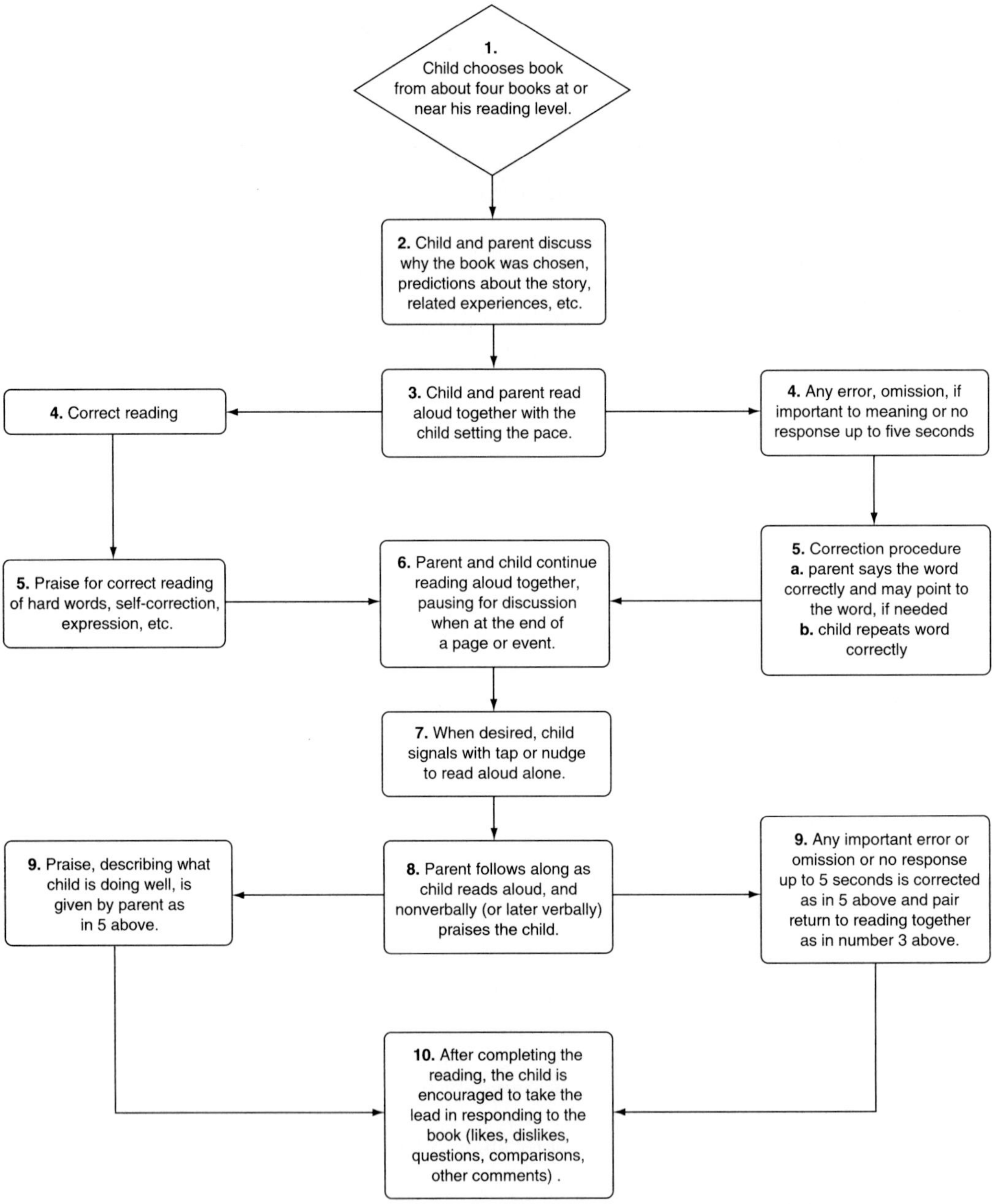

1.
Child chooses book from about four books at or near his reading level.

2. Child and parent discuss why the book was chosen, predictions about the story, related experiences, etc.

3. Child and parent read aloud together with the child setting the pace.

4. Correct reading

4. Any error, omission, if important to meaning or no response up to five seconds

5. Praise for correct reading of hard words, self-correction, expression, etc.

6. Parent and child continue reading aloud together, pausing for discussion when at the end of a page or event.

5. Correction procedure
a. parent says the word correctly and may point to the word, if needed
b. child repeats word correctly

7. When desired, child signals with tap or nudge to read aloud alone.

9. Praise, describing what child is doing well, is given by parent as in 5 above.

8. Parent follows along as child reads aloud, and nonverbally (or later verbally) praises the child.

9. Any important error or omission or no response up to 5 seconds is corrected as in 5 above and pair return to reading together as in number 3 above.

10. After completing the reading, the child is encouraged to take the lead in responding to the book (likes, dislikes, questions, comparisons, other comments) .

Adapted from K. Topping, 1987.

six- to eight-week Paired Reading projects said that the children gained greater confidence as readers; read more and a wider variety of materials; enjoyed reading more, and were more interested in and willing to read; read more fluently, more accurately, and with more expression. Some parents noted improvements in their children's behavior, particularly in cases where there were behavior problems. Many parents reported more positive relationships with their children, and often the children said they were getting along with their parent(s) better. In a study of students in the third grade in a Canadian school, this author used a similar questionnaire and obtained similar positive results.

Topping and Whiteley also had the children complete standardized reading tests before and just after the Paired Reading projects. Their scores on these tests showed that the children achieved an average of three times the normal gain in accuracy of reading words and four times the normal gain in reading comprehension. Scores on another set of reading tests, given seventeen or more weeks later, indicated that the children who had had Paired Reading experiences were still reading better than what would have been expected without that special reading experience. In other words, for most children Paired Reading did seem to boost their reading ability, and this gain was maintained.

Getting Started

Paired Reading is a suitable strategy for reading with a child who recognizes enough words to read most of an "early reader" or "easy" book. If your child can recognize only a very few words, it may be better to read to your child instead of trying to do Paired Reading too soon. Encourage your child to discuss what's being read and to chime in on parts she has memorized or when she recognizes a word, and start Paired Reading when she knows enough words so that she can really read. Some children may be ready for Paired Reading sooner, but for most it seems better to try this approach when your child is near the end of Grade 1 or even in Grade 2 or 3. The technique is helpful for many children who are older, but not reading fluently or not choosing to read very much.

You can begin Paired Reading with your child by using the directions that follow. I've found that initially parent and child need to focus on "doing it right." Getting into the routine is more task-like only for the first few days. Some of the things you'll likely have to work on are synchronizing the pace of your reading with the child's; ensuring that you are praising genuinely and not criticizing; helping by just supplying the words and by conversing calmly rather than trying to teach directly; and, deciding what comments to record. After a few sessions you'll find these parts of the process will have become almost automatic and that it is easier to relax and enjoy these special reading times with your child.

What You'll Need

Books Use books from home, school, or the public library. Read parts of magazines or newspapers, too. For early readers, look for stories that follow a predictable pattern like "The Three Bears" or "The Longest Journey in the World." Look for books that are about 24–32 pages in length and contain a moderate amount of print and plenty of illustrations. Fantasy, a realistic fiction about children and families, humor, easy poetry, and "all about a topic" nonfiction books are all suitable. Have a number of books on hand so that your child can choose a book before it's time to read, or choose from four or five. If your child gets tired of a book, rather than finishing it, encourage him to select another. Continue with the same book from day to day only if the child really wants to. Rereading familiar books is fine, even up to six or eight times. Your child will read with more expression and more enjoyment, and develop greater confidence in his or her own reading ability.

Time Try to read together daily at least five days a week, for 10–15 minutes. Setting a regular time for reading helps make it part of your daily routine. Don't Pair Read for more than 15 minutes at a time unless your child really wants to continue; reading aloud for much longer than this can be very tiring. If your child is anxious to hear the end of the story, you can offer to read the rest of it to your child right then.

Place Find a place that's quiet, away from the TV, radio, phone, and other people. Sit comfortably side-by-side looking at the book together. If you are right-handed, sitting on the left of your child tends to keep the child in control of the book.

Ways of Helping in Paired Reading

When your child gets a word wrong or can't say a word, just say what the word is. Then the child should repeat the word. Don't make the reader struggle or break it up or sound it out. This is not the time to teach reading skills or to treat reading like a puzzle.

When your child figures out a word without your help or makes a logical guess, smile and give praise for the effort. Praise the reading of hard words, getting all words in a sentence right, and for self-correcting.

Encourage Talking and Thinking before Reading, between Parts/Pages, and after Reading. If you need to encourage talk, ask what might happen next, or what your child thinks about what she has just read, or what it reminds her of. Questions like these have no one right answer. Rather, they serve as springboards for thinking and discussion about the story. Listen to each other and enjoy your conversations . . . and let your child do most of the talking.

Keep a Reading Log or Diary

A sheet or booklet should be prepared for recording notes at the end of each reading session. Keep a record of: what was read, for how long, who the helper was (if more than one parent or someone else helps), how the reading is improving, how you are doing in following the Paired Reading instructions, and the occasional note about what the child can do to improve his reading. If your child is willing to take over the writing, have him do the recording after you discuss together what is to be written down.

It is important to include comments that describe what the child has done well in each day's reading. Readers of all ages grow in reading ability by building on and recognizing their strengths. A good guideline is "three positive comments for every one area needing improvement." If your child is quite sensitive about criticism, perhaps it's better to just talk about the one thing that might be improved rather than to write it down. As the record of strengths builds, you and your child will be proud of your child's progress and the amount of reading done.

The format and examples that follow can be used as a guide in setting up record pages and making the entries.

Paired Reading Record Sheet

Name _____

Week of _____

Day	*Book Title & Pages*	*Minutes*	*Helper*	*Comments*
Sun.	*Brown Bear, Brown Bear* (all, 29 pages)	10 mins.	Dad	Lots of expression and uses pictures, colors, and rhyme to guess new words. Read alone smoothly at the end.
Mon.	*Bedtime* (all, 30 pages)	12 mins.	Dad	Told about being afraid in the dark. We need to read at same rate when reading together.
Tues.	*Red is Best* (all, 22 pages)	15 mins.	Mom	Used pictures and sounds of some letter to guess new words. Good expression.
Wed.	Didn't read because too tired after swimming lesson.			
Thurs.	*Frog and Toad Together* (pp. 1–29)	14 mins.	Mom	Talked about the silly parts like toad yelling at plants to make them grow.
Fri.	*Frog and Toad Together* (pp. 30–64: 24 pp.)	16 mins.	Mom	Read their talk with expression, shouting when they shout, etc. Guessed "beaks" when reading about birds taking cookies.
Sat.	Didn't read—went shopping and to the movies.			

Questions
Parents Ask

Q: I'm not very good at reading out loud myself. What if I make mistakes?

A: You don't need to read perfectly. Actually it's good for beginning readers to see that others "fix up" mistakes or miscues as they read to make sense of what they're reading.

Q: The books my child picks seem too hard. What should I do?

A: Make more and easier books available. Have your child "try on" the book briefly on his own. Or as you read a page or two to him, have him point to the words he doesn't know. In this way, help him decide if this book is for Paired Reading or perhaps for you or someone else to read to him.

Q: My child picks easy books and ends up reading "solo" nearly all the time. Is this all right?

A: Wonderful! Reading with confidence and fluency is great for your child. Praise your child and keep up the supply of books—easy ones and some others that are a bit more challenging.

Q: My son hardly ever taps the book to read alone. Is reading together helping if he doesn't want to read more on his own?

A: Reading together is probably helping him gain confidence in reading and in dealing with new words. Maybe he will want to read "alone" with easier books or after you've been doing Paired Reading for longer. If he chooses to reread some favorite books he may want to read solo more of the time.

Q: My daughter tends to "fade out" when we're reading aloud together. What can I do differently?

A: You might try reading more quietly yourself. If that doesn't work, jokingly let her know you can't hear her reading. If she's choosing quite difficult books, you'll find you need to lead and support more than follow. Make sure easier books are available and encourage her to reread some she's really liked.

Q: My child says, "Let's just read!" when I ask a question to try to get him to talk about the book. What should I do?

A: In general, follow the child's wishes. He may be just eager to read the story or perhaps he feels you are testing him. Another time you might try a less direct approach such as making a comment or two of your own to model that you are thinking about and enjoying what you are reading with him.

Q: Is it wrong to make any changes in the way we read together after we've been doing Paired Reading for awhile?

A: In observing parents and children as they do Paired Reading, I've found most make some adaptations, sometimes without realizing it. Of the changes I've seen, some I recommend are:

- When you know your child knows a word, encourage him or her to self-correct by just pointing to the misread or omitted word. Give the correct word only if you need to.

- If you feel your child is able to "read alone" and is not signaling to read alone, you can stop reading aloud until your support seems needed. Remind the child to signal in future session by including a comment about this when making an entry in the reading diary.

- When the child is not using the context of the story to predict new words, draw attention to picture cues during your pauses for discussion. Encourage making a "good guess" if your child is hesitant to try to read new words. Be sure to praise good approximations as well as correct guesses.

Q: How long should we continue to use Paired Reading if my child "reads alone" most of the time and doesn't want me to join in after correcting a word?

A: After four to six weeks of Paired Reading (or sooner for some readers) if your child doesn't seem to want or need all of the help that Paired Reading provides, talk with your child and make a decision about whether you want to do Paired Reading only with hard books and to use a different approach for easier ones. Remember Paired Reading is a bridge between reading to your child and your child reading on his or her own.

Paired Reading is especially appealing for use with beginning and nonfluent readers:

- It's quite easy to learn and do.

- It's a risk-free way for your child to practice reading what he or she wants to read. Help is "right there" when it's needed.

- It emphasizes key elements of good reading: fluency, use of context and other strategies to make good guesses about words, and comprehension of what's being read.

- It puts the child as the reader in control, by having the child choose the book and set the pace during reading.

- It guides the parent to "follow the child" by

  (a) ensuring the child's interests come first in choosing books,

  (b) focusing on what the child wants to talk about when you are reading together, and

  (c) having the child decide when to end the reading session.

- It helps the parent respond positively to what the child does while reading, rather than criticizing, pushing, or being unresponsive.

- It helps your child with learning to read better—to read words more accurately, to read with more expression, and with richer understanding.

- It encourages readers to find a suitable place for reading, one where they can concentrate on reading with few interruptions and to read in a tension-free environment.

- It's a flexible approach, one that can be adapted to your child's needs and wishes as your child becomes able to read more confidently and independently.

Summing Up: Some Advantages of Paired Reading

*References
and Other
Readings on
the Topic*

Videotape Package

Paired reading: Positive reading practice. A videotape and training package for using Paired Reading with school-age children and adults. It demonstrates the technique and gives examples of Paired Readers in action. Suggestions are given for organizing projects. Samples of adaptations, letters, and evaluation sheets are included. Produced by the Northern Alberta (Canada) Reading Specialists' Council, 1991 and distributed by:

International Reading Association, 800 Barksdale Road, Newark, Delaware 19711, U.S. (Order no. 663-437—$100 in U.S.) Tel. 800-336-READ, ext. 266; from outside North America call 302-731-1600, ext. 266.

Filmwest Associates, 2399 Hayman Road, Kelowna, B.C. V1Z1Z7, Canada ($115.56 Canadian, including GST) Phone: 604-769-3399 or FAX: 604-769-5599.

Articles

Barrett, J. (1987). Paired reading–psycholinguistics in practice. *Reading, 21,* 152–158.

> Describes theory about the kinds of information and strategies used in reading. Includes factors and issues such as: the use of reading schemes, the role of phonics, the importance of time spent reading, and how Paired Reading can support more reading at home. Some sections are fairly technical while others are understandable to those not trained in early reading education.

Gillam, B. (1986). Paired reading in perspective. *Child Education, 8–9.*

> Describes advantages of Paired Reading and how this technique helped a group of the poorest readers in top infant and first year junior (Gr. 1 & 2) catch up and even overtake their peers in reading ability.

Prentice, J. (1987). Real books and paired reading in context. *Reading, 21,* 159–168.

> A teacher describes how reading materials, parents, and teachers motivate, or discourage, children to become readers. Paired Reading is recommended as a way for parents to support their children in reading and learning to read.

Topping, K. (1987). Paired reading: A powerful technique for parent use. *Reading Teacher, 40* (March), 608–614.

> Describes Paired Reading and how to implement school-based projects with parents.

Topping, K. (1989). Peer tutoring and paired reading: Combining two powerful techniques. *Reading Teacher, 42* (March), 488–494.

> Describes the Paired Reading used in school with pairs of students having differing reading ability.

Topping, K. and M. Whiteley. (1990). Participant evaluation of parent-tutored and peer-tutored project in reading. *Educational Research, 32* (Spring), 14–27.

> A summary of studies of 2,760 children participating in Paired Reading projects in Huddersfield, England.

Chapter 9

Reading Aloud to Older, Independent Readers

Daniel Woolsey

D
aniel Woolsey has been a classroom teacher and college professor for
more than 15 years. Currently an associate professor of Education at
Houghton College in Houghton, NY, he teaches children's literature, reading, and language arts. He holds a Master's Degree in Children's Literature from
the Center for the Study of Children's Literature at Simmons College and a Ph.D. in
Children's Literature, Reading, and Language Arts from Ohio State University. He
is convinced of the power of positive interactions between children, adults and
books and often conducts seminars for parents and teachers on reading and talking
about good books with children.

I t is not difficult to convince most people of the pleasures in reading stories aloud to children. Most of us have experienced the powerful effect of a well told story, laughing and crying with our children at the escapades and struggles of characters in favorite stories. Many of us are equally aware of the multitude of benefits that regular read-aloud experiences can offer children, enhancing oral language, reading comprehension and writing abilities and promoting positive attitudes toward books and reading. These benefits are well documented in various studies and reported in widely known books such as Jim Trelease's *Read Aloud Handbook* and *For Reading Out Loud!* by Margaret Kimmel and Elizabeth Segal.

Unfortunately, as children develop independence as readers, many parents and teachers conclude that they no longer need to read aloud to them. Some think that children need to practice their reading skills, fearing that continued reading aloud will encourage laziness. Even more potentially harmful is the assumption that once children are independent readers, the adult's role shifts to that of monitoring the child's oral reading accuracy and comprehension. We have sounded the death knell of enjoyable shared reading when it becomes a performance in oral expression followed by a comprehension quiz. Other parents realize the importance of continued reading aloud to older readers, but give up in frustration when faced with the challenges of selecting books for older children and the increased complexity of family schedules as growing children get involved in more activities outside the home.

The basic premise of this chapter is that the ability to read independently does not quench the desire to hear stories read aloud, nor does it reduce the benefits of those experiences. In the pages that follow I will develop a rationale for reading aloud to older independent readers and then consider relevant issues such as how to set the stage for regular read-alouds, finding time to read aloud, principles for selecting books, and tips for reading aloud effectively.

Why Read Aloud to Independent Readers?

Enjoyment and Pleasure

An important reason to read aloud to older children is simply that it continues to be an enjoyable and rewarding experience for reader and listener alike. The enjoyment of stories in a communal setting is an experience as old as the human race itself. Whether those stories have been heard in a tribal setting around a crackling campfire or on the front porch of a farmhouse after the day's work is completed, listeners of all times and places have found pleasure and satisfaction in the captivating performance of a skilled storyteller or reader. The unique opportunities offered to listeners of all ages by the read-aloud experience are well summed up by the youngster who explained his enjoyment of hearing stories this way: "If your eyes aren't busy, your imagination is free to roam." (Mendoza, 1985, p. 527).

To Foster a Positive Attitude toward Reading

Jim Trelease argues that regular reading aloud is an effective "advertisement" for reading because it "allows a child to sample the delights of reading and conditions him to believe that reading is a pleasurable experience" (1989, p. 9). Throughout childhood, reading aloud continues to serve as an appetizer, stimulating a desire to read these books (or others like them) independently. Older readers need to be enticed into recreational reading because of the powerful lure of television and video games and the increasing responsibilities of preadolescence. The stiff competition for an older elementary child's time is illustrated by a study conducted by Linda Fielding and her colleagues (1984). They surveyed fifth graders' out-of-school activities and determined that 50 percent of the children read books for an average of only four minutes or less per day. In contrast, these children averaged 130 minutes per day watching TV. Regular, lively sessions of reading and chatting together about carefully chosen books is one of the most powerful tools that parents have to ensure that reading and books get the same loving attention as do Nintendo games and Nikes.

To Broaden and Deepen Children's Reading Interests and Experiences

Reading aloud to older children enriches their reading experiences, stretches their interests, and widens their literary horizons. Young readers typically have narrow reading tastes, showing devotion to certain authors, series, or topics. Ongoing read-aloud experiences can entice them to a wider range of authors and literary genre and strengthen their capacity to handle the complexities of more challenging novels. For example, many children are interested in mystery stories such as the familiar Hardy Boys and Nancy Drew series. Many of these children would be unlikely to pick up a historical fiction novel. However, they might change their minds after hearing Avi's exciting sea yarn *The True Confessions of Charlotte Doyle* (Orchard, 1990) in which a 13-year-old girl finds herself caught up in a dangerous drama on board a nineteenth-century sailing vessel manned by a rebellious crew and captained by a mysterious and murderous man.

To Improve Reading and Writing Skills

As children are expanding their interests and deepening their literary understandings through read-aloud experiences, they are also improving their independent reading skills. Children's capacity to understand and enjoy the language they hear is generally ahead of their ability to read that same language. Thus, the opportunity to listen to a book provides children with access to content, vocabulary, and literary styles that are beyond their current reading abilities and interests. It broadens the range of books in which they are interested and increases their chances for later success in reading those books independently. Reading aloud also helps children to internalize the rich language of literature and this, in turn, contributes to their growth as writers.

To Foster Family or Classroom Togetherness and Create an Arena for Discussion

Whether at home or at school, the communal enjoyment of stories establishes common ground and builds a genuine bond among the participants. For most families, finding time simply to talk and listen to each other is no easy matter. This is particularly true as children mature into adolescents and their days are filled with school, sports, and friends. Arthea Reed cites statistics indicating that, on average, American parents talk to their children only about 12 minutes per day, and ten of those precious minutes involve giving instructions (Reed, 1989, p. 82). Certainly these few minutes are not enough if we want to maintain good relationships with our children, relationships that allow us to talk about things that are important to them. Sharing Eleanor

Family reading fosters family togetherness.

Estes' *The Hundred Dresses* with my second grade daughter provided an opportunity to enjoy this gentle story of a poor Polish immigrant girl who struggles to fit into an American classroom. It also stimulated a thoughtful discussion about the difficulties of being different, something my daughter understood because of her left-handedness. Reading and discussing this story drew us together and opened up lines of communications which are difficult to establish in other ways.

Setting the Stage for Regular Read-Alouds

Hopefully, you are convinced of the mutual pleasures and benefits of reading aloud with older children, even up through middle school or as long as they are interested and willing. Let us now move on to the more practical concerns of actually implementing such a practice in your own family. Many families with preschool children have already established regular read-aloud rituals. Of course, the best way to form the read-aloud habit with older children is to simply never stop, but to alter these rituals as necessary to fit the evolving schedules and interests of the child.

How do you initiate regular read-alouds if you've gotten out of the habit or if you've never started? Arthea Reed (1988) suggests that a good way to get started is to take advantage of special family occasions and gatherings such as holidays. She also suggests taking books along on long car trips, noting that "if you can locate a good book about the place you are going to visit, reading it aloud in the car is natural. The ensuing conversation makes the miles speed by" (1988, p. 83). I can attest to the power of this simple practice. My family's recent trip through the rugged terrain of Montana was complemented by a reading of Kathryn Lasky's *The Bone Wars,* an adventure story set in the old west. In this exciting novel a pair of adolescent boys find themselves caught up in the schemes of two devious paleontologists who are each determined to receive credit for the dinosaur fossil discovery of the century. This fast paced story also includes a wealth of information and this provided an excellent information base for our appreciation of the dinosaur exhibits at the Museum of the Rockies in Bozeman, Montana. Consult Kimmel and Segal's *For Reading Out Loud!* (1983) to find a helpful appendix which lists books in which setting plays a major part and arranges them by location.

Finding Time to Read Aloud

Once a family begins to read aloud on these special occasions, it is natural to suggest that it continue on a more regular basis, at least several times a week. The key to success in any significant family venture is to work at it consistently and to help all family members feel a sense of ownership in the venture. Reading aloud is no exception. In order to succeed, oral reading needs to occur regularly and with the agreement of all concerned. Read-aloud sessions should be scheduled at times that are convenient for all family members and for only as long as everyone is enjoying them. Enforced oral reading in competition with a favorite television program or while most of the other neighborhood children are squealing with delight in the neighbor's swimming pool will surely doom the project to failure.

Read-aloud schedules need to be tailor-made for each family's particular lifestyle. Most families find that the best times are those when children are relaxed and receptive, such as around meals and at the end of the day. Some parents allow children to delay bedtime briefly with a cozy session of side-by-side reading as well as independent silent reading. Read-alouds can make family chores like washing dishes or cleaning the bedroom less unpleasant. They can also make a daily trip to school or a long wait in the doctor's office less tedious. Whatever time works best for your family, the important thing is to read aloud regularly. Once or twice a week is a good start, but in many instances the book itself will prompt your children to more frequent readings once they are caught up in the story.

Selecting Books to Read Aloud

There are many readily available books that provide guidance on book selection. Some of these guides, such as those by Cullinan, Hearne, Kimmel and Segal, Kobrin, and Reed and Trelease, offer helpful annotated book lists. These are listed in the Resources for Further Reading section at the end of the chapter. The following principles will guide your thinking as you select books.

Choose Books with Child-Appeal

Always keep in mind that the purpose of reading aloud is delight and enjoyment. Some elements are sure winners with children, such as humor, animals, and mystery. Children look for a fast-paced plot with plenty of suspense, one that concentrates more on action than on description. They also want engaging and memorable characters with whom they can identify. An example of a story with many of these elements is *Stone Fox.* In this short novel Willy and his sled dog, Searchlight, attempt to defeat the legendary Indian racer, Stone Fox, in a dog sled race. The breathless excitement of the race scenes and the heartbreaking conclusion is guaranteed to have intermediate grade children asking for more. Good follow-up read-alouds include Scott O'Dell's *Black Star, Bright Dawn,* about a modern teenage Eskimo girl who takes part in the famous thousand-mile Iditerod race, Jack London's *Call of the Wild,* or two Alaskan survival novels with teenaged protagonists: *Julie of the Wolves* by Jean Craighead George and Gary Paulsen's *Dogsong.*

Choose Books That Have Literary Merit and Ones That Children Might Not Choose on Their Own

The best stories for reading aloud include many of the elements that children enjoy, but they also have the language and style that characterize the best writing. Stories with nonstop action and cardboard characters may survive silent reading by children, but they often fall flat when we attempt to read them aloud. Well written stories flow almost effortlessly off the tongue, while poorly written ones can cause us to read clumsily, stumbling over words and failing to make sense of awkward sentences. One important purpose of reading aloud is to stretch our listeners' ability to savor and appreciate good literature. Since we only have time to read aloud one or two longer books per month, we shouldn't waste read-aloud time on books that children will mostly likely devour on their own. Look for books and authors which have won the prestigious Newbery Award for excellence in writing or talk with your child's teachers and librarians to learn about authors who are critically acclaimed in the world of children's books. Soon you and your children will develop your own list of favorite stories and authors.

Choose Books Which You Enjoy Yourself

If the goal is shared enjoyment of books, then it is important that *you* find delight in the books as well. The best stories offer satisfaction and pleasures for readers of all ages. It is counterproductive to devote read-aloud time to stories which you find tedious and boring; your dislike will be transmitted in the reading and this will send mixed messages to your children.

Build Variety and Balance into Your Read-Aloud Selections

If we want to stretch children's reading interests, then we need to read widely as well as selectively. Children need to hear classics like *The Secret Garden* and *The Adventures of Tom Sawyer* as well as popular contemporary works by the best authors writing today, such as Natalie Babbitt, Katherine Paterson, and Walter Dean Myers. Along with engaging narratives, they need to discover the pleasures of well written informational books such as Russell Freedman's *Lincoln: A Photobiography* and *Living with Dinosaurs* by Patricia Lauber. Be sure to also use reading materials other than books. Popular magazines such as *Sports Illustrated* and *Reader's Digest* provide short stories and articles that are full of the drama of the human experience and topics in which children are interested. Older readers will also enjoy newspaper columns such as the offbeat and hilarious columns of Dave Barry or the human interest stories of Paul Harvey.

It is especially important to include poetry in your read-aloud selections. The best poems offer a precise use of language and a powerful expression of human experiences and emotions. Poetry is especially appropriate for reading aloud since it is meant to be heard as well as read. Few children will be able to resist the melodic rap-like rhythms found in Eloise Greenfield's *Honey, I Love and Other Love Poems* or the hilarious narrative poems of Shel Silverstein and Jack Prelutsky. All home and school libraries should include a few anthologies of children's poetry for informal browsing and enjoyment. Two of the most complete anthologies for younger readers are *The Random House Book of Poetry for Children,* compiled by Jack Prelutsky, and *Sing a Song of Popcorn,* edited by Beatrice Schenk de Regniers. Young adolescents would probably prefer the poems found in *Reflections on a Gift of Watermelon Pickle and Other Modern Verses,* compiled by Steve Dunning and others, or *The Place My Words Are Looking for,* a collection compiled by Paul Janeczko which offers an excellent variety of contemporary poems and brief essays by each of the poets.

No matter what the age of the listeners, we should be reading both chapter books and picture books. Older children need to realize that picture books are not just for babies. A look at such recent favorites as David Macaulay's *The Way Things Work,* Chris Van Allsburg's *Two Bad Ants* or Jon Scieszka's *The True Story of the 3 Little Pigs* should convince anyone that some picture books offer delightful stories and illustrations and a sophisticated sense of humor which often goes over the heads of younger children.

Don't Be Afraid to Stop Reading

If it becomes obvious on the first reading that you have made a poor choice, don't be afraid to admit it and move on to another book. This process of evaluating books is in itself an important one for maturing readers. Children need to know that when a book is not satisfying or interesting it can legitimately be put aside. At the same time, they need to learn that some books need time to engage the reader and that the rewards of persisting in challenging reading can be great. Thus, the decision to stop reading should be made easily but not thoughtlessly.

Many of us have heard the dramatic interpretations of favorite stories recorded by professionals. Few can match the virtuoso performances of these actors, but all of us can enhance our ability to read aloud effectively. Kimmel and Segal remind us that "reading aloud, although not a theatrical experience, is a performance. The reader must be aware of audience reaction; of creating a mood that allows the listener to respond to the story. This interaction between reader and listener, between story and audience, is a key to success" (1983, p. 34).

This suggests that read-aloud sessions should take place in a location that is comfortable and relatively free of distractions. Be aware of the physical aspects of the read-aloud setting, taking care that you have adequate light and ventilation. Make sure that children can see and hear you and that they can see the book if the illustrations are an important element of the selection you are reading.

Eye contact between reader and listener is an essential ingredient in supporting the interaction between reader and listener and between the child and the book. This eye contact helps to keep children involved in the reading and affirms the bond between reader and listener, allowing you to share a giggle or a nod of recognition. It

Strategies for Reading Aloud Effectively

also enables the reader to monitor the involvement and reactions of the listener. Be sure to read only as long as the child is interested.

Another important strategy for involving children in oral reading is to prepare yourself and the children for the reading. Jim Trelease emphasizes the importance of previewing a book before reading it aloud. This allows you to "read it the second time to the class or child with more confidence, accenting important passages (and) leaving out dull ones" (1989, p. 65). Previewing also allows you to consider the best places to break off reading. These stopping points should leave the story intact, but reserve enough unanswered questions to entice children back for more reading.

Familiarizing yourself with a text before reading it aloud also allows you to think about how to introduce the book to your listening audience. Some books need little or no introduction. A simple mention of the title and author are lead-in enough and off you go. However, like an unknown guest at a party, some books need a careful introduction so that children can make personal connections to the text. This is especially true of stories with unfamiliar settings or characters whose experiences and motivations are far removed from those of your listeners. For example, *Sarah, Plain and Tall* is a moving and beautifully written story, but some children will need an explanation about mail-order brides in the days of the western frontier. Michael Dorris's *Morning Girl* is another short novel which is too good to miss, though it makes definite demands on the reader. The setting on a fifteenth-century Caribbean island just prior to the arrival of Christopher Columbus and the unique perspectives of the Taino Indian narrators will need careful introduction, as will the unusual structure in which the point of view alternates between two characters. Of course, this is not to suggest that the reading of these books be preceded by a formal history or literature lesson, just that children sometimes need simple explanations in order to get off to a good start in listening with understanding and delight.

As you read, strive to be a good model of fluent and expressive reading. Most of us will be most successful if we use our natural voice rather than attempt to vary the tone and pitch of our voices for each character. On the other hand, our reading will be more interesting for our listeners if we are aware of the dramatic possibilities inherent in the story, varying the volume and pace to fit the demands of the story. What is most important is to read clearly and at a pace that holds the listener's interest but also allows them to hear without straining. A common mistake in reading aloud is to read too quickly. Jim Trelease recommends that you "read slowly enough for the child to build mental pictures of what he just heard you read" (1989, p. 81). Reading more slowly also allows listeners to interject comments and questions if they feel so inclined.

Perhaps the most important principle in effective reading aloud is that during the reading and afterwards we must respect both the book and the listeners. Thus, we must be willing to let the story speak for itself at times, allowing for silences as children reflect and respond to stories. Following the reading, be careful not to break the spell of the story with trivial questions or by asking the listener to rehash the plot. Children need time and space to reflect on the story, to make personal connections and to offer thoughtful responses. Aiden Chambers points out that children's reactions to a story will vary depending on the nature of the book: "Some books provoke vocal responses—a kind of literary effervescent effect—while others seem to turn people in on themselves, when they prefer to say nothing but savor the reading in silence . . . On the whole, the stronger the emotional power of the writing the less children want to say about it" (1983, pp. 143–144).

Of course, many texts stimulate spontaneous conversations between reader and listeners. These discussions should be informal and natural, involving an easy give-and-take of reactions and opinions. When it's going well, the dialogue will feel more like a conversation among friends who have just seen a powerful movie and less like the interrogations and recitations which masquerade as discussions in some classrooms. Of course, the adult needs to lead the way at times, but it's better to do this through the modeling of ways to respond to literature rather than through direct questioning which may feel too much like a formal reading lesson. For example, the adult may share some thoughts and feelings about a certain character and reflect on what he or she might do if faced with a similar dilemma and then ask listeners to reflect on what their reactions might be. Sometimes questions are appropriate, especially if they are open-ended and invite personal reactions and connections. For example, we might ask:

What did this reading make you think about? How did it make you feel?

Do you see any connections between this book and your own life?

Does this remind you of any other books or stories you have read?

What parts of the story did you enjoy most? Least? Why?

Was there anything in this story which puzzled you?

These are the sorts of questions that can stimulate lively interchanges and help both reader and listeners to develop and express their personal understandings of a story.

Whether we are teachers or parents, we have in reading aloud a proven formula for stimulating our children's literacy skills and leading them into the pleasures of good literature. The good news is that reading aloud is inexpensive, easy to do, and, best of all, fun for all involved. How can we do anything other than commit ourselves to reading and discussing books with our children throughout their school years?

References and Other Readings on the Topic

Chambers, Aiden. (1983). *Introducing books to children.* Boston: The Horn Book, Inc.

Cullinan, Beatrice. (1992). *Read to me: Raising kids who love to read.* New York: Scholastic.

Fielding, L.G., P.T. Wilson, and R.C. Anderson. (1984). A new focus on free reading: The role of trade books in reading instruction. In T.E. Raphael and R. Reynolds (Eds.), *Contexts of literacy.* New York: Longman.

Freeman, Judy. (1992). Reading aloud: A few tricks of the trade. *School Library Journal, 38,* 26–29.

Hearne, Betsy. (1990). *Choosing books for children: A commonsense guide.* New York: Delacorte.

Kimmel, Margaret and Elizabeth Segal. (1983). *For reading out loud! A guide to sharing books with children.* New York: Delacorte.

Kobrin, Beverly. (1988). *Eyeopeners! How to choose and use children's books about real people, places and things.* New York: Viking Penguin.

Mendoza, Alicia. (1985). Reading to children: Their preferences. *Reading Teacher, 38,* 522–527.

Reed, Arthea. (1988). *Comics to classics: A parent's guide to books for teens and preteens.* Newark, DE: International Reading Association.

Trelease, Jim. (1989). *The new read-aloud handbook.* New York: Viking Penguin.

Children's Books

Avi. (1990). *The true confessions of Charlotte Doyle.* New York: Orchard.

Burnett, Frances Hodgson. (1987). *The secret garden.* Boston: David R. Godine (1911).

de Regnier, Beatrice Schenk, ed. (1988). *Sing a song of popcorn.* New York: Scholastic.

Dorris, Michael. (1992). *Morning girl.* Westport, CT: Hyperion Press.

Dunning, Steven, Edward Leuders and Hugh Smith. (1966). *Reflections on a gift of watermelon pickle and other modern verses.* New York: Lothrup.

Estes, Eleanor. (1944). *The hundred dresses.* New York: Harcourt.

Fleischman, Paul. (1988). *Joyful noise: Poems for two voices.* New York: Harper & Row.

Freedman, Russell. (1987). *Lincoln: A photobiography.* New York: Clarion.

Gardiner, John Reynolds. (1980). *Stone fox.* New York: Harper & Row.

George, Jean Craighead. (1972). *Julie of the wolves.* New York: Harper & Row.

Greenfield, Eloise. (1978). *Honey, I love and other love poems.* New York: Crowell.

Janeczko, Paul, selector. (1990). *The place my words are looking for.* Scarsdale, NY: Bradbury.

Lasky, Kathryn. (1989). *The bone wars.* New York: Morrow.

Lauber, Patricia. (1991). *Living with dinosaurs.* Scarsdale, NY: Bradbury.

London, Jack. (1968). *The call of the wild.* New York: Dutton (1903).

Macaulay, David. (1988). *The way things work.* Boston: Houghton Mifflin.

MacLachlan, Patricia. (1985). *Sarah, plain and tall.* New York: Harper & Row.

O'Dell, Scott. (1988). *Black star, bright dawn.* Boston: Houghton Mifflin.

Paulsen, Gary. (1985). *Dogsong.* Scarsdale, NY: Bradbury.

Prelutsky, Jack, editor. (1983). *The Random House book of poetry for children.* New York: Random.

Scieszka, Jon. (1989). *The true story of the 3 little pigs.* New York: Viking.

Twain, Mark (Samuel Clemens). (1989). *The adventures of Tom Sawyer.* New York: Morrow (1876).

Van Allsburg, Chris. (1988). *Two bad ants.* Boston: Houghton Mifflin.

Chapter 10

Becoming Readers and Writers Together

JoBeth Allen

J oBeth Allen is an associate professor of Language Education at the University of Georgia. Her interests include how teachers and parents promote children's early language and literacy development.

R achel turned five two weeks too late to enter kindergarten. She cried because she wanted to go to "real school," even though she loved her preschool. As I comforted her, she looked up at me and pleaded, "Mommy, please, couldn't *you* teach me to read?"

For so many children, going to school means learning to read. They don't realize that they have been learning to read since birth if they have been in environments that are rich in both oral and printed language. Children listen to the soothing, repetitive rhythm of lullabies. They watch their parents sigh with pleasure as they finally relax with the evening paper. They observe the many functional uses of print, such as distinguishing "Sugar Frosted Oat Loops" from "Bland Bran." They observe and eventually help with letters to Grandma, instructions for the babysitter, and family memos on the events of daily life. Denny Taylor, a parent, teacher, and researcher, has written several interesting books describing these home literacy events: *Family Literacy, Family Storybook Reading,* and *Growing Up Literate.* These books show that even when parents are not intentionally teaching their children literacy, many children become readers and writers because those around them read and write.

Many parents, however, want to know how they can help their children learn to read. And many children, like Rachel, beg to be taught. People who have studied how children become readers do have some advice about both planned and unplanned literacy events.

Becoming a Reader

Be a reader yourself, and let your child see you reading. When my three children were young, it was hard to get them to respect their dad's and my right to read the newspapers and novels that were an integral part of our lives. As new parents, we sometimes felt guilty about taking this private time. But researchers have documented the importance of adults as "models of joyous literacy." So sometimes we read side by side, they with their books and we with ours. Sometimes we had family read-alouds. Always we promised to read to them as soon as we finished a chapter. But they knew reading was an important, pleasurable, engrossing part of life.

One day our son Paul brought a new friend home. As he showed him around the house, he pointed out, "There are books in every room of this house—even the bathroom!" Books and other reading material can "litter" your house even if you are unable to spend a lot of money. A friend of mine has a special shelf at her house with books from the public library that is well used and replenished every two weeks. Her five-year-old daughter's library shelf is right below. Other sources of inexpensive books are the used book sales that are annual events for many libraries; also, garage sales yield tremendous book bargains.

The single most important thing parents and literate others (including older siblings, care givers, other adults in the home) do for their children as literacy learners is to read to them. They read as often as possible every day, often at the child's request. Many families have some honored ritual time, usually at bedtime; in our family, Dad was the bedtime story reader or teller. Another great time is when one person is fixing a meal, and another reads, thus providing that close, quiet time that (1) gives the cook a break, (2) gives the reader special one-on-one time, and (3) settles an often cranky child down. As older children become readers they often read to younger siblings; admittedly, I read less to my third than to my first, so thank goodness for Rachel moving into the reader role.

Researchers have found what children have always known: It's important to read favorite books and poems over and over. When Elizabeth Sulzby, another parent, teacher, and researcher, studied how children learn to read, she discovered some very interesting things about favorite storybooks. Young readers often follow a general pattern with these books. At first, children create their own version of the stories from the pictures. They label or comment on each picture; at a later date they tell a story from the pictures. Many children eventually tell the whole story much as they have heard it read to them—they memorize phrases or the whole book. They emerge as readers at different rates; these changes occur after months or years.

An odd thing may happen next. The same child who has memorized/read beautifully from her favorite books for months may suddenly say, "I can't read." This is really a very exciting insight, because if it occurs at this point in development, it usually means that the child has realized that it is the print, not the pictures, that "real" readers read. This was the point Rachel had reached when she begged for instruction.

Dorothy Butler, a children's bookstore owner, and Marie Clay, a respected New Zealand researcher, offer very sound advice when a child reaches that point. In their excellent book for parents, *Reading Begins at Home: Preparing Children for Reading before They Go to School,* they suggest that parents or other caregivers

1. choose familiar books with about a line of simple writing per page, preferably books the child knows well;

2. read slowly as you run your finger smoothly under the words;

3. encourage your child to repeat each phrase or sentence after you, or to join in with you, as you run your finger under the words;

4. encourage your child to use her finger for guiding the reading when he or she expresses interest;

5. *use* language about books and print, like "front of the book," "word," "sentence," and "top of the page," but don't *teach* these terms.

Such guided reading is in addition to, not in place of, the reading and discussion of children's story choices (and yours) that are longer and more complex. This procedure is not all-at-once advice, but a slow process of repeated readings of simple books that you and your child enjoy. If either of you stops enjoying the process, starts fidgeting, gets discouraged, QUIT. Do something fun together. Wait for your child to ask to read again, and ask, "Do you want to help me read it, or just listen this time?" They learn a lot from just listening. My son Luke taught me that.

I was reading several of Bill Martin's wonderful *Instant Readers* one day to Rachel, then five, and Paul, not yet one. Luke kept running in and out of the room, exploring, riding the dog, climbing, all his favorite three-year-old activities. I tried persuading him to sit down and read with us. The book we had been reading several times, *When It Rains, It Rains,* was perfect for "instant reading." The simple pattern, "when it _____, it _____," was great for the kind of language play Martin encourages, where children make language structures their own. I wheedled, "Come read with us." "I can't read," he called over his shoulder. "You can read these books," I explained. "The guy that wrote them made them especially for children to read." He wheeled around, put his hands on his little hips, and shouted, "When I hate it, I hate it!"

He had obviously been listening, but I hadn't. Luke didn't like to read then, and he doesn't like to read now, at 19. He'd much rather be actively involved in something than reading about it. This was hard for me to accept, but Luke taught me that you can be a happy, contributing member of society and not be an avid reader. I think the important thing is to follow the child's lead, create initiations and opportunities (Luke loved the family read-aloud *Where the Red Fern Grows* when he was 11), and then enjoy their individuality. No two children are alike—even in families that read.

The Lukes of the world aside, most children love to be read to. As you and your children read together, you'll notice that they take more and more responsibility for the reading. They will chime in with rhyming words, or repeated phrases, or words at the end of the sentence. Pause as you read, just long enough to give them the chance to join in. For this reason, it's important to read books with predictable language structures such as rhymes, refrains, questions and answers, familiar sequences such as days of the week, and other easily learned patterns.

When we start thinking about "reading together" sessions as "learning to read" sessions, parents sometimes forget that we read to children for a wide variety of purposes. We read to entertain, to learn about interesting things, to play with language, and for many other reasons. So while simple, predictable books support children's early reading, we want to continue reading and discussing a wide variety of fiction, informational, and poetry books.

Often parents think that as soon as children begin reading to themselves, they are not interested in being read to. Some of my most treasured literary memories are whole family read-alouds; when the children were in elementary and middle grades, we savored classics like *Island of the Blue Dolphin* and Dad's favorite, *The Education of Little Tree*. A good resource is Jim Trelease's *Read Aloud Handbook,* which suggests books for different ages and interests, and tells you a little about each.

Probably the single best resource for parents, available at a bargain price from Scholastic, is Bernice Cullinan's *Read to Me: Raising Kids Who Love to Read.* She provides suggestions for home reading events and good literature for preschoolers through 12 year olds, and a great chapter called "Tips for Busy Parents."

Becoming a Writer

When I decided it really was time to help Rachel learn to read, we not only read together, we wrote together. People who study literacy development have documented that reading, writing, and talking are closely related. Learning in the three areas is similar in many ways, and development in one area often lays a foundation for learning in the others. For example, when children experiment with writing, they often stretch their concepts of oral language (e.g., they learn what a "word" is).

So writing together is important not only for introducing your child to the creative, expressive, informative world of writing, but also as a pathway to reading. Rachel and I wrote together in three main ways, depending on what she felt like (she usually insisted on all three each day). At times, she drew pictures and dictated long, creative stories to me which I printed for her to read, with my support. At times, she asked for a special word (usually one a day, often one from her dictated story) to be printed on a sturdy card and placed on her own Word Ring. She read through her ring at least once a day.

Third, Rachel created her own pictures and text, with my support. That support included talking about language, letters, sounds, and written forms, but not doing the writing for her. Remember how your children learned to talk, when every new sound they made sounded kind of like "Daddy" or "cookie" or "Bye-bye"? But sure enough, with your interpretation and encouragement and answers to their questions, those sounds did indeed become meaningful communication. You didn't tell them they were wrong to say "dada" or "gookie." You modeled the word ("Yes! There's Daddy" or "You want a cookie?") and responded to the message. That's just the kind of support young writers (and readers) need.

Two wonderful books for understanding and helping young writers are Marie Clay's *Writing Begins at Home,* and *What Did I Write?* She explains that what may look like scribbling and random marks are meaningful attempts to "invent" written language. Early writing includes playing with forms such as lines and circles, distinguishing "drawing" from "writing," and making lines of "scribbles" that may look distinctively different if they represent labels, a letter to Grandpa, or Daddy's shopping list. Next, you might see forms that look kind of like letters, but with variations—backwards E's, or M's with seven humps. Soon the letter forms become more stable, but they still might not "stand for" words with that letter: PEQMA might be "doctor."

An exciting breakthrough in writing occurs when oral and written language team up and the child begins hearing sounds in words, and writing letters to represent those sounds. Children usually hear beginnings of words, later ending sounds, and then sounds in the middle; so the evolution of "cat" might be K, then KT, then KET, KAT, and finally CAT. Vowels are difficult, especially if they do not "say their name," so they are often the last letters children attempt as they invent spellings. Children may be able to write certain words with correct spellings also during this time of experimentation and invention—words such as their names, STOP, Mom.

It is essential that parents and teachers encourage the invention of writing, rather than insist on the "correct" form from the beginning. When children begin to use letters to represent actual sounds, respond to their questions about spelling with "write the sounds you hear in the word." Help them hear more sounds in words, and provide other prompts that encourage independence. Sometimes children may demand correct spellings, and it's fine to write or spell out words occasionally, as long as the children don't become totally dependent and stop trying words on their own. When they can write most of the sounds they hear, children are ready for more information about spelling patterns. A good way to help at this point is to make lists, with the child, of words that fit certain patterns (e.g., and, sand, land, band).

There are several other important things you can do to help your child become a writer. Be a writer yourself, and let your child see you write for a variety of purposes. Supply your child with a variety of writing materials, such as felt markers, finger paints, real stationery and stamps, etc., and invite their frequent use. Let him or her write the grocery list, then use it as you shop together. Write notes to friends and go to the post office together to mail them. Support exploration and invention on the typewriter or computer. Encourage your child to compose stories orally into a tape recorder and act them out for company.

These suggestions, from my own experience as a parent and from many researchers of literacy development, are offered for children from birth to perhaps second grade. During much of this time, you will not be the child's only teacher. Preschool and elementary teachers will be very interested in what you and your child are doing at home, and are usually very helpful in recommending other ways to complement school instruction. Children learn to read and write in many different ways. Rachel learned as recounted here; Luke learned from a loving first grade teacher and a basal textbook; and we don't know how Paul learned—one day he just started reading along with us.

However, if you see your child developing a negative attitude about reading, writing, or herself as a learner, it is time to talk seriously with the teacher about what is going on in the classroom and at home. What is making the child feel pressured, insecure, unable, bored, or frustrated? Work together to change the situation. You risk turning a child off for life to the joys of literacy. You risk not getting the call I got last night.

"Mom, help!" 20-year-old Rachel pleaded from far-off California. "I just finished *Prince of Tides* and you have to tell me another book that good!"

References and Other Readings on the Topic

Butler, Dorothy, and Marie Clay. (1979). *Reading begins at home.* Portsmouth, NH: Heinemann.

Carter, Forrest. (1976). *The education of Little Tree.* New York: Delacorte.

Clay, Marie. (1975). *What did I write.* Portsmouth, NH: Heinemann.

Clay, Marie. (1987). *Writing begins at home.* Portsmouth, NH: Heinemann.

Cullinan, Bernice. (1992). *Read to me: Raising kids who love to read.* New York: Scholastic.

Martin, Bill, Jr. (1976). *Instant readers.* New York: Holt, Rinehart and Winston.

O'Dell, Scott. (1960). *Island of the blue dolphin.* New York: Dell.

Rawls, Wilson. (1961). *Where the red fern grows.* New York: Bantam.

Sulzby, Elizabeth. (1985). Children's emergent reading of favorite storybooks. *Reading Research Quarterly, XX*(4), 458–481.

Taylor, Denny. (1983). *Family literacy.* Portsmouth, NH: Heinemann.

Taylor, Denny, and Catherine Dorsey-Gains. (1988). *Growing up literate.* Portsmouth, NH: Heinemann.

Taylor, Denny, and Dorothy Strickland. (1986). *Family storybook reading.* Portsmouth, NH: Heinemann.

Trelease, Jim. (1989). *The new read aloud handbook.* New York: Penguin.

Chapter 11

Demystify the Written Word and Make Writing a Lifelong Adventure

Sally Hudson-Ross

S ally Hudson-Ross is an assistant professor of language education at the University of Georgia. With the help of children, parents, and teachers, she collected the writing of 40 avid young writers in two research studies to explore children's perceptions of the home and school situations in which they write. This research was funded in part by grants from the Research Foundation of the National Council of Teachers of English and the University of Northern Iowa.

At age three, Andrea etches her name on the side of the house with a rock. At eight, Lewis sits on the sidelines finishing a story before his soccer game begins. Second grader Jonathan and his first grade buddy Robbie make up stories on the bus; Jonathan writes and Robbie illustrates their endless daily books. Ten-year-old Kathryn plays waitress, doctor, poet, playwright; she begs her father to dictate letters and works beside her teacher-mother in the evenings as both create lesson plans. One mother of an avid young writer laughs, "We use a lot of paper around here."

These children, all avid writers, love to write. They write freely, and they write everywhere. They write with most anything they can get their hands on. As parents with more than one child know, some children seem to take naturally to writing while others do not. After interviewing parents of 40 avid young writers, I have come to realize that parents and others can help to inspire and nurture avid young writers, as well as their less eager peers.

Truly avid young writers do have some common characteristics. Often they are the eldest or an only child. Many began school older than their peers due to late birthdays. Most thrive in the structure of a school setting, especially one that allows frequent and extended time and support for their writing. Most—but not all—also love reading.

Some, like Jonathan, are perfectionists. Says his mother, "He just likes things to be there, in case he were to need them again." Lauren who loves school, "is very orderly, very disciplined. She follows all the rules and everything." But just as many are extremely messy. "If you go up to Andrea's room," according to her mother," you'll find all kinds of scraps of paper and pages, and you know, it's everywhere. It's like a rumpled college professor's office."

To their parents, these children have seemed driven by curiosity since birth; as Andrea's mother says, "She has to know everything." They love to learn, often stay with projects or subjects for extended periods of time, and entertain themselves happily with reading and writing. His mother recalls when Lewis became enchanted with myths: "When he gets on a track, he pulls out every encyclopedia, every book we have, and he quizzes both his dad and me on what do you know about myths? Why was this? Who was that? Then he takes off with that idea, and he kind of plans down the road. . . . Once he decided it was going to be a myth, he wasn't going to have just one or two mythological people . . . , he was going to incorporate them in an appropriate way."

Some parents express concern that their children who write a lot aren't "social" enough. "I would really prefer her to spend this time socializing with her friends rather than writing. I mean, she has spent all day doing that, but this was her idea, and she bought it [a notebook and pen] with her own money . . . ," but Lauren's mother also sees that her second grader's "whole horizon is expanding." By upper elementary grades, young writers generally turn toward peers as collaborators, characters in, and audiences for their writing. The solitary nature of early writing becomes a cooperative effort to explore more adult-like genres and purposes for writing. Nicole, for example, was an almost reclusive writer in second grade, partly because her family lived near no other children. She wrote "for my puppies" and filled bookshelves with her work. But by sixth grade, in a new, friendlier cul-de-sac, she emerged as a neighborhood leader, the one who kept records, planned meetings, and wrote and delivered notices with her friends for upcoming "girls' club" gatherings.

At the other extreme, some children seem to have no interest in writing at all. These children don't have the patience to sit still long enough or to get every word correct when it appears on paper. They can't think of anything to write about, or they find absolutely no reason to write in their busy worlds. Asking them to sign their names on Christmas cards can be as traumatic as potty training. Yet even these children can become engaged in writing—primarily if we adults help change definitions of what writing *is* and *can be.*

Parents can best encourage children to become writers by supporting every child's natural desire to play—alone or with others. When children amuse themselves with imaginary role-playing as teachers, waitresses, store owners, leaders of army battalions, writing may support their play. Within their "pretend" worlds children find reasons to write much as adults do. When interesting materials and writing tools attract them, they invent and explore new ways of writing and new roles. Forms to complete, cards and invitations, announcements and signs, calendars, diaries, notes, lists, records of scores and activities all provide natural outlets for children as they contemplate the world around them and how it works. Writing, for children as well as adults, is far more than creating stories.

Young writers do not, however, thrive in a vacuum.

The following guidelines can help parents, teachers, and other adults encourage writing as a creative outlet and as a habit for all children.

Acknowledge All Forms of Writing As Valid

The variety of written forms that children invent is simply amazing. When he isn't drawing skateboard designs on his jackets and shoes, Mark devises club rules and certificates of membership for neighborhood friends. Allison hangs a sign on the upstairs bathroom, "Just Women." Lewis and Michelle pass colorful, detailed love letters, while Nicole and her girlfriend write extensive maps and plans for how to trap a boyfriend on the playground (by dropping a dime to entice him).

Fred and a buddy label every item in his room with numbers on slips of paper, "playing store and those were the prices for things," he later informs his baffled mother. Lauren's daily play school involves long lists of friends' names, now imaginary students, with their assignments and grades. Emily and her cousins play restaurant or cafeteria and have birthday parties for their dolls complete with invitations. Emily and her brother invent a millionaire for whom they work, and for weeks they keep records of their purchases and expenditures as his fantasy life emerges. Instead of writing "stories" on their own outside of school, most children write to make their worlds work. James Britton (1975) calls this *transactional writing,* writing "to get things done." Although children's explorations of written forms often appear in childlike ways, they serve real, children's purposes. As anyone might guess, Kristy's attempts to persuade her parents in Figures 11.1 and 11.2 were quite successful. Children's uses of writing to pretend and to communicate should be recognized as major strides toward writing in very real worlds. After all, adults construct many of

Figure 11.1

KRISTY WANTS A GREATER ALLOWANCE

the same types of writing when we need to meet our goals. Likewise, children will adopt or invent new adult forms when they have a need for them as well.

Provide Materials for Writing without Spending Lots of Money

Mark's dad brings home free pens, markers, business cards, and forms from his pharmaceutical conventions that keep Mark busy for days. Lauren loves all kinds of stationery and spends hours at a simple desk in her room. Kristy and her friends play "insurance office" with an adding machine and typewriter picked up at garage sales and unsolicited blank forms that arrive in the mail. Abby's mom, who works in a bank, brings home discarded, colored copy paper and discontinued forms and checks: "When she sees me pay bills, she always wants the cover to a blank check book to record her own checks."

Figure 11.2

KRISTY WANTS A HUG

Children have a natural affinity for filling out forms, albeit one we soon out-grow, and enjoy the feel and potential of every new writing tool. They love to fill in the blanks and use "real" papers such as letterhead, business forms, and carbon paper as they explore and invent their own forms. Adults with an eye to nurturing young writers can find free or cheap materials everywhere: garage sales, paper-recycling boxes at work, local businesses who advertise with pens and notepads, and those willing to set aside discarded writing materials for children's use. Most stores, doc-tors, mechanics, post offices would be willing to spare one extra form for a child's play. Learn to see the ubiquitous materials in your world—pencils for golf scores; outdated, unused office machines that take up space; junk mail—as outlets for a child's experimentation and growth. Decorate baskets of such goodies for gifts that intrigue and entice children into writing in delightful ways. If you are a classroom sponsor, collect 30 sets of these materials and present one to each child in September. Just watch the writing begin!

Encourage Children to Play Indoors with Friends in an Environment Full of Writing Materials

Children play with the materials around them. The avid young writers I interviewed lived in homes rich in materials, places for writing, and opportunities. Papers and pencils were accessible in every room, not tucked away in drawers or hidden in high, unreachable cabinets. Such spaces where papers and pens compete with toys cannot help but lead to inventive play.

Because the materials were available, Lewis and his sister set up a complete veterinary clinic in her room one Saturday complete with check-in counter and sign-in form, hospital and visitors' passes, and bed chart labels to explain her stuffed animals' ailments: "Sam fell down out of a tree and got parilised," "Sarah has a broken ear." Lisa and her friend Crystal "sell stuff," explains Lisa's mother, "One day, before I could catch them and knew what they were about, they were down the road and went and asked Micky, a neighbor, if she would like to buy a poem or a birthday card. So she gave them ten cents and they wrote a poem for her husband. It said, 'I love you George' and all this stuff. It *was* real cute, but you've got to watch those two!" "Gregg would 'kill me' for telling this," said his mom, but she explained that "the boys play a lot of GI Joe games. He writes up their secret words. They're into playing army, and he loves to do the codes."

Just about any imaginary game can include writing, but it isn't as likely to do so if the materials aren't convenient. At the same time, *suggesting* that children include writing in their play can destroy the inspiration, the momentum that builds when children find their own ways to include writing in the many environments they construct. Provide the materials and the space, and let children explore for themselves.

Take Children to Work. Let Them See the Writing You Do at Home

Lisa's mother is a teacher. "She has a toy typewriter, and so she would pretend that she was typing when I was typing or she would want my typewriter when I finished and she would try to type out stuff."

Elizabeth's parents gave her early practice in a family business. "When we started our business, it was in a little place. When Elizabeth was in kindergarten, she was pulling orders for me and packaging orders. And now, in third grade, when I get her in there on my typewriter, she types letters: 'Dear Mike and Libby, I received my order. I was missing . . . blah, blah, blah.' I have been there when she would have her dad on the other side of the counter, and she would say, 'May I help you?' And he would tell her he would like to place an order, and she would ask and write down what size, what style, all the questions I would ask, you know? And then she would turn around and say, 'We'll ship it out UPS just as soon as possible,' and I would crack up!"

Lewis's family is a family of letter writers, thanks to parental models. Says his mother, "Letter writing is always something they've seen me do. They see me leave notes to them, and so they leave notes back to me. That's what I've asked them to do when I'm on the phone; if it's really urgent, write it to me." In one short period, Lewis' notes around their house included,

I'm ready!

Do you want me to take a bath?

Cut the grill cheese in half I'll be back later ok! I'll be out-side with Justin.

They won't fit in my dror!

When are we going to make the deviled eggs? Love, Lewis the Great

Today! channel 07, 8:05 Eastern *A CRISTMAS STORY* it's funny.

Children learn about how writing matters in adult lives by what they see. Fourth grader Mary Elizabeth thinks that "adults write lots of stuff. Checks, bonds, directions, lists, documents, contracts, and notes so they can remember things. Grownups have to write their wills too." However, according to avid writer and second grade wit Nicole, "Grownups don't write. They may write opinions, but most of them don't write stories. My teacher writes, but very seldom. My parents? No way!"

If children are to expand upon their own reasons to write, they need to see the wide range of reasons adults find for writing: to record, to communicate, to share information, to express themselves. Children who see adults as writers, see writing as a productive enterprise.

Avoid the Urge to "Teach" Children to Write

Research shows that children come naturally to writing, often before they are reading. Says Lauren's mom, "She was doing pretty much before school. You just couldn't read any of it, you know. . . . there was lots of scribble and that kind of thing." Any parent is bound to be excited about the first gestures toward forming letter-like shapes. However, parents who attempt to build on this initial interest, to teach or coach their children, usually meet only frustration and can turn a delightful activity into work. Fred's mother learned from her son how to let him go.

She heard that children were doing journals in kindergarten so she decided to have Fred keep a daily diary during the summer before he started school. "He would just decide what he wanted to say, and I would print or write it, and he would draw a picture. And I thought that would help him not to freak out about doing this at school." Instead, they often reached loggerheads—and tears—when Fred insisted he had nothing to say.

A year later, looking at her son's rich kindergarten journals, she realized that it was her own "teaching" that had been too demanding. "I was trying to have him keep what *I* thought was a diary, so I would try to get him to say just one thing about his day, but some days there just isn't anything a child has to say." Once in school, in a daily writing time, Fred wrote about the special events in his life—going fishing, having the chicken pox, his dad's visit to school—often repeatedly. The everyday events his mother insisted upon had only frustrated him. To Fred, these mundane events simply weren't important enough to make note of—as any true diarist will agree.

On the other hand, programs that encourage children to write freely can be an incentive to continue. A local bookstore's summer program tied children's literature to writing and allowed Lewis to be as inventive as he pleased; as a result, he believed early that he *could* write and, in fact, that he was good at it. He too could mimic or create stories like those in the books he loved. He gained confidence and by third grade was widely recognized as a major classroom author. Said his buddy, Jonathon, "Lewis has great ideas. He reads a lot of books. He has like a whole library of books in his house. I read one book, and he writes sorta like that author writes!"

As we all know, we usually *can* do what we, and others, believe we can do. However, without a foundation of confidence nurtured in our early years, many people enter life with a fear of writing. And unintentionally, we pass on this fear through inappropriate demands on ourselves and others.

Don't Expect Adult Perfection, and Don't Embarrass Children by Worrying about or Laughing at Their Developmental Mistakes

Writing, in all forms, is a very personal and precarious endeavor. We all fear the critic when we put words on paper. Yet parents, ever vigilant, tend to worry that every mark on paper is a sign of delay.

"What I remember at first," says Andrea's dad, "is that we wondered if she was dyslexic because she made letters backwards. When we asked around a little bit, we found that was very common, and, you know, what mattered was just that she was trying to do it. She was looking one way and her hand was going another, but she was trying." Instead of worry, Andrea's parents decided to celebrate her newfound interest in copying and writing letters, and she continues to be an avid writer.

Once children begin to write, teachers today encourage children to "invent" spelling of words they are unsure of; they help children see that people can look up words or ask for help when a piece is ready for sharing with others. Insistence on perfection at all stages, in fact, may hinder growth. According to Harste, Woodward, and Burke (1984), "To live within existing rules and predictable patterns is not to grow. . . . By penalizing the language user for engaging in risk-taking, teachers or would-be teachers potentially convince the language learner to play it safe or, worse yet, encourage nonengagement." When a child is encouraged to think through spelling that seems to make sense rather than slavishly memorize, "he or she finds himself or herself in a setting where calculated guesses and 'what-I'm-ready-for' are allowed to evolve" (p. 136).

Jenny's mother recognized the difference in her own children:

> He was more interested in learning about [writing]; she was a little bit later, but she seemed to learn it all at once. She brings home these little short stories—two or three little sentences but they are stories—and the fact that she'll write it and she doesn't care about the spelling. . . . My little boy, he was always concerned with how the word was spelled and how the letters were made and if it was down correctly on the paper and where the punctuation goes and everything, and as a result, he was more hesitant to put anything down. Now [with invented spelling], it's really opened up both of them because now I see Joey is writing more too.

Unfortunately children's tentative, expanding sense of spelling can result in funny meanings. Try to envision the pain you would feel if a superior laughed with others over your private and unintentional slips. Instead of laughing, help young writers save face by searching for their intended meaning. Discuss how adults write—often struggling and revising until they get their ideas just right—and then edit carefully before sending out their work. Otherwise enjoy what is written and marvel at the truly amazing natural growth that occurs in a child's writing in a year's time. Can you say as much for your own?

"Last year we were going to send out Christmas cards to grandparents and aunts and whatever," says Lauren's mom, "and the children were just not interested in signing a typical card. Since they loved to cut, draw, paste and color, I just gave them some construction paper and cookie cutters to get some patterns, but they thought that was cheating. It had to be freehand to be theirs, and they really seemed to enjoy doing it that way."

Encourage, Accept, and Enjoy All Writing That Children Produce

Parents of avid writers know when to get out of the way, but they also know how to encourage. They hang writing on the refrigerator, mail it to family members, and seek out writing contests and other ways to publish children's writing. They carefully save children's writing, and now and then they take out old boxes to celebrate the growth that written products reveal. They begin book-binding projects at their schools to celebrate all children's best written products. Most of all, they are on call to listen when a young writer's new ideas are born.

Parents of avid writers also value writing and help their families see how writing can be meaningful to real audiences. When Emily expressed an interest in a newspaper article about kudzu, her mother encouraged her to write to the man being interviewed. This avid defender of the South's most hated plant not only wrote back but made Emily the vice president of his new kudzu fan club. For each of her two children, Irene has maintained a journal from the day she found out she was pregnant. A professional typist, she doesn't write every day, but at least weekly she takes a few minutes to record the major events of each child's life on a separate file. Already in elementary school, her children love to hear "their" stories. Could there be any better holiday gifts than family-written collections of memories about each other? Family heirlooms in the making.

Just as successful novelists may have greatness in their blood, avid writers may come prepackaged to some extent. However, home, school, and community environments that demystify the written word and invite children to participate in their own ways encourage writing as an accessible, life-long adventure. Once they—and we—experience the awesome power and potential of the written word, it is hard to go back. The most important step, then, in encouraging a young writer is simply to take off *with* her or him down that uncharted course of possibility and delight in all that has been and has yet to be written down.

Bissex, Glenda L. (1980). *GNYS AT WRK: A child learns to write and read.* Cambridge, MA: Harvard University Press.

Britton, James, et al. (1975). *The development of writing abilities.* London: Macmillan.

For Further Reading: Children and Early Writing

Harste, Jerome C., Virginia A. Woodward, and Carolyn L. Burke. (1984). *Language stories and literacy lessons.* Portsmouth, NH: Heinemann Educational Books.

Hudson-Ross, Sally, Linda Miller Cleary, and Mara Casey (eds.). (In press). *Children's voices: Children talk about literacy.* Portsmouth, NH: Heinemann Educational Books.

Newkirk, Thomas. (1989). *More than stories: The range of children's writing.* Portsmouth, NH: Heinemann Educational Books.

Temple, Charles, Ruth Nathan, Nancy Burris, and Frances Temple. (1988). *The beginnings of writing* (2nd ed). Boston: Allyn and Bacon.

Chapter 12

The Role of Lists in Family Literacy

Nancy Padak
Timothy Rasinski

N ancy Padak is an associate professor of Curriculum & Instruction at Kent State University where she also directs the Reading and Writing Center. She has worked extensively with several Even Start Family Literacy programs in Ohio.

Tim Rasinski also teaches literacy education courses at Kent State University and has been active in supporting family literacy programs in Ohio.

One of the most fundamental forms of writing is lists. In nearly every form of human activity lists are present. Lists are abundant in most homes—grocery lists, menus, lists of household chores or things to do at work, lists of new books to read, lists of messages from the answering machine. Adults have different list-making preferences. Gary Padak and Tim Rasinski, for example, make lists all the time, little "to do" lists to keep organized and, perhaps, provide a sense of accomplishment as the items on their lists are scratched out. Nancy Padak, on the other hand, rarely makes "to do" lists. When she does, it usually means that she is too busy, that she's afraid she'll forget something important. In fact, if she notices too many lists on her desk at work, it's a sign to slow down. Kathy Rasinski keeps a list of her children's activities on a calendar—on Monday, Mike has cross-country practice from 4:00 to 6:00 P.M. and band from 7:30 to 9:00. Emily has soccer from 5:30 to 7:00.

So each of us has our own way with lists. But for each of us, lists are an important and functional type of writing.

So it is with our children. They, too, are natural list makers. To some extent, their lists reflect their ages. Nancy's daughter Katy, for example, who recently moved into her first apartment, left behind a pages-long list of household items that she hoped to accumulate. Not too long ago, Katy used lists for other functional purposes, such as her list of reasons why she should be allowed to stay up later than 9 P.M. (Reason #1—I'm the ONLY kid in third grade who has to go to bed that early.) Sixth grader Emily Rasinski keeps a special notebook in which she records her daily homework assignments. As a new first grader, Mary Rasinski made a list of things to buy for school (see Figure 12.1). Even as a toddler, Mary made her own version of her mother's grocery list (see Figure 12.2). Over time and with encouragement, those lists become much more conventional in form. By the time she was in kindergarten, Mary's grocery lists began to take on a more conventional form (see Figure 12.3).

Our children's lists also reflect their interests. Matt Padak is a sports nut; he always has been and he probably always will be. Most of his lists have something to do with sports. Each year, for example, he compiles a list of current baseball players called "My All-Star Team," which he compares to those voted upon by fans. He recently developed a list of his "All Time Best All-Star Team" (see Figure 12.4). Mike Rasinski uses lists when he and his cousin put on their own version of the "David Letterman Show." Lists such as "Ten reasons why summer vacation should last through September" or "Ways to drive your teachers crazy" are the heart of these shows. At the beginning of the summer, six-year-old Mary made a list of things she wanted to do (see Figure 12.5). Like their parents, our children use lists in their own functional ways, for their own purposes.

Our family members are pretty typical as list makers, both in terms of the reasons we make lists and the types of lists we make. We make lists to remember and to keep ourselves organized; we make lists to record our wishes, either concrete like birthday gifts or abstract like bedtimes; we make lists for fun. Some we share with others, and others we write for ourselves. Lists are just a part of life in our homes, as they are in many others.

Figure 12.1

MARY'S SCHOOL LIST

Figure 12.2
MARY'S TODDLER VERSION OF MOM'S GROCERY LIST

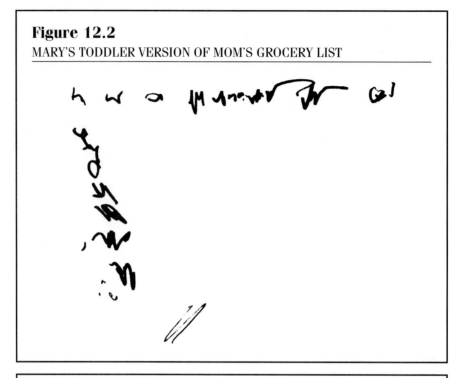

Figure 12.3
MARY'S KINDERGARTEN-AGE GROCERY LIST

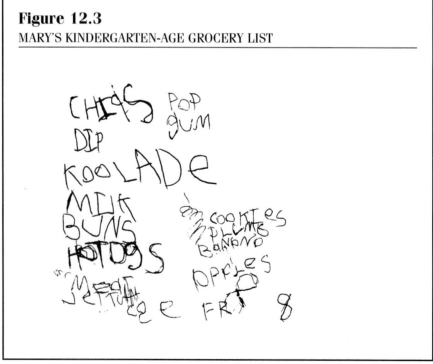

Figure 12.4

MATT'S ALL-STAR TEAM

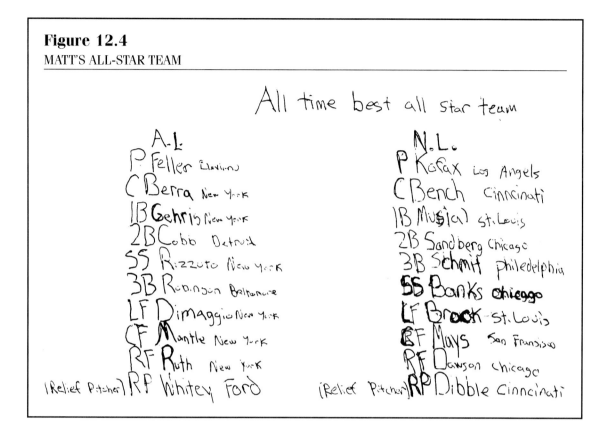

List making may be the most natural, authentic, and prolific type of writing we do at home. For this reason, lists are a good choice for parents and children writing and reading together. Some ideas about encouraging children to make lists are presented in this chapter, as are suggestions for using lists as the basis for more elaborated writing.

Especially if the adults they live with are listmakers, children can and will make lists at home. Whether based in reality or fantasy, children's lists are as real and functional as adults' lists. For some children, listmaking is a spontaneous activity. Matt makes his sports lists, for example, just because he wants to. Over the years, his lists have become more complex. He has recently begun using the computer to make lists of his sports cards (see Figure 12.6), using different computer files for different types of cards (e.g., "best cards") and creating categories that capture what he considers important information (e.g., number of cards, condition of cards).

Other times, parents can offer assistance by suggesting that children make lists. When Emily was preparing to go to camp this past summer, she worked with her mother to develop a list of things to take with her. "Why don't you make a list?" is also a good response when the inevitable barrage of birthday wishes begins to dominate conversations.

Children and Lists

Figure 12.5
MARY'S SUMMER ACTIVITY LIST

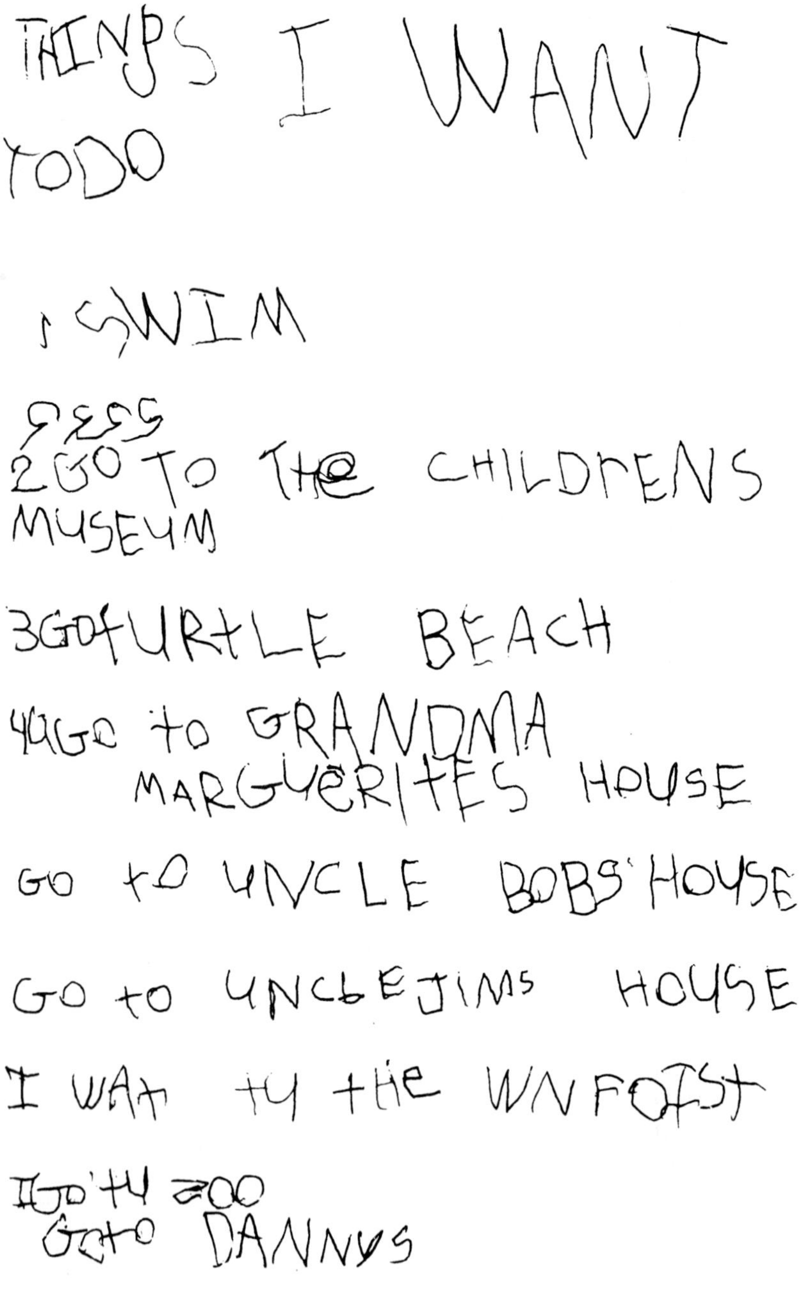

THINGS I WANT
TODO

SWIM

2 GO TO THE CHILDRENS
MUSEUM

3 GO TURTLE BEACH

4 GO to GRANDMA
        MARGUERITES HOUSE

GO to UNCLE BOBS HOUSE

GO to UNCLE JIMS HOUSE

I WAA ty the WNFOTSt

I GO ty ZOO
GOto DANNYS

Figure 12.6

MATT'S SPORTS CARD LIST

BEST CARD

Player	Year	Brand	Num.	Cond.
R. Clemente	1967	Topps	1	EXC
A. Dawson	1977	Topps	1	EXC
T. Seaver	1975	Topps	1	EXC
O. Smith	1980	Topps	1	EXC
F. Thomas	RK90	Topps	3	EXC
F. Thomas	RK90	Score	1	MINT
F. Thomas	1992	ToppsSC	1	MINT
W. Stargell	1973	Topps	1	EXC
W. Stargell	1970	Topps	1	EXC
J. Bench	1973	Topps	1	GOOD
D. Gooden	RK85	Topps	1	MINT
G. Sheffeild	RK89	Topps	1	EXC
T. Glavine	RK90	Topps	3	EXC
S. Avery	RK90	Topps	3	EXC
N. Charlton	RK89	Topps	4	EXC
J. Canseco	RK89	Topps	2	EXC
D. Justice	RK90	Topps	2	MINT
A. Benes	RK89	Topps	3	EXC
R. Clemens	RK86	Topps	1	MINT
W. Clark	RK87	Topps	1	EXC
S. Avery	RK90	DNRS	1	MINT
B. Jackson	RK87	Topps	1	EXC
J. Gonzalez	RK91	Topps	1	EXC
M. Surkont	1955	Topps	1	GOOD
G. Stephens	1955	Topps	1	GOOD
J. Gonzalez	RK90	Topps	1	MINT
R. Santo	1965	Topps	1	EXC
R. Sutcliffe	RK80	Topps	1	EXC
S. Avery	RK90	UD	1	MINT
G. Maddux	RK87	DNRS	1	MINT
K. Griffey Jr.	RK89	DNRS	1	EXC
M. Mcgwire	RK87	Topps	1	EXC
F. Viola	RK83	Topps	1	EXC
L. Walker	RK90	Fleer	1	MINT
T. Fryman	RK90	CMC	1	MINT
M. Mantle	1982	ASA	1	MINT
R. Martinez	RK89	Topps	1	EXC
G. Olson	RK90	Topps	1	EXC

Parents can also promote list making as a way to solve problems. Before the last holiday season, Matt (then 11) agonized over whether he should ask for a Super Nintendo (SNES) or a Sega Genesis entertainment system. After hearing him go back and forth on his choice for a few weeks, his parents finally suggested that he list the strengths and weaknesses of each system. He did (see Figure 12.7) and ultimately made a decision. The list helped him to solve a problem that was very real for him. Mike monitors his performance in school by keeping lists of assignment grades and test scores for each of his classes and periodically calculating his current grade.

Figure 12.7

MATT'S COMPARISON OF SUPER NINTENDO AND SEGA GENESIS

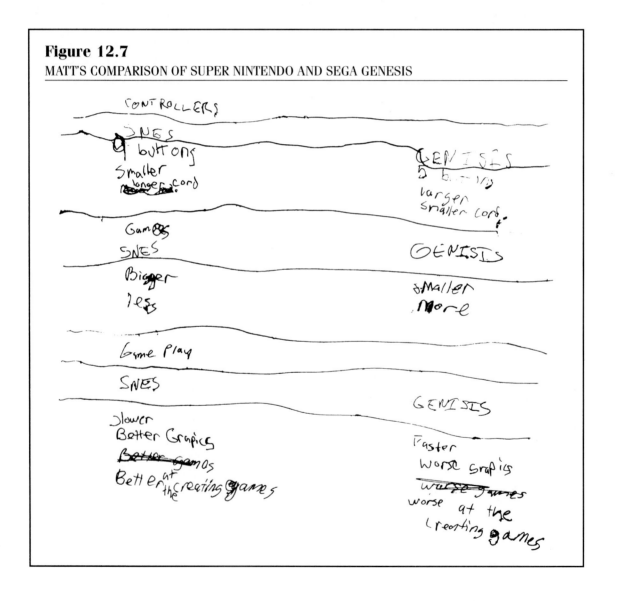

Parents can encourage children's list writing, as well as all other types of at-home writing, by adhering to a few simple rules. First, children need easy access to writing materials—pens, pencils, crayons, markers; lined and unlined paper of different sizes. If these materials are readily available, such as in bedrooms or play areas, children will be able to write lists whenever they want. Other materials such as magazines and merchandise catalogues can be the sources of inspiration for children's list writings. Emily's birthday gift list (Figure 12.8), developed when she was eight going on nine, came from the toy section of a store catalogue.

Having a place to keep or display lists is important, too. At some houses, lists end up under magnets on the refrigerator. Other families have bulletin boards for displaying lists and other family-generated writing. Some children like spiral notebooks for saving their lists and other types of writing.

Parents support children's list making by making their own lists and involving children in their development. For example, when planning a shopping trip, a father and son might survey the house or apartment looking for items that need to be purchased. Then together they can make a shopping list that reflects the family's needs. And if they go shopping together, they can check items off as they find them or tear the list in half, with each person finding items on his half. Although this activity may seem simple and commonplace, it sends the child a powerful message: Grownups make lists because they are useful.

Parents can assist young children in their efforts to make lists by taking dictation. This simply involves writing down exactly what the child wishes to say in her

Getting
Started
with Lists

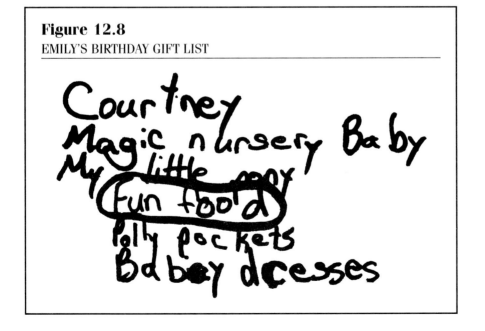

Figure 12.8
EMILY'S BIRTHDAY GIFT LIST

own words. The child should sit where he can see the words as they are written, and the parent should read the finished list to be certain that it says what the child wants it to say. These simple techniques have the added benefit of graphically showing young children how written language works. Figure 12.9 shows a list of toys that Mary dictated to her mother when she was a five year old. Note how Kathy Rasinski took Mary's dictation verbatim—even in number nine. Incidentally, just the process of list making can be a powerful model for children's own writing. As Kathy was taking dictation from Mary, her three-year-old sister, Jennifer, wrote her own list of toys (see Figure 12.10).

Finally, an attitude of acceptance is critical for encouraging children's list making. Young children's lists may be scribbles (Figure 12.2) or pictures. For example, Mary's initial list of school supplies for first grade was a set of drawings (see Figure 12.1). Nevertheless, they were quite clear and specific. Invented or made-up spellings may also appear. Parents should accept the physical appearance of their children's lists instead of expecting perfect, adult-like formats. Especially for something as informal as making a list, the content of the list and the child's interest in writing it are far more important than the list's surface appearance.

Lists as a Springboard for Writing

Lists have value all by themselves, of course. In a recent *Newsweek* article about lists, Robert Samuelson (1993) suggested that "We love lists because they satisfy our craving to count, collect and categorize" (p. 55). He also speculated about the many functions lists can serve—to entertain, educate, surprise, or simplify.

Lists can also serve as springboards for other, more elaborate forms of communication. Adults frequently make lists to prompt their oral communication—lists of points to make during an important telephone call or at a critical meeting. We make lists to keep track of what we want to say and to ensure that we don't forget anything.

Likewise, lists can facilitate written communication. An outline for a story or report, for example, is nothing more than an organized list. Because we know the value of lists, we outlined our ideas before writing this chapter. Having our ideas in list form on paper allowed us to organize our thinking, which made it easier to have this chapter say what we wanted it to say.

Children can use lists in much these same ways. And they will, especially if they have learned the value of lists, both reading them and writing them. Figure 12.11, another illustration of Matt's list making, shows how children can use lists to develop their own writing. In this case, Matt had read one of those magazines, published before a new professional sports season, that recaps the previous season and offers predictions about the one to come. The articles in these magazines typically contain ranked lists of teams. Matt didn't like the ones he read, so he made his own (see the left side of the figure). Then, mimicking the articles in the magazine, he developed written rationales for his choices (see right side of the figure). The lists that he read gave him ideas for his own lists; the related articles that he read and the lists he had written gave him ideas for his own writing.

As with the making of lists, encouraging children to expand their lists into more elaborated writing is not difficult. Sometimes a simple suggestion will do the trick: "Maybe you could make a list of the things you want to write to grandma about. That

Figure 12.9
MARY'S DICTATED TOY WISH LIST

TOYS I WANT

1. STARLOVE

2. MAGIC JEWEL DOLL

3. EGG

4. FLOWERS

5. DOLLY

6. STACEY'S TWIN BROTHER

7. STACEY

8. JEWELERY

9. I DON'T KNOW WHAT
   ELSE I WANT

way you won't forget anything" or "What do you want to say to grandma? Tell me and I'll make a list for you so you don't forget." Suggestions like these may prompt children to see the value of lists for organizing their thoughts.

More elaborate writing activities, such as stories or school reports, may require more involved lists, such as outlines. Here, too, parents can assist children by showing them how lists can help them. One way to do this is to suggest that the child

Figure 12.10
THREE-YEAR-OLD JENNIFER'S TOY WISH LIST

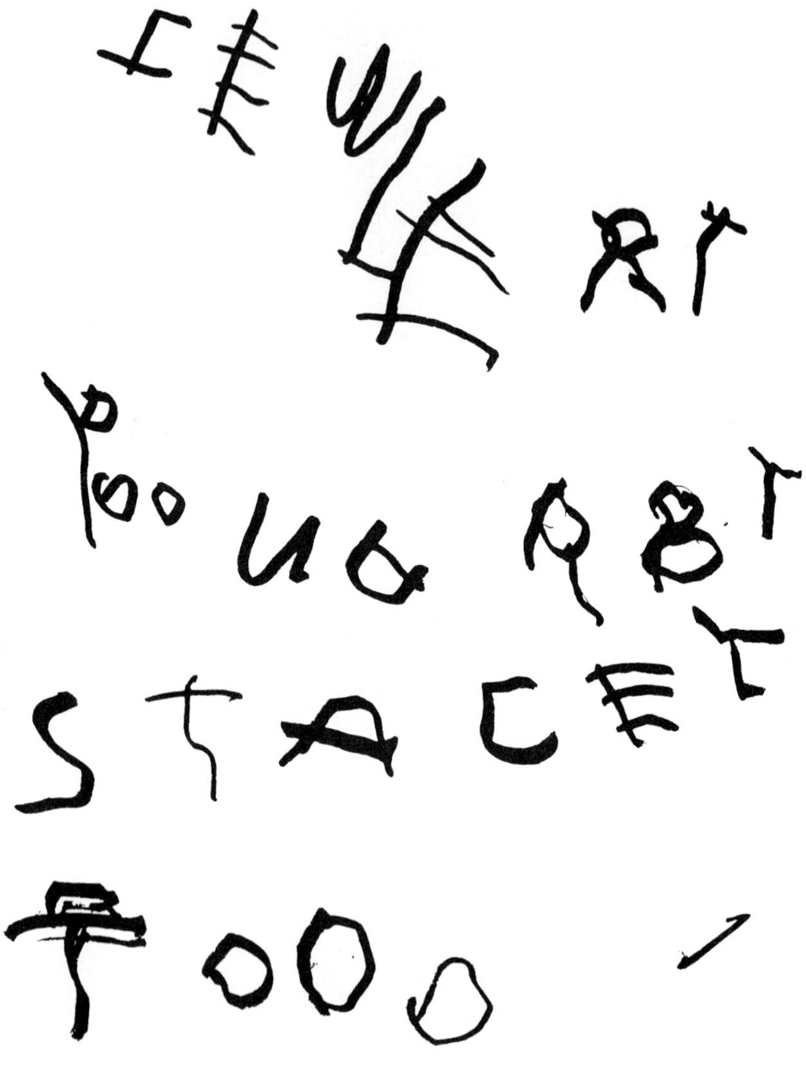

number the items in her list to correspond to the order in which they will appear in writing. Another alternative is to label several pieces of paper with major topics (events or episodes in a story or major sections of a report). Lists of points to make about each major topic can then be made on the pieces of paper and, if necessary, renumbered as above. Either way, parents can show children how useful lists can be for organizing their thoughts before writing.

Figure 12.11

MATT'S BASEBALL PREDICTIONS

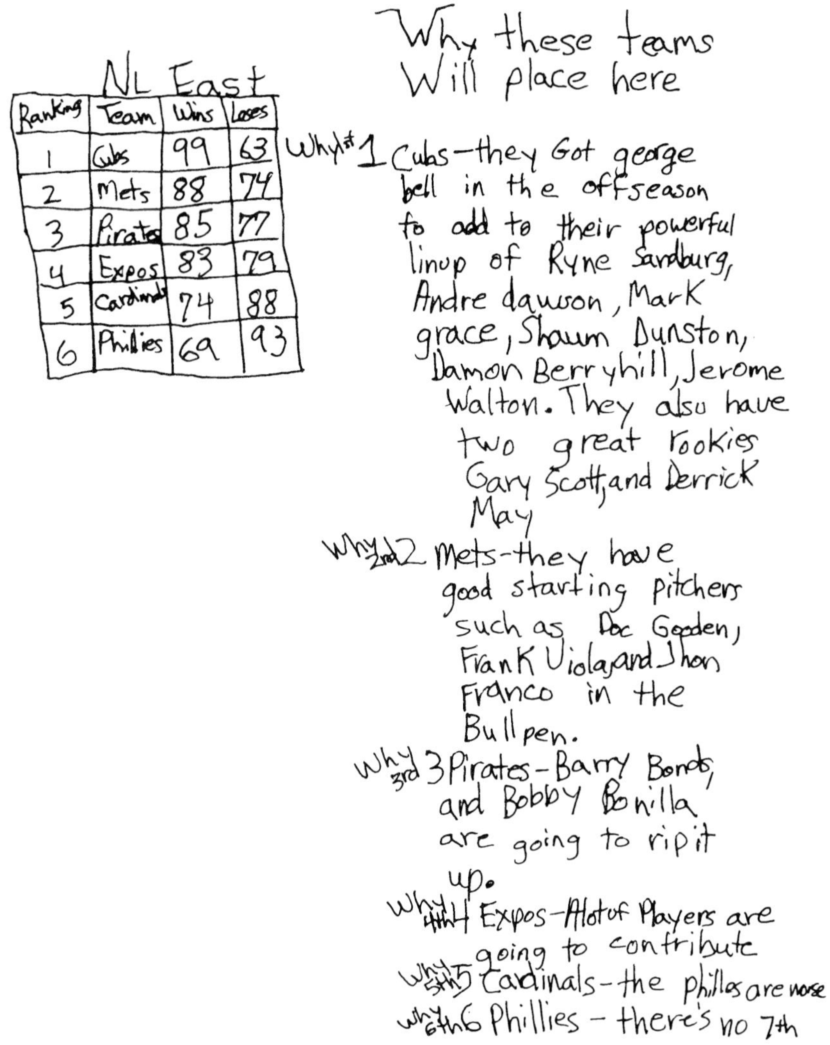

Why these teams
Will place here

Ranking	Team	Wins	Loses
1	Cubs	99	63
2	Mets	88	74
3	Pirates	85	77
4	Expos	83	79
5	Cardinals	74	88
6	Phillies	69	93

NL East

Why #1 Cubs—they Got george bell in the offseason to add to their powerful linup of Ryne Sandburg, Andre dawson, Mark grace, Shawn Dunston, Damon Berryhill, Jerome Walton. They also have two great rookies Gary Scott, and Derrick May

Why 2nd Mets—they have good starting pitchers such as Doc Gooden, Frank Viola, and Jhon Franco in the Bull pen.

Why 3rd Pirates—Barry Bonds, and Bobby Bonilla are going to rip it up.

Why 4th Expos—Alot of Players are going to contribute

Why 5th Cardinals—the phillies are worse

Why 6th Phillies — there's no 7th

Conclusion

Why are lists such a pervasive form of writing? Perhaps because they're useful; perhaps because they're easy; or perhaps, as Robert Samuelson suggests, because they satisfy people's inherent need to count and classify. Whether we're jotting down our own ideas or reading someone else's, we encounter lists frequently in our daily lives, probably because they serve important, functional purposes.

Parents and children can make lists together, and parents can encourage their children to make lists on their own. This simple and natural family literacy activity nurtures, firsthand, the development of children's writing abilities and helps them see the value of this ubiquitous form of writing.

Reference

Samuelson, R.J. (1993). The glory of (yes) lists. *Newsweek* (July 19), 55.

Chapter 13

Helping Develop Competent Spellers: Parents and Children Working Together

Jerry Zutell

J erry Zutell is an associate professor in the Graduate Program of Language, Literature and Reading at Ohio State University, where he teaches courses in Advanced Reading Methods, Corrective Reading, and Clinical Reading. Zutell's major area of interest is the study of children's acquisition of word knowledge in reading and writing. He has done research and written articles about assessing students' oral reading fluency, the stages of spelling development, connections between word knowledge in spelling and reading, and instructional practices for making students better readers and spellers. He is also a senior author of the spelling textbook series, *Spell It—Write!*, published by Zaner-Bloser Educational Publishers.

S pelling is one of the most visible and permanent products of literacy instruction. Much of what happens during reading happens "in the head" of the
reader, or at least in the quickly passing stream of oral language. But because
it is part of the written record, both correct spellings, and especially misspellings, are
fixed on the paper to be easily and repeatedly examined. Moreover, the standards we
have for accuracy in spelling are remarkably high. The one word out of a hundred
that is misspelled grabs our attention and has, at the least, a subtle effect on our assessment of the care, education, and intelligence of the writer and the validity of that
writer's message. State and national politicians and members of the general public
often simplistically use misspellings as indicators of the general failure of schools to
help students master basic literacy skills.

Spelling instruction has long been one of the cornerstones of the elementary
school curriculum because of this visibility and because the plan for spelling instruction has remained fairly consistent over the years: Pretest over an assigned class
list from the spelling book on Monday, study and practice on worksheets during the
week, formal test for a grade on Friday. Many teachers and parents have liked the
simple, straightforward nature of this routine. Teachers have felt comfortable in
sending word lists home for practice, and parents have believed that in helping with
their spelling assignments they have a positive way of participating in their child's
education.

But many students have been frustrated by their lack of success on such activities and what they see as the mindless drudgery of the tasks required of them. For the
parents of these children the weekly test has become a source of anxiety and stress,
and home practice a source of family conflict.

As ideas about child-centered and literature-based literacy instruction have become more popular, more school systems and individual teachers have begun to incorporate spelling instruction into other areas of the school curriculum. Children are
reading more "real" books, writing down their own thoughts and ideas more frequently, and revising their writing on a regular basis. In this context formal spelling
instruction may be viewed as less important; recent research has shown that learning
to spell is a developmental, complex process rather than simply rote memorization,
so students will learn the spellings of many words from the writing-revising cycle;
when lists of spelling words are assigned they are more likely to be individualized
and come from children's own writing than from an assigned list.

While many parents are heartened to see instruction closer to their children's interests and abilities and students' enthusiasm for real reading and writing increase,
many may still feel uneasy about the change in spelling instruction from what they
themselves experienced in school. As increased wide reading has expanded student
vocabularies, frequent writing has provided students with the opportunities to use
these new words on their own. Since students are writing more and are trying out
more new words, parents are likely to see more spelling errors in their children's work,
which seems to confirm their fears that spelling is not being given adequate attention. But many of these misspellings are of words that students previously wouldn't
have even tried. For example, a teacher recently told of a grandfather who was quite
disturbed that his third grade granddaughter had misspelled *enthusiastically* in her

writing, a great word for her to use in expressing her thoughts, but one that would be unlikely to appear on a third grade spelling list.

The following sections of this chapter address parent concerns about spelling by answering some common questions parents have, providing some ideas about how to create a home environment that supports word learning, and suggesting specific ways of helping children become more positive about and successful with spelling list assignments.

Why is English spelling so hard?
We often think of English spelling as hard to learn because there doesn't appear to be a straightforward and consistent match between the sounds in words and the letters we use to represent them. A single sound may be spelled with different letters or letter combinations (*f*or, *ph*one) and a single letter or combinations of letters may be used to represent more than one sound (*ch*air, *ch*ampagne, *ch*orus).

There are complex historical reasons why this is so. One reason is that English pronunciations have changed dramatically over time, thus changing the matches between pronunciation and spelling in complex but systematic ways. For example, the *k* and *gh* in *knight* were once pronounced, but are now silent.

Another reason for this complexity is that although English began as a dialect of early German, many French words and spellings became part of the basic vocabulary after the Norman Conquest (1066 A.D.) (*beef, soldier*). Many scientific and scholarly words are constructed from Latin and Greek elements, often keeping the letter combinations and sometimes, but not always, the pronunciations from those languages. When the "f sound" is spelled *ph* the word is usually formed from a Greek root (*telephone*). The same is true when *ch* is used to spell the "hard c sound" as in *chorus*. French words that have been borrowed directly may represent the "sh sound" with *ch*, as in *champagne.* Throughout their history, the English-speaking people have continued to borrow and adapt words from languages all over the world (e.g., *rodeo, spaghetti, polka, kimono*) to meet their conceptual and linguistic needs. But a side effect has been to import aspects of other languages' writing systems into English spelling.

Another way we can think about this issue is to recognize that there is much more to a spelling system, especially that of English, than simple sound-letter matching. Spellings are also based on sets of letter combinations that form *visual patterns* (bri*dge*), on *meaning units* that preserve their spellings but change pronunciations (n*a*tion + al = n*a*tional), and how and when the word was created for or imported into the English language (*c*ello borrowed from Italian in which *c* is pronounced "ch").

English spelling is hard because it is complex. There are clearly "irregularities" and idiosyncrasies, but there is often more predictability than we realize. These facts have at least two important implications for learning and teaching: (1) both teachers and parents should recognize that it will take children time to make sense of this system; we must be patient and understanding with them, and not expect perfect spelling from the very beginnings of writing; and (2) we should help students

Some
Questions
Parents Ask

recognize predictable patterns and meaning connections as best we can so that the system makes as much sense to them as possible.

Isn't learning to spell just a matter of rote memorization?
Recent analyses of children's spelling attempts have shown that as children gain in spelling skill they do more than memorize individual words. They form concepts about how words work—what letters can go together under what conditions, how syllables are joined in relation to sound and meaning, etc.

Learning about spelling appears to be conceptual and developmental. First, while highly familiar and/or personal words may be learned individually, with less familiar words some *word types* are easier to learn to spell than others. For example, young children are usually able to spell the short vowel words like p*e*t and l*a*nd correctly before they can consistently use "silent e" and vowel combinations accurately in long vowel words like sp*a*ce and ch*ai*n. Control over how syllables are joined (whether to double a consonant or drop a "silent e" before adding an ending) comes much later.

Second, as children increase their spelling vocabulary and gain a greater understanding of the system, *how* they misspell unknown words changes as well. Consider, for example, the following attempts at the word *commotion:*

KMOSHN   CAMOSHIN   COMOSTION   COMOTION

The child who created the first attempt spelled the word phonetically, doing a good job of matching letters and the sounds heard distinctly in the word's normal pronunciation. The child who produced the second attempt has become visually sensitive to the use of the letter *c* for the "k" sound. That child is also spelling more by syllables, having learned that each syllable must include a vowel, even when the syllable is unstressed and the vowel element is barely heard. The third attempt reveals considerable familiarity with some of the more complex class of words spelled with the *-ion* suffix. This spelling is particularly interesting because of the inclusion of both *s* and *t* with *-ion.* On the surface it may appear that the child has either mispronounced the word or made a bad letter–sound match. However, the child is more likely to be working on balancing how to represent what is heard as "sh" with the known *-tion* visual pattern, so elements of both are included. The child who produces the fourth attempt has resolved that problem, but has not yet figured out how prefixes added to a root sometimes create a double-consonant pattern at the beginning of the word.

Changes in both what words are spelled correctly and how unknown words are tried tell us that children do not simply memorize words in rote or arbitrary ways. Familiarity with words leads to seeing connections and patterns in spelling. These understandings, in turn, make the spellings of new words easier to remember. Learning to spell is, to a large degree, a problem-solving process.

Will producing misspellings in their writings make it harder for children to learn those words later on?
The answer to this question is based directly on the ideas in the answer to the previous one. Since learning to spell is conceptual and developmental, children need the opportunities to experiment with spelling that are provided by frequent, meaningful

writing in a nonthreatening atmosphere. Spellings of unknown words move toward correct form as the child's experiences and concept development allow. There is no evidence to show that misspellings in writing are the *cause* of later spelling difficulties. However, during writing conferences with students, teachers can encourage students to locate misspellings in their work and learn the correct spellings of words they use regularly. Good teachers challenge their students to become word-conscious, but they also know which words are in their conceptual grasp, and focus their attention on a manageable number of these.

Why do children sometimes continue to misspell words in their writing that they have spelled correctly on tests?
To make sense of this fact we must first take into account the differences between the two situations. When students take the weekly test they know the words they are to be tested on, they have already spent time practicing those words, and their full attention is on spelling. In authentic writing activities, students focus mainly on the ideas they want to communicate and how to best express those ideas. Word choice is based on appropriateness, not spelling practice (though writers may sometimes pick a synonym to avoid using a word they are unsure of). While writers focus mostly on ideas, young learners may also have to concentrate on other aspects of production like handwriting and spacing, as well as spelling. Thus spelling is only one factor among many in writing, and it is not the primary focus of attention. Writers also know that they can change what they have done during a revising or proofreading stage in the process, so they may be less concerned about spelling during initial production.

One might then ask, if spelling practice and tests are so different than spelling in real writing situations, is there any value to formal instruction and testing? More organized, focused spelling activities are instructionally useful in that they give students the opportunity to step back and examine words and see the connections between them in order to make more sense of the system and make spellings more memorable. Students need to have easy command of a wide spelling vocabulary in order to make writing fluent. Organized practice can help students build spelling fluency and develop strategies for trying unknown words. But, in order for such instruction to be effective, it must be combined with many opportunities for real reading and writing, students must see the connections between practice and the words they use, words chosen should be appropriate to the writing needs and the conceptual level of the students, and testing should be used as a means for giving students positive feedback about what they are learning, not as a means to compare students and thus mark many as failures. Formal instruction should spark and encourage student curiosity about words and their written forms, not dampen and discourage it.

Creating a Home Environment

There are many positive things parents can do at home to foster an interest in words and to provide the setting and the information students need to become active, successful word learners.

Reading to and with children and encouraging them to read on their own are valuable for many reasons. For spelling, it gives students multiple encounters with an extensive vocabulary and familiarity with a variety of visual forms that makes learning to spell so much easier. A large reading vocabulary also provides students with the necessary examples that help them make sense of the many complex patterns that are part of the English spelling system.

The vast majority of words we learn to read and spell are not taught to us directly in school. If students were taught 25 new spelling words every week 40 weeks a year, for the eight years of elementary school, a total of 8,000 would be covered. (This is clearly a very generous estimate, not accounting for review and repetition and assuming every word taught is learned.) Yet the literate adult has at his or her command many times that number. Most words are learned through the many encounters we have with them in wide reading and frequent writing. Schooling can provide specific activities with a basic vocabulary and should provide numerous opportunities for such reading and writing. It should also help us develop a way of processing words that make the new ones we encounter easier to remember. But the fact remains that wide reading outside of school probably accounts for the greater proportion of our word learning.

Similarly, the value of regular, meaningful writing experiences at home as well as in school cannot be overestimated. These serve as natural opportunities for children to develop fluency in spelling known words and as a means for them to use their understandings of the system to attempt less familiar ones. A recent study in first grade classrooms indicated that those students who wrote regularly, even with misspellings, did as well or better than students who did not. Most important, writing activity was particularly beneficial to the less accomplished students.

Parents cannot and should not force their children to write regularly, but they can encourage writing by having materials conveniently available in the home, using writing as a natural part of daily life (taking phone messages, writing out grocery lists), encouraging their children to do the same, and accepting and praising their children's efforts.

Of course, the presence and regular use of a *dictionary* and *thesaurus* in the home directly conveys a sense of interest in words and their meanings. There are also many books available that explore the meanings and origins of individual words, phrases and idioms. Along with modeling how to use such materials for specific purposes (finding the meaning or spelling of an unknown word or locating synonyms for writing), parents can model and encourage browsing through these books. In doing so, they demonstrate a basic curiosity about words and the pleasure and satisfaction that can come from learning something new.

It is also especially helpful to have available and to use *books and other materials that play with words.* For example, in the *Amelia Bedelia* stories (by Peggy Parish) humorous situations are created when Amelia misinterprets everyday expressions and idioms. For example, when told to dust the furniture, she applies a fine coat of dust to tables and chairs. Several books by the late Fred Gwynne (for example, *The King Who Rained* and *Chocolate Moose for Dinner*) use illustrations and spellings to play with the use of homophones (words that sound the same but have different meanings) and figures of speech. Others might combine illustrations and word forms to create clever misunderstandings, as in *Daffy Definitions* by Joseph Rosenbloom (for example, chargeable—what the toreador does). Joke books for children often use puns and plays on words as the basis of their humor. Such books are not only enjoyable, they help children step back and look at words from new and often unusual perspectives. They help children develop a sense of exploration that underlies their ability to examine patterns in language, especially in words.

Other sources of information and pleasure are the many word games available in stores and often present in daily newspapers and magazines. (I well remember as a child working together with my parents to solve the JUMBLE in the daily paper as dinner was being prepared.) Many of these are aimed at or have special editions for younger children. Crossword puzzles, scrambled letter games, Scrabble, Boggle, Perquackey, Wheel of Fortune, and others focus specifically on how letters and letter combinations are arranged within words, a direct connection to building spelling skill. Both oral and word boardgames can serve as important learning experiences as well as pleasant diversions to pass the time.

Helping with Schoolwork

Many parents are more specifically concerned with how they might best help their children with their schoolwork and homework assignments that are directly related to spelling.

Of course, the first thing to do is to create a positive attitude towards schoolwork and to build the child's confidence in himself or herself as a reader, writer, and speller. When children bring home completed written work, parents should focus on what the child has done well. A first response to writing should be to the content of the piece, the ideas being expressed and the amount of thinking and effort that the child has put in. If a parent does decide to draw the child's attention to spelling, the focus should be on correct spellings, especially of words the child struggled with on other occasions.

The most common way that parents work with children on spelling is by helping them practice and learn the weekly word list. To many this may seem a straightforward, simple task. On the other hand, for parents of children who consistently do poorly on spelling tests, it is often a constant source of frustration. There are, in fact, several things that can be done to make interactions more positive, learning easier, and success more likely.

A first step is to communicate with the teacher, making him or her aware of the support the parent provides and the effort the child puts into his work. Poor spellers are often stereotyped as careless or lazy when, in fact, they may well expend more time and energy than the good spellers for whom the task is quite easy. When the same list is used for all students, poor spellers are expected to learn many more words than good spellers who may very well already know how to spell most of them.

Parents can also check with the teacher to find out how spelling words are selected. Words may come directly from a spelling book, from a core list, from a theme the class is studying, from students' own writing, or from some combination of these. Many teachers are now giving students the responsibility of choosing some of their words themselves. Knowing the sources and reasons for word selection can be useful in at least two important ways: (1) parents can reinforce the connection between the words children are studying and their own reading and writing; students are often more willing to put an effort into spelling activities if they see the relevance to everyday activities; (2) if the word list is organized around spelling patterns or principles parents may be able to help children make the connection between the spellings of individual words and those patterns so that the spellings make more sense and are thus easier to remember.

When a parent does choose to work with a child directly on a spelling list, there are several things to keep in mind and use in order to make their work together more enjoyable and productive:

1. Keep the atmosphere positive by focusing on the child's successes. Whether they state it directly or not, most children value highly and seek their parents' approval; if a child is working on an activity with which she usually has mixed success, working with the parent may only increase stress and anxiety, sure roadblocks to learning, if the parent becomes visibly exasperated or frustrated. It is often better to let the child work alone or with someone else rather than under such conditions.

2. There are two simple ways to check the difficulty of the assigned words for your child: Use a rearranged list or a set of index cards to see if your child can read the spelling words accurately and easily, or give the child a quick test over the words to see how many can already be spelled correctly. (This information may be available from the teacher's own pretest.) If a child struggles with reading many of the words or misspells half or more of the words on a long list (for example, 10 out of 20 words), then correct spellings are going to be difficult to produce and retain. If the list of words seems too hard for your child, discuss this fact with the teacher so that adjustments can be made for future assignments.

3. Play games like Go Fish and Concentration that require careful attention to visual form with assigned words on cards to build familiarity in a positive way.

4. Use study/practice time to work on the words with which your child has difficulty; do not spend much time practicing words she or he already knows. But do make the connections between the spellings of known words and unknown words that follow the same patterns.

5. If the word list is organized around one or more spelling patterns, discuss those patterns and how either pronunciation, special letter combinations, or meaning can be used as cues to spelling. *Examples:* words that have a vowel that "says its name" (long vowel words) are usually spelled with the vowel, a consonant, and "silent e" (c*a*me) or with two vowels together (r*ai*n); Long i plus final "t" is often spelled -*ight* as in r*ight;* past tense verbs are spelled with an -*ed* even when the final sound is "t" (miss*ed*). Encourage your child to decide which words follow which patterns. (Don't be thrown off by words that are

exceptions if they are included on the list, for example, *love,* but do point these out as words that may need special visual attention.)

6. Help your child make connections between patterns in words he knows how to spell and new words or words that are difficult—*Examples:* words that begin with the same sound, rhyming words. Spelling "by analogy" is a conscious strategy that many good spellers use. Poor spellers often have no strategy besides listening for individual sounds.

7. Pronounce words clearly and in an articulate way, but do not distort them. Sounding out words letter by letter is highly overrated. Beginning writers do need to become aware of the phonetic principle that each "sound" in a word needs to be represented by a letter or combination of letters moving left-to-right across the word. But this is a fundamental concept that most children learn early on, sometimes before formal schooling. Spellers must move beyond sound to visual patterns and spelling-by-meaning connections in order to control a large spelling vocabulary. Poor spellers often seem to perseverate on sound, exaggerating pronunciations and sometimes adding letters because of their exaggerations. Telling these students to carefully "sound it out" often reinforces an ineffective strategy that they are already overusing.

8. When your child misspells a word, help her compare the spelling to the correct version. Write the correct spelling above or below the misspelling and discuss which parts of the word the child spelled correctly as well as the parts that caused trouble. Most misspellings are off by only one or two letters. Comparing the spellings allows the child to see how much of the word was handled correctly and the part or parts that need direct attention. It helps make the learning task more manageable.

9. Writing a word several times can be good practice, but not if done as mindless copying. It is best first to let the child look at the correct spelling, then cover the spelling up and have the child visualize the word in his or her mind, then have the child try the word from memory. The correct spelling is next uncovered, and the child compares the attempt with the correct form and tries the word again if necessary.

10. Focus on the child's successes, the words learned rather than those missed. Encourage your child to keep a notebook or log of new words learned. Thus, even the less successful speller can be proud of his learning and build self-confidence over time.

Conclusion

Accurate spelling is important because it serves as a courtesy and aid to the reader and it supports fluent writing focused on the communication of ideas. Students learn many of the words they need from wide reading, frequent writing, and teacher support during the writing process. Focused spelling instruction is also beneficial because it supports student development of concepts that help them make sense of the complex "logic" that underlies the spelling system, making the spelling of individual words more memorable.

Parents can contribute to word learning in a variety of ways: by having a positive, supportive attitude towards their children's writing and spelling efforts, by creating a home environment that stimulates curiosity about words, by having available the resources necessary to satisfy that curiosity, and by playing with words and language with their children in informal, everyday settings. When children need help with more formal spelling assignments parents can use the suggestions presented here to make those activities productive and to build children's spelling skill and self-confidence.

References and Other Readings on the Topic

Bates, D. (1993). *Word games.* Melbourne, Australia: Longman Cheshire.

Geller, L. (1985). *Wordplay and language learning for children.* Urbana, IL: National Council of Teachers of English.

Gentry, J.R. and J.W. Gillet. (1993). *Teaching kids to spell.* Portsmouth, NH: Heinemann.

Henderson, E. (1990). *Teaching spelling.* Boston: Houghton Mifflin.

Chapter 14

Using Computers to Promote Literacy

Linda DeGroff

L inda DeGroff, a former first grade teacher, is now an assistant professor in the Department of Language Education at the University of Georgia where she teaches and does research in children's literature and language arts.

A few years ago my sister and her husband acquired a home computer for their three children who were then in kindergarten, second, and fourth grades. My sister's family lives across the country so I relied on the phone to learn about how they were enjoying and using their new equipment. Over the course of several months I heard about how they set up the computer, tried some of the software that came with it, and tested some games loaned to them by friends. But as the months went by reports became less frequent and I began to suspect they were using the computer less frequently as well.

I thought then that I should write down some suggestions for computer use in the home. But, as we often do, I put this off as other demands filled my time. So I was pleased when I was asked to write this chapter, pleased that I would finally get to share with my sister's family and other families the following suggestions for how to promote literacy with computers in the home.

Provide for Social Interaction

Children learn language, both oral and written, by interacting with others. As youngsters, they learn to talk by listening and speaking to siblings and parents during play and routine events in the home. In school, they learn to read and write by talking about books and creating pieces of writing with peers and teachers.

Interaction around the computer comes naturally in schools where there are many students and fewer computers. Out of necessity or choice, children work in pairs as they collaborate on tasks. Sometimes interaction is spontaneous as passersby interact with computer users, commenting on what they see on the highly visible screen.

Learning through social interaction also can take place around the home computer. Siblings, parents, and friends are the partners with whom children interact. By placing the home computer in a spot where two or more chairs are readily accessible, parents can facilitate interaction. Parents also create environments conducive to language learning when they invite children to share in adult or family computer activities or accept children's invitations to join them in child-initiated activities.

Read and Write for Authentic Purposes, Texts, and Audiences

Words on flashcards, spelling lists, sentences to diagram, multiple-choice questions about main ideas—if these sound familiar, it is because these tasks have been the basics of traditional literacy instruction.

Today, we realize that curling up with a good book, writing in a diary, or corresponding with a friend or grandparent living in a distant town are types of experiences that lead to lifelong reading and writing. Children are motivated to read and write when they are engaged in meaningful or authentic reading and writing activities. Children, like adults, read in order to laugh, cry, be held in suspense, or to find answers to their questions about dinosaurs or volcanoes. Words on flashcards can't fill these needs, but good books, real children's literature, can. Likewise, when children compose in order to store their thoughts, send messages to others, or create stories and poems, they create texts to be read by real audiences—people other than the lone teacher with a red pen.

When children work with computers, they also need to engage in tasks with authentic purposes, to work with meaningful pieces of texts, and to communicate with a variety of real audiences. In schools, students read stories or information stored in computers, write their own stories or reports, print their work to be read by peers, send letters to individuals outside the classroom, and sometimes send messages through electronic mail to audiences near and far. Children can work with computers in the same ways at home, reading and writing for the same purposes and for similar audiences.

Another recent change in literacy learning and instruction concerns the importance of focusing on the processes of reading and writing as well as the products. In the past, we often focused solely on products—flawless oral reading, correct answers to multiple-choice comprehension questions, or final drafts of written pieces.

Value Processes

Today, we recognize that processes, knowing how to go about reading and writing, are essential to literacy development. For readers, this may mean understanding how to adjust strategies required for reading different types of texts. For example, we don't read poetry and newspapers in the same way. For writers, this may mean knowing how to find topics, create a rough draft, revise, and edit.

The many types of texts (stories, information lists, games, directions for operating software) available on computers give children opportunities to engage in diverse reading processes. Likewise, writing with word processors facilitates processes, particularly revising, editing, and publishing. Parents can support the development of reading and writing processes at home by working with children *as* they read and write, by talking with children about strategies they use, and by demonstrating their own successful reading and writing strategies.

Reading and writing are activities that take time. When I'm reading a good book, I like to have hours of uninterrupted quiet so that I can become absorbed in the experience. Likewise, I choose to write when I know I have big chunks of time to immerse myself in my thoughts. I like to be free of distractions when I read and write. I don't read and write with a stopwatch running. I set my own pace and it's often a slow one.

Provide Time and Choice

I also choose what to read and write. Of course, I get lots of suggestions about good books from friends. But, in the end, I make the final selection. Likewise, I write what I choose. I decide when I am going to write letters to friends. And I develop the ideas for pieces of writing—like this chapter.

Children also need time and choice in their reading and writing. School can provide both, but home may do it even better. The hours at school are short and curricular demands often place pressures on time. The hours at home are likely to be more flexible. Given the current arrangements in most schools, it's often difficult for a child to have an hour or more to engage in a reading or writing activity. At home, this is not a problem. After school hours, evenings, and weekends are filled with extended chunks of time for reading and writing. The home environment is also conducive to choice. Home is without a curriculum. Home is an ideal place for children to pursue their very unique interests in reading and writing.

Computers are particularly well suited for providing time and choice. While you may have some images of computers beeping and buzzing to rush you on or to prompt you to enter specific information, this is not the case with word processing and data base software, two basic software tools for writers and readers.

When writers use word processors or databases they work at their own pace, writing and rereading as quickly or slowly as necessary. When writers compose with word processors or fill databases with information, the computer is open to all ideas, forms, and styles. Computers allow young readers and writers to control time and choice—just as you and I like to control time and choice in our reading and writing experiences.

Support Risk Taking

When I think of risk taking, I reflect back to a photography course I took in my early adult years. The instructor calmed our fears and supported our risk taking by explaining that even professional photographers took hundreds of shots in order to get one picture that was completely satisfying.

For children to learn, they too must be free to take hundreds of shots at reading and writing without fear of failure. Children reading and writing with word processors and databases find that computers are very accepting and uncritical. For example, when the young child writes "dnsr" for "dinosaur," the computer accepts this delightful attempt and supports the writer's effort to get ideas into print. The parent's role is to be equally accepting and supportive.

Issues of Equity

Parents reading this chapter are concerned about computers and literacy for *their* children. But if we are to have a healthy and productive society, we must be concerned about *all* children. And, research shows that all children do not have equal access to computers or equal opportunities to use them in constructive ways. Girls and children from economically disadvantaged homes or schools do not have the same opportunities to work with computers that boys and more economically advantaged children have.

What can we do about inequities for girls and economically disadvantaged children? To begin, awareness helps. Share your awareness of equity issues when you talk to school personnel about instruction, programs, and equipment purchases. Let teachers, administrators, school board members, and other parents know about your concerns. Encourage them to think critically about computer access and use in your school. Speak up about concerns for your daughters and other parents' daughters. Speak up about your concerns for *all* children.

Conclusion

The above suggestions describe general attitudes that can help guide our use of computers with children. In the final section, I offer a list of specific activities—all of which can and should be pursued with an eye toward providing for social interaction; reading and writing for authentic purposes, text, and audiences; valuing processes; providing for time and choice; and supporting risk taking.

Ten At-Home Computer Literacy Activities

The following activities can be done using word processing and/or data base software. The activities involve writing. Reading often takes place when children reread what they have written. It's important not to overlook the value of these rereading experiences.

1. Develop family or individual lists of friends' and relatives' names, addresses, phone numbers, birthdays, and anniversaries.

2. Keep a personal diary.

3. Make "wish lists." Wish lists might include gifts children would like to receive, places they would like to visit, activities they would like the family to pursue, or titles of books they would like to read.

4. If your child is a collector (e.g., souvenirs, baseball cards, glass figurines) or an observer (e.g., birds at the backyard feeder, sports statistics, weather watching), work with him or her to develop a system for organizing information in computer files.

5. Write thank-you notes, invitations, friendly letters, letters of request (e.g., for an increase in allowance), or letters to express opinions (e.g., a letter to the editor of the local newspaper about the need for more recycling drop-off points).

6. Write personal or family memories. Children can write about their own experiences or record stories told by relatives.

7. Write imaginative stories, poetry, plays, etc.

8. Write reports based on collection and observations

9. Record favorite recipes. A parent may want to work with a younger child. One can read the recipes from cards or cookbooks while the other transcribes.

10. Create a household inventory for insurance purposes. List important items, their description, and cost, for example.

Chapter 15

Television and Literacy

David Reinking
Douglas Pardon

D avid Reinking is head of the Department of Reading Education at the University of Georgia, where he is also a researcher at the National Reading Research Center funded by the U.S. Department of Education. He has published widely in the area of technology and literacy. Reinking has three school-age children and was an elementary school teacher for eight years prior to his career as a university professor.

Douglas Pardon is an assistant professor of education at Westminster College. He received his Ph.D. in Reading Education from the University of Georgia, and prior to that was a public school teacher.

P arents and teachers share many concerns about children. One of those shared concerns is the effect television viewing has on the academic development of children. Their concerns take the form of questions such as, Does television viewing adversely affect reading achievement? Would children read more if they watched less television? Does television create children who have shorter attention spans or who are more inclined to seek immediate gratification in their learning? In this chapter we approach the topic of television and literacy as a parent, as former elementary school teachers, as educational researchers, and no less important, as individuals who watch a fair amount of television and who are ourselves products of the television age.

One difficulty in addressing this topic is the mixed feelings that many adults have about television. On the one hand we complain about the many examples of television's shallow, seemingly addictive characteristics and on the other we enjoy its ability to entertain, to enlighten, and to motivate learning. Television has produced both the "Beverly Hillbillies" and a widely viewed documentary about the Civil War that subsequently increased the sales of books about that period of history.

Our mixed feelings about television can be translated into mixed messages to our children about television. For example, it may be difficult for children to understand adults' apparent love-hate relationship with television. In our roles as parent and teacher we have discouraged our children from watching television one day and strongly encouraged them to view a particular program the next day, all the while watching a good deal of television ourselves. Parents have been known to rally against television viewing to their children, but then use it as a method for rewarding or punishing certain behaviors. And, what parent has not occasionally used television as an electronic baby-sitter? The teacher whose car displays the bumper sticker "Fight prime time, read a book" may also be the one assigning students to view an educational program to be discussed in class.

As these examples suggest, concerns about television and reading cannot be reduced to the issue of whether or not to watch television. Few would suggest that television viewing should be abolished entirely, although some parents have done so, usually on a temporary basis and often in response to the pleas of educators. Noticeably absent from many discussions about television and reading are findings from research. The discussion of any issue should begin with the relevant facts or at least the best available information. In this chapter we provide a brief overview of the best available information about the relation between television viewing and reading. We believe that the evidence provides useful information to help parents and teachers make informed decisions about television and reading. We also provide some suggestions about using television viewing to enhance children's literacy.

What We Know about Television and Reading

One thing is clear: Children in the United States spend a great deal of time watching television. A study by the National Institute of Mental Health found that the typical high school senior has spent more time watching television (approximately 15,000 hours) than attending school (approximately 11,000 hours). This fact led researchers interested in studying the effect of television on reading to ask a logical question: *Are children who watch more television poorer readers than those who watch less televi-*

sion? This question has not been as easy to answer as one might expect and has led to some surprising results. For example, children who watch a great deal of television tend to come from homes that are not very enriching in many other ways. So, it is hard to tell whether television or other factors such as having few reading materials around the house are to blame for poor reading. When such factors are taken into account, researchers found something surprising: Reading achievement tends to *increase* slightly as children watch more television, at least up to the national average of about two to three hours per day. However, as the amount of TV viewing increased above the average, reading achievement dropped sharply. Moderate levels of television viewing may help some children, especially disadvantaged children, become more aware of the world around them, which translates into increased understanding during reading and perhaps increased motivation to read.

A group of researchers led by Richard Anderson at the Center for the Study of Reading at the University of Illinois looked for a relation between reading achievement and a wide range of out-of-school, free time activities including watching television. Their findings suggest that television viewing was weakly related to poor reading achievement. Interestingly, however, activities such as talking on the phone and listening to music were more strongly related. The researchers wisely cautioned against jumping to conclusions based on these findings. Nonetheless, there seems to be no evidence clearly suggesting that moderate levels of television viewing (an *average* of two to three hours a day) is having a widespread, negative effect on children's reading achievement in this country. On the other hand this finding does not offer clear guidance to parents and teachers who are interested in making specific decisions about children's television viewing. For that sort of guidance it is necessary to dig deeper into the research.

Not surprisingly, many studies, including the one just described, have found that children who read for pleasure outside of school tend to read better than their classmates who do not. This finding leads to another question about television and reading: *If children watched less television, would they read more books?* Underlying this question is an assumption that has not been clearly supported. Put simply, the assumption is that if you turn off the television, children will pick up a book to read. Theorists such as Susan Neuman of Temple University suggest that leisure activities like watching television fulfill certain needs. Television viewing and reading do not always fulfill the same needs. For example, there is often a social dimension to watching television. Children may sometimes see television viewing as a way to socialize with their friends just as adults may use a televised sporting event as a reason for a party. Turning off the television in such instances may lead children to seek out other social activities as opposed to read a book.

Although television viewing is clearly a popular leisure activity, it is only one among many activities that compete with reading. The bad news is that among all the things that children do outside of school, they spend relatively little time reading. Various studies estimate that on average the majority of school-age children read between four and 16 minutes a day outside of school (disturbingly, recent studies have found that children also read less in school than might be expected). The good news in these findings is that we wouldn't have to find too many extra minutes in the day to double the time that many children spend reading at home. To increase a child's reading from ten to 20 minutes a day does not necessarily imply significant changes in their television viewing habits. In fact, as we will highlight in the second section of this chapter, television can become the stimulus for more leisure reading if parents and teachers look for opportunities to help bring this about.

An important finding for parents and teachers to consider is that environment has a major effect on both leisure reading and television viewing. For example, children's reading for pleasure and television viewing seem to follow the pattern set by their parents. Parents who read little and watch television a great deal tend to have children who do likewise. As in many aspects of parenting, it is difficult to underestimate the power of our example. To decrease children's television viewing while increasing their reading, parents may need to think about changing their own reading and viewing habits. Teachers can play a role too. Research clearly supports the benefits of having a wide variety of reading materials available in classrooms and establishing a time when everyone reads, including the teacher.

Thus, there is no clear evidence that simply turning off the television will by itself significantly increase long-term leisure reading. Instead, the research suggests that efforts to increase the disturbingly little time that many children engage in reading outside of school should focus on creating an environment that encourages reading, not necessarily on finding ways to reduce the amount of television viewed. A good environment for stimulating reading will include adults who model the value of reading (perhaps at least occasionally in place of television viewing), a variety of interesting reading material, opportunities to discuss what family members have read or might read, and so forth. Given that many children spend so little time reading for pleasure, even small increases in the number of minutes they read each day are significant.

Another popular assumption about the effects of television on reading is found in the following question: *Are children who watch television less likely to read because television viewing leads to shorter attention spans?* Some researchers have tried to determine if the nature of television viewing may lead children to become more passive or impulsive, which may in turn lead them to read less. The research in this area is sketchy at best and the findings are mixed. In one relevant study, Gavriel Salomon at the University of Arizona found that children do seem to devote less mental effort while watching television but they also seem to adjust their mental effort to the demands of reading. Some studies suggest that children who watch television tend to be more impulsive in their approach to solving problems, while others suggest that watching some programs may increase their persistence. The connection between these findings and reading, however, is unknown. Again, there seems to be little cause for concern that television is having a widespread negative effect on children's approaches to learning or school, although this possibility has not been ruled out entirely.

In summary, there is no clear evidence that a moderate amount of television viewing has a strong harmful effect on literacy in general. Variables such as the type of program watched, a child's age, viewing habits (e.g., some people try to read and watch television at the same time), home environment and the like make generalizations difficult. Several researchers in this area have suggested that the lack of any clear findings condemning television viewing is due to the fact that some positive effects lessen the impact of the negative effects. Such a viewpoint leads us to a final question: *What are the potential benefits to reading that can be gained from watching television and how can parents and teachers use television to enhance children's development as readers?*

Because most research is focused on determining the potentially harmful effects of watching television, there are relatively few studies that directly address the potential benefits of television. In fact, several years ago David Reinking heard a presentation at a professional meeting in which a pair of researchers reported their findings that the vocabulary used in several popular children's cartoon programs was greater and more diverse than in several popular children's books. They were so surprised and distressed by this finding that they decided to suspend further research. Actually, this finding does not imply that children should watch more cartoons and read fewer books, but it does suggest the potential of using television viewing to enhance vocabulary development.

Another example of using television in a positive vein has been a series of investigations carried out by Patricia Koskinen and her colleagues at the University of Maryland. She has found some encouraging results in using closed-captioned television with young readers and readers experiencing difficulty in learning to read. Closed-captioned television was developed for the deaf to be able to read the dialogue of popular programs on the television screen. Koskinen found that some beginning reading skills were enhanced by using this feature for children without any hearing problems. Previously, the use of closed-captioned television has required the purchase of a special decoder, but some major manufacturers are currently including a built-in decoder as a standard feature.

The major conclusion we draw from looking at the best available research is that a moderate level of television viewing does not seem to be harmful to children's reading. Furthermore, watching a moderate amount of television might have some benefits for reading. These benefits might be enhanced by engaging children in reading and writing activities connected to their television viewing. In the next section we suggest how parents and teachers might look for such activities and we provide some examples.

Experienced teachers and many parents who take an active role in their children's education often recognize what has been called the teachable moment. A teachable moment is usually an unplanned opportunity for learning that occurs naturally during an experience in which a child has some personal involvement. For example, a parent or teacher taking a child to a baseball game might see an opportunity to point out how a player's batting average represents a chance of getting a hit each time at bat, thus introducing the concept of probability in a rich, motivating context. With practice, most teachers and parents can go one step further by extending teachable moments through informal games and activities. A common example would be the

Using Television to Enhance Literacy

informal games parents sometimes invent to keep children occupied during a long trip in the family car. For example, "Let's see who can find a sign with the name of an animal on it."

Similarly, television viewing can be seen as a potential source of such informal learning. In this section we offer a few examples that we hope might help parents and teachers creatively use television to enhance children's literacy. The possibilities are, of course, limitless, but at first they may be difficult to see. Once parents and teachers begin looking for connections between television and reading, they may be surprised by how many opportunities there are to connect rich reading and writing activities to television viewing.

Some opportunities are easy to identify and are a good place for a parent or teacher to start noticing the possibilities. For example, many television quiz shows require the use of language skills as viewers participate along with the contestants. Predicting words in a sentence from only a few letters in each word, as is done on "Wheel of Fortune," for example, is a motivating activity related directly to skills frequently included in the school's reading curriculum. Other game shows, such as "Jeopardy," require contestants to pit their knowledge against each other in specific categories such as sports, history, or movies. A debated answer on the show or among family members might lead to consulting an encyclopedia or other reference source.

A more elaborate extension of game shows might be to encourage children to create their own home version of the show, developing their own categories and questions. In fact, children often enjoy creating their own versions of other types of programs as well. Some will want to write their own scripts and commercials, perhaps using a video camera to tape their "program." This level of involvement may work best on a rainy summer day or other occasions when children have extended free time.

Commercial breaks can be a good time to engage children in brief conversations that reinforce reading. For example, making predictions about possible developments in a story's plot, a valued reading skill, can be reinforced during a commercial by asking children to predict what they think will happen next in a television drama and by informally asking them to give reasons for their predictions. They can learn aspects of how characters are developed in a story by looking for who emerges as the hero or heroine as well as the villain (*hero, heroine,* and *villain* are also good words to know and understand). A game-like activity would be to see whose predictions are most accurate from one commercial break to the next (the loser has to pop the popcorn).

Occasionally, there is a direct link between television and books. For example, some television programs are adaptations of acclaimed children's literature. "Reading Rainbow" aired on Public Television is one regularly scheduled program that has had this aim, and the series "Little House on the Prairie," often seen in syndication, is based loosely on books by Laura Ingalls Wilder. As parents and teachers skim television viewing guides, they can be alert for key phrases such as "based on the popular children's book . . ."

Watching such programs on television can lead to a variety of activities that may encourage reading and writing. The book upon which the program is based can often be found at a public library, which is a good excuse to visit the library. Many of the book club orders that are sent home from school may highlight books related to television programs. Connecting television and books may be especially effective in opening up the world of reading to reluctant readers. After viewing a television program, reluctant readers may be more open to reading a book related to the program. For younger children or readers having difficulty reading by themselves, parents or older siblings might also read the book aloud. Or parents might wish to use a VCR to record the television version and play it in parts as portions of the book are read aloud over several days. Comparing the versions of the story in the book and in the television program can also give children the opportunity to see the unique characteristics of each version. Such activities can illustrate the power in reading and listening to written stories that cannot be fully duplicated in a video presentation.

Television can also be used to motivate writing. For example, many television programs provide addresses that allow viewers an opportunity to respond in some way to the program: writing for further information about the content of the program, joining a fan club, and so forth. Children might also be encouraged to write a letter in support of a favorite program to prevent it from being canceled. Many of these letters are answered, which is itself motivating. Parents might ask their children to submit a written justification for staying up past an established bedtime to watch a particular program. Or parents who choose to limit the number of hours a child watches television each week might consider written explanations for extending the allotted hours one week. Children might also create a written summary comparing and contrasting the way different brands of the same product are advertised on television.

As suggested earlier in this chapter, television is a potential source for enriching children's vocabulary. In fact, when children hear new words on television, they often have the benefit of a rich visual context to help them determine the word's meaning. These opportunities build children's vocabulary and increase their interest in language. A simple approach is to draw attention to interesting words while watching television with children. A comment such as "that's a new word to me, do you know what it means?" or "that's an interesting word (or way) to describe . . ." may help children learn new words and expressions. Perhaps more importantly, such observations help children develop a lifelong awareness of the subtleties of language and verbal communication. They might also be encouraged to keep a log of their favorite or most interesting words heard during television programs.

A more elaborate, structured activity entails helping children conduct a scavenger hunt for words they hear while watching television. Children might be given a short list of words to listen for while watching television. To verify that a word has been found, a child would record the program, the date, and the context of each word heard. Bonus points could be awarded for hearing words having similar meanings (huge, enormous), opposite meanings (talkative, reserved), or that sound the same (blew, blue); or, bonus points could be awarded by predicting that a word on the list would be used in a particular program. Children could also generate lists of words describing favorite characters from television programs, their clothing, their personalities, and so forth. A children's thesaurus and dictionary could be used along with these activities.

However, the ground rules for competitive activities such as a scavenger hunt need to be established in advance to head off potential problems. For example, some children may get carried away with the activity and respond by significantly increasing their television viewing. Also, adults supervising this game should be willing to give as much information about the words' meanings as possible. It is not advisable to send children to the dictionary as the sole source of information about a word that is totally unfamiliar. Instead, give examples of how the word would be used appropriately in several different contexts, then ask a child to guess the word's meaning, and then look in a reference source to see if the guess is correct.

The previous examples are only a sample of informal activities that illustrate how television viewing can be used to enhance literacy. For such activities to be successful it is usually necessary that children perceive them to be enjoyable, nonthreatening, and not too distracting from their involvement in watching a program. Parents need to be especially cautious in proposing activities like the ones presented here. Children may be wary of "school-like" activities proposed by parents, especially when associated with valued free time activities such as television viewing. We do not advise parents to require their children to participate in activities like our examples. Doing so runs the risk of developing negative attitudes towards literacy. Instead, parents should make suggestions, provide support where necessary, and offer encouragement and reinforcement. They should also feel comfortable with the fact that not all of their suggestions will be greeted with enthusiasm.

A Concluding Word

Television is a powerful force in American culture and it is appropriate for teachers and parents to consider its role in shaping children's development. There is no shortage of worrisome issues when we consider television's potential to influence our children. We worry about television's influence on shaping children's values concerning issues related to violence, family life, and the importance of material things. We worry about whether unrestricted television viewing may turn our children into couch potatoes.

In this chapter we addressed the common worry that television has an adverse effect on children's acquisition and appreciation of literacy. Several conclusions seem warranted. First, there is little evidence to support the worry that moderate levels of television viewing will greatly harm children's development of literacy. A second conclusion proceeds from the first: to enhance children's literacy, parents and teachers should devote more of their energies to finding ways to engage children meaningfully in enjoyable reading and writing activities as opposed simply to restricting the time spent viewing television. A third conclusion is that with a little imagination parents and teachers can use television viewing constructively as a source for enhancing children's literacy.

We believe that these conclusions provide one base from which parents and teachers can make informed decisions about children's television viewing. Ultimately, however, the questions parents and teachers have about how television will affect literacy must be answered individually for each child.

Anderson, R.C., P.T. Wilson, and L.G. Fielding. (1988). Growth in reading and how children spend their time outside of school. *Reading Research Quarterly, 23,* 285–303.

Koskinen, P.S., R.M. Wilson, L.B. Gambrell, and S.B. Neuman. (1993). Captioned video and vocabulary learning: An innovative practice in literacy instruction. *The Reading Teacher, 47,* 36–43.

Neuman, S.B. (1991). *Literacy in the television age: The myth of the tv effect.* Norwood, NJ: Ablex.

Searles, D.T., N.A. Mead, and B. Ward. (1985). The relationship of students' reading skills to TV watching, leisure time reading, and homework. *Journal of Reading, 3,* 158–162.

Shoup, B. (1984). Television: Friend, not foe of the teacher. *Journal of Reading, 25,* 629–631.

References and Other Readings on the Topic

part two

Home and School: Working Together for Literacy Learning

Chapter 16

Understanding Changes in Beginning Reading (and Writing) Instruction

Susan Carey Biggam

S usan Carey Biggam is the Elementary–Reading/Language Arts Consultant with the Vermont Department of Education. She has been a classroom, Chapter 1, and special education teacher and has particular interests in early support for at-risk students, reading comprehension, and parent partnerships. She is currently a doctoral student in Educational Administration and Planning at the University of Vermont.

L earning to read and write is a real milestone. Parents know how important it is, and children know how important their parents think it is. It's definitely not something that happens overnight though. Like learning to talk and walk, learning to be literate happens gradually—sometimes with great leaps forward, but also sometimes with extended periods that feel like "plateaus," when youngsters are consolidating what they've learned. Both parents and children look forward to the point at which children can read and write in conventional ways, but are sometimes concerned when they don't appear to be progressing as expected.

What complicates matters a bit is that beginning reading and writing instruction "these days" may seem quite a bit different from when most parents were in school and learning to read. In many cases materials have changed, methods have changed, work that is brought home often looks different, and even report cards don't look the same. Terms such as "whole language," "literature-based instruction," "process writing," and "invented spelling" are increasingly used to describe what goes on in current reading instruction, and often need some explaining. Parents also need to know *why* these changes have been introduced—in response to a clearer understanding of how children learn to read and write as well as documented trends of many students toward avoiding reading or achieving only limited success in becoming fully literate.

Understanding some key ideas about beginning reading and writing instruction today can help parents support their youngsters' early reading and writing efforts, and work together with teachers to help their children take on new challenges and become independent readers and writers.

First, I'll address some of the key points about beginning literacy instruction today and then some common questions that parents often have.

What's Different Today, and Why?

Materials

Parents today will see fewer basal readers (graded instructional textbooks for reading) and fewer workbooks and worksheets when they enter the classroom or sit down for parent-teacher conferences. They are more likely to see trade books (commercially published children's literature), journals or logs, story maps, and projects that involve extensive reading and writing. Early reading books tend to be predictable, with more natural-sounding language and repetition than the "Look, look, see Puff jump . . ." of a few years ago.

Works of children's literature are used today for several reasons: Because of their quality, these books have more appeal for children; if carefully chosen, they are easier to read; and they lend themselves more naturally to real discussion and other forms of response. Moreover, in many classrooms children have a certain degree of choice over what books they choose to read. When children choose their own book they're more likely to read with enthusiasm and success.

Instructional Approaches

Students today spend less time in fixed ability groups (low/middle/high), have more choice in what they read and write, and spend less time learning skills in isolation. Instead, grouping tends to be more varied and flexible. Teachers often work with the whole class and teach mini-lessons of strategies and skills. Students read in a variety of settings. Sometimes they read with partners, sometimes they read and discuss in "literature groups" (often based on level of performance, but sometimes based on interest), sometimes they read with their teacher, and sometimes they read or respond to what they have read independently. There is more time spent reading "real," meaningful stories, more choice available, more opportunities to read alone or with others, and more time to discuss what is read—because we now know that these are essential ingredients for students' growth as readers.

Instead of waiting until youngsters know all their letters and sounds before beginning reading instruction, increasingly teachers today provide reading and writing experiences right from the start of kindergarten and first grade. Students still learn letter names and sounds, of course, but generally these are learned gradually, and *through* reading and writing experiences. For example, when a child is writing a note to the teacher about a block castle just completed, the letter "c" has real meaning, and is likely to be remembered if the teacher helps the child find a model of "c," form the letter, and connect it to the sound of "c."

Frequently children begin reading simple books while they still only know some of the letter names and sounds, and this allows both the teacher and the children to "ease into" reading, much the same way very young children learn to talk. When children learn to talk, they begin with fairly crude "approximations" of talking, but because they are surrounded with encouragement for their beginning efforts, lots of modeling, and supportive corrections, gradually they become more independent and conventional in what they say. When beginning reading, children often "invent" stories or read along with the teacher at first, but because of similar modeling, encouragement and supportive corrections, they gradually notice more and more about the way books, stories, letters, and sounds work. Youngsters take on more independence as they gain confidence and skill as readers.

Writing is a major part of beginning literacy instruction. The connection between reading and writing is now much clearer, and teachers spend a good deal of time having students write about what they have read or about other things they know or experiences they have had. Every time youngsters write they learn more about how the system of print works and how to sound like an author.

Skills are still taught, but in a different way. Less time is spent in the classroom on skill work taught through worksheets and workbook exercises, and more time is spent on teaching students to use skills and strategies in actual reading, in responding to reading, and in writing.

Reading outside of school is even more important than ever. Generally youngsters are expected to read at home every night. Reading to youngsters continues to be important even after they have learned to read themselves.

Student Work

When parents open backpacks or see folders of student work these days, they see fewer workbooks and fewer end-of-the-story comprehension questions. Instead, they will often see rewrites of familiar stories (children's own versions of stories), character maps, story webs or charts, and journal entries. If what parents see are first drafts or examples of daily (unedited) work, they are likely to see a good deal of temporary or invented spelling, because youngsters are writing a message using the spelling patterns that they currently have control over. Like early efforts at talking, these beginning spelling attempts need to be encouraged as students are gradually led to learn more conventional spelling patterns through mini-lessons, the editing process, and other forms of support from teachers, peers, and their classroom environment.

Assessment

In the past parents would learn of their child's progress in literacy chiefly through hearing of their placement in a reading group (often based on performance in end-of-the-unit tests that emphasize isolated reading skills) and occasionally from performance on standardized tests. Today, assessment in reading and writing is broader. It includes an emphasis on the process of reading (running records of reading behavior, notes on book discussions, reading interest and attitude surveys, and so on) as well as the products (story maps, logs of books that have been read, diagnostic inventories, etc.). The emphasis is on noticing students' actual reading behavior and work in and out of the classroom, looking at it for certain qualities or criteria, and then evaluating it both in terms of student growth and development over time and as compared to behavior and work of classmates.

Parents will increasingly see student folders or portfolios in which students' writing is kept. Upon examining their child's writing portfolio parents can see how their child's writing has changed from September to May and how one piece of writing improves as the child moves from first to final drafts.

They will find that, although assessment information seems more complex, it is also richer. And it places much more emphasis upon what students can *do,* as opposed to what they are not able to do. Most importantly, assessment information used today directly influences instruction. For example, when a first grade teacher takes weekly running records of a student's oral reading, he or she might observe that the youngster is just beginning to self-correct when what is read does not make sense. The teacher then focuses on this with the youngster, encouraging more self-correcting behavior, and also supporting it with additional appropriate reading materials and experiences.

What Questions Should Parents Ask?

With changes such as those just described, it is sometimes difficult for parents to think of sensible questions to ask about their child's progress and reading program. Some key questions they might begin with include whether or not the youngster is viewing herself as a reader and writer, whether or not she is progressing at an appropriate rate, and whether or not she is able to benefit from the regular classroom reading and writing instruction. Parents have a legitimate concern in this area—much the same as when their youngster was learning to talk. But, as when youngsters learn to talk, no single test score or age/grade level can adequately describe progress, attitude, or potential. Instead, parents and teachers need to work together to look at a variety of factors in order to get a whole and true picture of a child's developing literacy abilities.

Parents also might well ask about the balance of activities in the classroom. What happens during the language arts block? Is there time for oral reading and silent? Do students read with partners in groups and alone? Are some books selected by the teacher, some by the student? Do students write about what they read, and read their writing? How do they respond to what is read? Do they ever read or write nonfiction? poetry?

Absolutely, no question about it, parents should help. Parents and teachers need to work together, as partners, in supporting children's developing literacy skills. Just because parents learned to read using different methods and materials doesn't mean they can't help. Two important areas of help are needed—opportunities for practice and encouragement.

Should Parents Help?

Opportunity for Practice
Parents can set the stage for reading at home in lots of ways—having a variety of books and magazines available (from the school or public library or elsewhere), making reading a valued part of the day (by having a "quiet" reading time, reading together, etc.), and by sharing, with other members of the family, what they have read. Research has shown that reading together as little as ten minutes per day can have a significant and positive impact on children's reading.

Similarly, parents can promote writing at home. They can encourage their children to keep journals, make lists (grocery lists, lists of favorite foods, gift lists, etc.), write their own stories and poems, and write letters and informal notes to family members and friends.

Encouragement
Parents can encourage and support early readers in lots of ways too. When youngsters begin to read, parents are often unsure of how to listen to them read. With young readers, it's often helpful to read a story to the youngster first, then read it together or read alternating pages.

If there is a mistake, should parents tell youngsters the word? Have them sound it out? Ask questions at the end of a page? In general, the best advice is just to be a good audience—listen attentively, laugh at the funny parts, "wonder out loud" at confusing or intriguing points, and comment on what strikes you in the book. Equally important is to show appreciation of the child's efforts by noticing when the child uses successful reading behaviors. Don't spend time pointing out mistakes when doing so detracts from understanding and enjoying the story.

Here are some things parents can say to be a good audience:

"I love this picture too . . . it's like a jungle"

"I wonder if he'll find him there?"

"Hmmm . . . she really is curious, isn't she?"

"Ha! Look at that!"

"This part reminds me of that trip we took on the train once, remember?"

Here are ways parents can notice and praise successful early reading behaviors:

"That's great, how you fixed that up yourself . . ."

"How did you know that hard word?"

"Yes, you read that part so it sounded just like a bear!"

"Such smooth reading . . ."

"Nice work there . . . you really worked that one out"

"You really used your finger to check there, didn't you?"

"That didn't make any sense the other way, did it?"

But sometimes beginning readers do get stuck or make mistakes that change the meaning of the story. Generally, the best thing to do in this situation is to give the youngster time (three to four seconds) to work it out for himself, and then simply to *tell* the word. Encourage the child to keep reading so that fluency and meaning are maintained.

In writing, parents should respond to what their children write in meaningful ways. Respond to the message, not to the mistakes that may have been made in spelling or grammar. Remember, children write to communicate, not to be given lessons in proper spelling or writing mechanics. When children see their parents responding meaningfully and positively to their writing, they will continue to write and grow in their writing competence.

Things to remember:

- Instruction may have changed, but the process involved of learning to read and write hasn't—and parents are still important partners in helping youngsters learn to read and write. In fact, parents are probably the *most* important partners!

- The "label" for a teacher's reading and writing program or the name of the book a child is reading is not as important as the elements of a successful classroom literacy program. Some questions to ask include: Do youngsters spend a significant amount of time reading and writing each day? Do they use reading and writing to support each other and to explore other subject areas? Are they given help in using the strategies of successful readers and writers? Do they have access to lots of quality books, good models of reading and writing, and a stimulating environment filled with opportunities and materials for writing and reading?

- Parents provide key support for beginning readers by making sure time, books, and other materials are available for reading and writing; by listening attentively; and by encouraging youngsters' beginning literacy efforts.

- When in doubt, ask the teacher. Parents do have a legitimate need to understand what is going on, and how they can help. They should expect honest and helpful advice from teachers.

The following resources may be useful to parents or other family members who want to know more about whole language or literature-based approaches to literacy, and their role as partners in supporting beginning readers:

For Further Reading

Barron, Marlene. (1990). *I learn to read and write the way I learn to talk.* Katonah, NY: Richard C. Owen.

Hill, Mary W. (1989). *Home: Where reading and writing begin.* Portsmouth, NH: Heinemann Educational Books.

Vacca, Richard and Timothy Rasinski. (1991). *Case studies in whole language.* New York: Holt, Rinehart and Winston.

Chapter 17

Nurturing Children's Literacy Development through Parent-Teacher Conferences

Anthony D. Fredericks

T ony Fredericks is an assistant professor in the Department of Education of York College, York, Pennsylvania. A prolific writer, Fredericks is well-known for his advocacy of parents' participation in their children's reading and writing education. He is a past chairperson of the International Reading Association's Parents and Reading Committee and Parents and Reading Special Interest Group.

Helping children become successful and lifelong readers is a major goal of schools. When children are supported by parents AND teachers in their efforts to become effective readers, then that goal is more easily realized. Parents' support of their child's growth in reading has been shown, through educational research, to be one of the most significant factors in children's academic progress. In other words, parents do make a difference—a difference that can be significant, not only in reading growth and development, but also in every other subject as well.

In order to ensure that their children receive the best possible support and instruction—both in school and at home—it is important that parents and teachers share common goals and ideas on how to foster literacy development. For example, parents may receive a phone call or note from their child's teacher about some difficulties the child is having in reading. What can they do? First, it's important not to panic. Many children have difficulty in learning to read and write. Any panic by parents may be misunderstood by the child. Second, they should take time to talk with their child about any problems he or she may be having. It's important not to accuse or blame the child, but rather, discover some reasons why reading is difficult (*Note:* frequent conversations on a daily basis often can turn up minor problems before they become major ones). Third, parents should get in touch with the child's teacher immediately to set up a conference or face-to-face meeting in which difficulties and concerns can be shared. While notes, letters, and phone calls are positive ways to share information, parent-teacher conferences hold the promise of an honest discussion that is essential to the child's "reading well-being" and are often a significant link in the child's ultimate success in reading.

A conference is a wonderful opportunity to communicate with teachers about the child's reading/writing progress and work together to develop plans that can help the child achieve academically, emotionally, and socially. But, let's face it, most parents find the prospect of a face-to-face meeting with the child's teacher less than exciting. This "return to school" may conjure up some unpleasant memories of earlier educational experiences; it may create uneasy feelings about the fact that someone else is evaluating their child. Whatever the reasons, the parent-teacher conference often seems to be a formidable event.

However, these conferences need not be frightening nor intimidating. Indeed, they can be one of the most positive kinds of meetings between parents and teachers. With that in mind, I'd like to share some ideas that can make an upcoming meeting between parents and their child's teacher more productive and, hopefully, more successful.

A successful parent-teacher conference is built in layers. The first layer is what takes place prior to the actual conference, the second layer concerns the conference itself, and the third layer is what happens immediately after the conference. All three are important and will help ensure that parents and teachers communicate effectively.

Prior to the Conference

It is important to keep in mind that what takes place immediately before a conference can often determine the level of communication that takes place within the conference. Here are several tips and ideas for parents to keep in mind prior to a scheduled meeting with their child's teacher.

1. Confirm the actual date and time of the conference. Parents may wish to call the school or send a brief note to the child's teacher.

2. Conference times can sometimes be anxious times for teachers, too. Parents may wish to send the teacher a note indicating what they hope will be accomplished during the meeting as well as their desire to share some information and talk about educational goals for their child. This brief message can go a long way toward establishing a positive relationship with the teacher well before the meeting takes place. The note can also be used to relay any new information about the child that the teacher may not be aware of (for example, a change in a family situation, a recent illness, etc.).

3. Gather several examples of the child's work and make notes of her reading behavior over the past several weeks. What has the child been reading? Does the child read on his own at home? How often? What has the child been writing? Take some time to review your child's work and your own notes in order to understand your child's academic performance and progress during the academic year. It is especially important to review this work with your child so that both parents and child understand exactly how the child is performing.

4. Plan to arrive at the conference several minutes ahead of schedule. Mentally review the points you wish to cover in the conference while waiting. What do you really wish to communicate to the teacher? Conference times are usually hectic and when one group of parents is tardy, it tends to affect the time available to those who follow.

Of course, the emphasis in a parent-teacher conference will be on the information shared and the decisions made during the meeting with your child's teacher. Here are some tips to keep in mind.

During the Conference

1. Keep the emphasis and the discussion on your child and his or her reading and writing. Try not to compare the child's reading performance with that of other children. It is most important that the focus be directed to the child's own progress and needs.

2. Be sure to ask questions (parents should prepare several questions in advance of the conference and record them on note cards for use during the conference) about how the child is performing overall, as well as within reading and language arts. Does the child enjoy reading instruction? Does he or she read independently in school? How does she act during sustained silent reading in class? Parents should ask the teacher about the goals the teacher has for their child and make sure that those goals are compatible with their own.

3. The most productive conferences are those that emphasize a "shared partnership." That is, both teacher and parents need to be working on common ground and fully understand each other's motives. Parents and teachers need to ask the question, "How can we work together to provide

the best reading and writing experience and instruction for our children?" While it may be easy to blame the teacher for a child's academic shortcomings, it is far more productive for parents and teachers to arrive at mutually agreeable decisions of an optimal course of action for your child. In other words, be less concerned about "who did what" or "who didn't do something" and more involved in working together to seek answers and solutions.

4. Teachers may have limited information about the children they teach. It's important for the teacher to know about family conditions, changes in the health or attitude of their students, as well as any other pertinent data that may have a bearing on their scholastic performance. Be sure that data is communicated to the teacher; but don't burden the teacher with an extensive personal history.

5. If parents don't understand something the teacher is saying, they should stop the conversation and ask for clarification. Again, the emphasis is on establishing effective avenues of communication. Thus, if some information seems confusing, be sure to ask the teacher to explain it.

6. While there may be differences of opinion between parents and a teacher, it is important that parents and teachers establish some middle ground on several matters on which both can agree. Be sure to let the teacher know where there might be disagreement, but don't spend an excessive amount of time on those disagreements. It is more important to spend time productively on reaching mutually agreeable solutions and directions. Also, consider the need to remain calm and considerate during the conference. Engaging in arguments will do little to resolve potential difficulties regarding the child's achievement. It is more important to explore concerns in a spirit of mutual cooperation until agreement is reached.

7. When discussing what your child does or doesn't do, be sure to give the teacher specific examples. Telling the teacher that your child "doesn't seem to be interested in reading" provides the teacher with little information. Here's where documenting reading and writing behaviors at home really helps. It would be more useful to share information such as, "My child had trouble with the vocabulary in his/her reading assignment last week" or "My child really enjoyed the poetry that the class wrote and read last week."

8. Make sure that before you leave the conference, both parents and teacher are in agreement on future goals, plans, and actions. It is important that a consensus be reached on the best course of action for the child in the coming weeks and months. Be sure to summarize points of agreement and disagreement. Although not all problems will be solved at a single meeting, it is vital that parents and teachers understand the need for continuous, honest, and open communication. Ask for specific recommendations on what you, as parents, can do to nurture your child's

reading at home and to reinforce the reading and writing that is occurring in the classroom. Don't settle for only general recommendations such as "read to your child." Follow up such recommendations with questions such as "How long should we read together?," "Can you recommend any titles or authors?," or "What should we do when the child doesn't want to read with us?"

A successful conference doesn't end after parents leave the school. The conference can be a starting point for an effective bond between home and school. Here are some suggestions parents may wish to consider after the conference.

After the Conference

1. Upon arrival home, write down some of the important points that were discussed at the conference. Do they still make sense after having some time to think about them? It would certainly be appropriate to send a note to the teacher thanking him or her for the conference and mentioning a few of the items that were discussed in the conference. Let the teacher know that you wish to work closely with her or him to ensure your child's reading and writing progress.

2. Take time to talk about the conference with your child. It's important for students to know of the goals and/or decisions made in their behalf. Make sure that the child is aware of the information shared in the conference and the material discussed. Ask your child if he or she agrees with the recommendations and has recommendations of his or her own.

3. Above all, make sure that open lines of communication with the teacher are maintained. Don't let the parent-teacher conference be the only time when your child's reading performance is discussed. Take advantage of phone calls, letters, and notes to convey your feelings about your child's progress and request additional information throughout the school year.

4. If parents feel that there is still disagreement on several points, they may wish to consider some of the following:

   a. Request additional conferences with the teacher over the span of several weeks.

   b. Ask if the guidance counselor or principal can "sit in" during a conference to act as an impartial mediator.

   c. Ask if a friend, neighbor, or relative can accompany you to a scheduled conference to provide support and additional information.

   d. Write a letter to the principal outlining some of the points of disappointment and request a personal meeting with him or her.

   e. Ask to observe your child in the classroom to confirm your perceptions as well as those of the teacher.

Effective parent-teacher conferences involve a lot of information sharing and goal setting. Following is a checklist parents may wish to use prior to a scheduled parent-teacher conference to help make the conference a productive one.

_____ Be prepared; review your child's work prior to the conference.

_____ Talk with your child and solicit his or her input, too.

_____ Approach the conference with a positive outlook.

_____ Seek to establish a positive relationship with your child's teacher.

_____ Listen carefully to what the teacher is saying.

_____ If you don't understand something, ask questions.

_____ Try to reach mutual decisions on your child's academic future.

_____ Take time to ask questions about your child's work and the teacher's program.

_____ Make sure the teacher understands important family situations, but don't dwell on them.

_____ Discuss several examples of your child's work. Be sure you get a complete picture of his or her total academic performance.

_____ At the conclusion of the conference try to summarize the conversation between parent and teacher—make sure that the two of you are in agreement on important matters.

_____ Be sure to talk about any differences of opinion and try to reach some mutually agreeable solutions.

Successful parent-teacher conferences don't just happen. They involve some preparation on the part of both parents and teachers and should be geared toward establishing a positive and mutually supportive partnership. By working closely together throughout the school year, parents and teachers can make the conference an important event in the overall literacy success of their children.

Chapter 18

Literacy Is for All Languages: Building Literacy in Nonnative English-Speaking Homes

Sally Nathenson-Mejía

Sally Nathenson-Mejía is an assistant professor in the Language and Culture program at the University of Colorado at Denver. She teaches in the Reading and Writing Program and also works with teachers of bilingual education. Over the past six years she has done extensive research into the language development of children who are or are becoming bilingual. She has a special interest in the writing of these children and how teachers can help students improve their writing skills in both their first and second languages. She currently teaches courses on reading theory, writing theory, and effective instruction for linguistically different students.

Vietnamese	English translation
Doc caí nãy cho con, má.	Read this to me, Mama.
Russian	**English translation**
Что здесь написанно, папа?	What is written here, Daddy?
Spanish	**English translation**
¿Cómo escribes la palabra 'científico'?	How do you write the word, Scientist?

The language may differ from home to home, but the requests are consistently similar: Read this to me, what does this say?, how do you write . . .? When children are surrounded by print, exposed to the reading and writing of adults, at home and in school, they need and desire to become involved in the world of print themselves. As parents and teachers, we can encourage and build upon those desires, welcoming our children into what Frank Smith calls the "literacy club."

Working together, parents and teachers can nurture excitement and discovery about reading and writing. This will create a strong foundation of literacy for our children. Using what is normally found in any home, children can become actively involved in the world of literacy. You don't need expensive educational materials, you don't need to spend hundreds of dollars on new books, you don't even need a perfect knowledge of English. Development of literacy *in any language* will help children understand how written language works, and this will help them to succeed in school (Cummins 1979).

Language is a social activity. Involvement in written language is just as much a social activity as speaking. Children notice print in their world at very young ages. Two year olds readily identify fast food logos and their favorite cereal and cookie boxes. They come to realize that adults use this print in helping them make decisions about their lives. Children want to make connections between themselves and others. They want to be like the people they love. Children can use written language to connect with others just as they use oral language.

Thus, we have the three year old who brings us a book at 6:30 Monday morning and says, "Read to me" or the five year old who wants to hear the funny pages read on Sunday. Taking the time to honor such requests allows children into the literacy club. It doesn't matter that the three year old doesn't "really" understand the moral implications of "The Little Red Hen" or that the humor in the funny pages is over the head of the five year old. What matters is the human connection, that two human beings who love each other are involved in a pleasurable activity that involves language in both oral and written form.

Written Language Concepts

Families that speak languages other than English at home can give their children a wealth of literacy experience in their home languages. When children become involved in any written language they learn important concepts about language meaning and use that will support their academic success. The fact that print *has meaning* is a concept that comes from involvement with print in any language. The fact that the meaning within print has tremendous communication potential also crosses language boundaries. And, the fact that children can both create their own print and learn to interpret the print of others is true whether children are involved with Vietnamese, Spanish, Navajo, Hebrew, or Russian.

These three ideas—(1) that written language has meaning, (2) that written language has communication potential, and (3) that children can create and interpret written language—transfer from one language to another. Having realized the power of literacy and felt their own control of literacy in their home language, children can come to school confident in their ability to learn to control the new language. Learning the new language will take time and it will definitely take understanding and help from adults, but the knowledge that it is possible can give a child the confidence to persevere.

Literacy Building Activities at Home

As was mentioned earlier, you don't need fancy materials. You can use materials in any language to create an effective literacy club at home. It is important to involve children with the language they use daily so that they look for meaning in print using the language they know best. By drawing children's attention to the print they use and create everyday, parents invite children into the literacy club. Food containers, newspapers, magazines, grocery lists, letters, and books, are all effective materials for involvement in print.

Here are a few activities in which children and parents can become involved in print-related activities. The main idea is to have fun and be together while creating a relaxed learning environment.

Grocery Shopping

Whether you shop at a large supermarket, a corner grocery store, or a family-owned ethnic market, shopping for food is an activity all families engage in. Children love to help decide what will be purchased and find it in the store. Young children can help decide what should go on the grocery list. Older children can actually do the writing (see Figure 18.1). Everyone can get involved in looking through the cupboards to see what is needed.

As children participate in grocery shopping they also use a number of thinking skills which support literacy development: making direct connections between what is said and what is written, recognizing logos and print on packages, categorizing items (fruit, vegetables, soup, cereal, etc.), predicting what will be needed and figuring out what is missing. Children understand that food and grocery shopping creates a meaningful, supportive environment for learning.

- Look through cupboards to see what you still have and what you need.
- Have young children tell older children what to put on the shopping list.
- At the store, look for items on the shelves.
- Read over the shopping list and cross out items as they are found.
- Match coupons with item labels.
- Discuss how items are grouped together (all the soups, all the cereals, all the dairy, etc.).

Figure 18.1

GROCERY SHOPPING LIST FOR KING SOOPERS

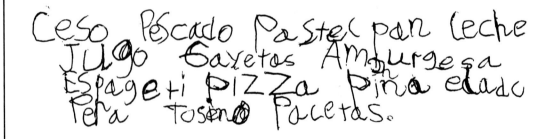

- Once home, figure out where different items are stored, which items are stored together.
- What did you forget? Start a new list and keep adding to it during the week.

Reading Together

Spending a bit of time reading with children *everyday* is one of the best ways to bring children into the world of literacy. Ten or fifteen minutes daily spent reading one book together is worth more than one hour of reading only once a week. When children read with their parents everyday it is the shared experience that makes the biggest impression. The comfort and support of regular time together makes it possible for children to focus on the meaning of stories and print.

Children love to hear the same books over and over again. Every time they hear a familiar book they learn something new. Primarily, they learn that books are meaningful and sources of pleasure. Once children know a story by heart they begin to notice other things about written language that will help their literacy development. They notice that the words are the same everytime the book is read. They notice that the illustrations complement the story. They begin to notice features of print such as words that are written bigger or darker than others. They recognize letters, words, and the direction one moves while reading. By choosing a favorite book over and over, such as *The Very Hungry Caterpillar* by Eric Carle, a supportive environment for learning is created.

Using the Library

The number of children's books published in language other than English is increasing every year. Libraries are realizing the need to have books available for nonnative English-speaking families. The more parents check out and use these books, the more libraries will be inclined to increase the size of their collections. You may also want to make specific requests to the librarian to purchase particular books or books on particular topics.

Going to the library and getting a library card is an exciting event for a child. Creating the opportunity to use that card on a regular basis demonstrates to children that libraries are comfortable and important places to visit, that their family values books and reading, and that belonging to the literacy club means being able to spend time enjoying wonderful books and stories. The librarians who work with children's literature are more than happy to help families acquire library cards, find books and magazines in their home language, and select appropriate books for children to take home. Books at the library are free and can be checked out over and over again. Many libraries also have a "story time" for families. You can take your children to hear the stories and even volunteer to tell stories and tales from your own culture, as well.

Creating Native Language Books at Home

Though publishers are continually putting more non-English books on the market, there still are not enough books available in all the languages our children speak. One possibility for increasing the amount of native language literature in the home is for families to create their own.

Many families treasure traditional stories that come from their native countries and cultures. Families also have favorite stories of special family events. Parents can write these stories down and make them into family books that children can illustrate themselves. Family books may become some of the children's favorites—to be read, shared and even taken to school. Two or three families may even want to get together for story and book-making projects.

Making family books requires a minimum of materials, used notebook or computer paper work quite well, and the text and pictures can be put on the unused side. Two used pieces of paper can be taped or stapled together so that the used sides are hidden. These books don't have to be fancy to be effective and loved. Teachers often use old computer printouts to create blank books for children. This not only saves money, it helps save the trees and teaches our children good environmental conservation strategies.

Once the paper has been found it can be folded into book form. Parents can write the story, leaving space for the children to illustrate. This activity not only reinforces all of the literacy behaviors already discussed, it also demonstrates to children that they can be involved in *creating* real literature. Children between four and seven who wish to write the stories themselves can be encouraged to do so. Their creative spelling should be accepted as a normal part of learning how written language works. What they will learn from the experience of creating literature is more valuable than correcting a few spelling errors. Creating family literature gives children a wonderful sense of control over written language. This sense of control helps develop the confidence they need to become proficient readers and writers in any language.

Building Bridges between Home and School

Homework activities can help build bridges for children between home and school (Enright & McClosky, 1988). The best activities do not create a "time for language drill and practice, but a time for meaningful language play and discovery" (p. 264). Parents and children should be able to look forward to engagement in these activities. It is important for children to feel that their home and school worlds work together. When parents and teachers *both* reach out to close the gap between home and school, children are the winners.

Many literacy building activities can be done at home and then shared at school. Students can be encouraged to create a display of grocery lists from home. This display can be used not only to compare languages, but also to compare the kinds of foods families eat. Children may be motivated to bring in some special foods from home for everyone to taste.

Family books can be brought to school. For the younger children, a parent or older sibling may be able to read the story in their home language. Perhaps the child or other family member can tell the story in English. What truly matters is that the child has been able to share a special piece of her- or himself with the teacher and classmates. One school in Elgin, Illinois, enlists parents and children in creating bilingual stories which become part of the classroom library.

Much can be shared. Families can make maps of homes and neighborhoods which can be displayed at school. Traditional recipes can be brought to school. A study of names, their meanings and origins can be done. Family trees can be drawn and displayed. Stories and maps of family migration routes can be compared. Some very powerful stories have been written by children about their journeys to this country and the adjustments they've had to make. By sharing these stories, maps, family trees, and recipes, children are able to say to those in their school world, "This is me, this is what I'm all about." At the same time, the teacher and classmates are able to celebrate the child and tell her or him, "Thank you for sharing yourself with us. We think you're wonderful."

When children and parents become involved together in literacy building activities in their native language, children learn concepts that will improve their academic learning in *any* language. Activities done at home do not need to be complex or involve elaborate, expensive materials. The most successful activities are those that can be done with materials at hand, in the context of normal daily living, and in which everyone is happy to participate. The best invitation to the literacy club we can give children is to share our involvement in literacy with them, in any language.

Conclusion

Enright, D. Scott and Mary Lou McCloskey. (1988). *Integrating English: Developing English language literacy in the multilingual classroom.* Reading: Addison-Wesley.

> Full of ideas for teachers working on literacy development with multilingual children. Excellent ideas on making literacy connections between home and school.

Lamme, Linda Leonard. (1985). *Growing up reading.* Washington DC: Acropolis Books.

> Practical suggestions for parents on supporting literacy development in the home. Good information for parents of very young children through elementary school.

Trelease, Jim. (1985). *The read-aloud handbook.* New York: Penguin.

> Widely acclaimed and very readable book. Many ideas for parents on how to read aloud, why to read aloud, and excellent lists of suggested books.

For Further Reading

Carle, E. (1969). *The very hungry caterpillar.* New York: Philomel.

Cummins, J. (1979). Linguistic interdependence and the educational development of bilingual children. *Review of Educational Research, 49,* 222–251.

Enright, D.S. and M.L. McCloskey. (1988). *Integrating English: Developing English language literacy in the multilingual classroom.* Reading: Addison-Wesley.

Smith, F. (1988). *Joining the literacy club.* Portsmouth, NH: Heinemann Educational Books, Inc.

References and Other Readings on the Topic

Chapter 19

Reading, Writing, and Giftedness

Beverly Shaklee

B ev Shaklee is an associate professor at Kent State University, Kent, Ohio, where she teaches courses in gifted education and teacher education and is coordinator of the Curriculum and Instruction program. She has recently directed two research projects on alternative methods for identifying and teaching gifted children in the regular classroom.

Sam is a second grade student in a suburban elementary school. He is also a gifted child. The intellectual ability that Sam displays is well beyond his seven years. He is curious, questioning, sometimes demanding, and he reads with the ease of a much older child. Recently, Sam became interested in the "democratic process." He decided to petition the school board for a salad bar in his school lunchroom. Sam wrote the petition, collected signatures, and spoke for about twenty minutes before a packed audience at the Monday night meeting. Although he spoke eloquently, his petition was denied. In frustration and unable to understand his adult behavior, he cried.

Sam exemplifies the paradox of a gifted child. Perceptive, aware, and sensitive, Sam is intellectually advanced, but emotionally still seven years old. This discrepancy between intellectual ability and social/emotional/physical development is commonplace for gifted children. Intellectually they are developmentally advanced beyond their peers. Socially, emotionally, and physically they are apt to be more age appropriate. Oftentimes, the areas of social, emotional, and physical development do not appear to "catch up" until late adolescence.

Knowing that they have a complex and delightful human being in their home usually makes most parents feel as if they have to "do something special" to continue to nurture this development. In the case of a gifted child who is also an avid reader, parents may question their own ability to promote intellectual development. And yet, if the child is gifted and an avid reader, parents must have been doing something right all along! Unfortunately, most parents are not sure they have been doing anything at all!

Reading can have a profound effect on a gifted child. Furthermore, reading can guide the intellectual and emotional development of gifted children. Guiding a gifted reader can be a joy and a frustration at the same time for parents and teachers. Concerns are usually expressed in the light of several questions:

How can I identify giftedness?

How do I guide a child in the appropriate selection of content?

Should I be concerned about the amount of time my child devotes to reading?

How can I talk to my child's teacher about reading?

Looking at Giftedness

For many parents the first indicator of "official" giftedness comes when the school system requests permission to test their child and the test scores meet criteria defined by the state. Some parents have previous knowledge that their child is exceptional because they have had the opportunity to compare his or her performance with some developmental standard. For example, watching their child play and interact with other children of the same age or reading a parent handbook on development which describes certain behaviors that are typically reached at certain ages are excellent ways to determine advanced development. A gifted child can best be described as a child who demonstrates significant advanced development when compared to age-mates.

In addition to advanced development when compared to other children, the gifted child may also have an exceptional memory and advanced comprehension (understanding unexpected things), or learn many things easily. The gifted child may demonstrate an exceptional use of knowledge, demand reasons for unexplained events, or reason extremely well when solving problems.

Awilda is a good example of a child who reasons well when compared to her age-mates. She and her classmates in kindergarten are discussing shapes. Awilda is curious about shapes and observes, "A hexagon has six sides—a snowflake is a hexagon! Hey, when you fold a hexagon in half, you get a trapezoid!! Trapezoids are one of my favorite shapes!" Awilda's knowledge, verbal skills, and logical thinking are highly developed for a five year old.

Another attribute of gifted children is the ability to use symbol systems in an expressive and complex manner. There are many symbol systems in our culture, including numbers, words, and sign language, to name a few. Gifted children often have a large vocabulary; they like to "play" with words, using complex sentences and expressing elaborate ideas. Billy, in a discussion of careers, expressed his ideas in this manner: "I like the whole field of science. I think I will be a paleontologist or perhaps a botanist." Billy is nine years old.

In addition, a gifted child's language is often more colorful, giving nuances, comparisons, or using words creatively with rich imagery. Kindergartners who describe the sky as "a silver shadow" or the color pink as "the color of a Japanese person stepping out of a hot bath," demonstrate a developmentally advanced ability to use language and create visual images.

A cautionary note for us all is necessary. It is neither desired nor demanded that the gifted child be advanced in all areas. In fact, a more typical description of a gifted child suggests advanced development in one area (e.g., reading, language development, self-expression), with other areas developing in a more or less normal fashion.

These abilities—to acquire and use language fluently, to explore the unknown, to challenge the typical levels of development—are all part of the gifted child. Combine these with a child who loves to read and we have a delightful and sometimes challenging human being in our lives. How can parents and teachers nurture in children their giftedness through reading and writing?

Guiding Gifted Readers is the title of a book by Judith Halsted that accurately represents the nature of working with gifted readers. Guiding, not directing or requiring, is the key word.

Guiding Gifted Readers

Selecting Appropriate Reading Material
Like all children, gifted children are a blend of their intellect, emotions, and physical attributes. According to Nancy Polette, gifted readers are children who read earlier, more, and better than average readers. They may choose a greater variety of materials to read; however, their choice of reading material is often age appropriate. Gifted readers usually select material that they are emotionally ready to read. Pushing a child to select reading material that is intellectually and emotionally advanced can

backfire. Many children will not appreciate and take pleasure from such material. Moreover, children could be "turned off" to reading in general by such an approach.

For example, although Meredith can read at a significantly advanced level, she still chooses to read books that are her childhood favorites and not unlike the books other children are reading. As teachers and parents, we should continue to expose our gifted readers to a wide variety of reading topics, but we should not be concerned if the child returns time and again to old favorites. It is usually best to help children select books they are emotionally ready to read.

Parents and teachers can help children discover what they like to read and discuss with them why they like those particular selections. It is also important to find out what kind of reading children have been doing. If we acknowledge that reading goes beyond the decoding of words and construction of sentences, and we recognize, as Nancy Polette notes, that reading is "the creation of visual images" (p. 39), then we need to explore what our children are reading and what they are thinking.

Helping gifted children select books that describe the lives of other gifted persons is also beneficial. Among my favorites is a series of books by Ibi Lepscky which contain stories about the childhood of famous people like Albert Einstein and Leonardo da Vinci. Lepscky begins his book about Albert Einstein in this way:

> About one hundred years ago, there lived a boy named Albert Einstein.
> Albert was a strange boy.
> Always absentminded.
> Always messy.
> It was a difficult job for him to tie his shoes.
> But he knew how to play the violin very well.
>
> (1982, pp. 3–4)

The book tells us about growing up as a gifted child. Children need to know that they are unique and that others who are unique have overcome obstacles, developed loving relationships, and have been successful in the world. Reading can sometimes provide an outlet for understanding differences between people and the unique abilities they themselves possess. Two other excellent resources about reading and gifted children are Judith Halsted's book, *Guiding Gifted Readers* and *Books for the Gifted Child* by Barbara Baskin and Karen Harris.

Beverly Otto, a researcher of young gifted children and emergent or beginning literacy, recommends that parents and teachers also involve gifted children in story writing activities as a means to communicate what they are thinking and learning. Books often provide gifted children with new information and ideas that can be expressed through writing activities. She recommends that parents and teachers involve them in regular opportunities for writing individually and in small groups, sharing and reading selections, and developing journals so that they can document the "history" of their own development as readers and writers. For young gifted children, it is important for parents and teachers to remember that "writing" may be found in the form of illustrations, invented spelling, or even wavy scribbling. The critical element is that young gifted children have the opportunity to integrate their own experiences with their imagination through these prewriting activities. A good resource for parents and teachers of young gifted children is Jackie Saunders and Pam Espeland's *Bringing Out the Best: A Resource Guide for Parents of Young Gifted Children.* It is an excellent guide to nurturing gifts in young children.

Unfortunately, many gifted adults who have the ability choose not to read! If we are not reading and writing, we restrict our thinking. In Nancy Polette's words, "a simple, nongrowing vocabulary equals a simple, nongrowing mind" (p. 39). Developing a love of and pleasure in reading and writing will help the gifted child continue on a lifelong path of growing and learning.

Certainly, all of the positive habits of literacy should be modeled for and shared generously with gifted readers. These include: reading aloud to the child, yourself reading at home, showing pleasure in and enthusiasm for reading, and informal sharing of reading materials. The key element is to demonstrate the pleasure and reward you yourself receive from reading and writing which in turn will be a model for your gifted child.

Reading "All of the Time"

Parents of gifted readers often express concern over the amount of time their children devote to reading. It may seem as if every moment the child has a book in his or her hands! Often when invited to take part in other activities or learning opportunities the child defers in preference to a book. For parents and teachers the question becomes not how much time the child spends reading but why do they spend so much time, and is this alright?

If the child is reading a wide variety of materials, continues to engage in other intellectual, physical, and social activities, and seems happy, then the amount of time spent reading is a personal preference that should be honored (even when it interferes with dinner!). However, a far more significant concern is when the gifted child only reads and refuses to participate in other activities. In this situation, it is important for parents and teachers to talk with the child to determine the reasons why reading has become such an obsessive activity in his life.

Matthew is a good case in point. He reads voraciously and constantly. When invited to play outdoors, ride a bike, or participate in other activities, he often refuses to join in, citing, "I am at the best part of my book, maybe tomorrow." Matthew's parents and teachers have noticed that "tomorrow" never comes and eventually other children stop asking. While there is no need for Matthew to give up his pleasure and success with reading, and he certainly does not have to become a social butterfly, if he is using reading as a means to avoid social interactions or develop physical skills, then parents and teachers need to intervene to help Matthew achieve balance in his development. In fact, in this particular situation Matthew was avoiding riding his bike because he did not feel he rode as well or as "courageously" as his friends. Gifted children can also demonstrate perfectionism, which can inhibit their willingness to take a risk with something new. In this situation, Matthew felt far more secure reading his book than riding his bike.

Reading and School

Children who demonstrate advanced abilities in reading sometimes experience conflict in the school setting. This was dramatically displayed for me when I asked

Robyn, a fifth grader, what she liked to read in school. Robyn replied, "I don't read in school. We do workbooks. I read at home." Fortunately, many schools and teachers are recognizing the singular importance of authentic or real reading in school and out.

Two concerns are most prevalent among parents of gifted children. One emerges if the child is an early reader (and not all gifted children are early readers). The second concern appears during the course of reading instruction itself and the alternatives suggested by school personnel.

When a child is an early reader (i.e., reading fluently before entering formal educational settings) parents are often concerned about the focus of reading instruction during the early years. Classrooms which use a lock-step curriculum (i.e., all students must do the same things at the same time) and ignore individual differences are not beneficial settings for any child, but especially young gifted readers. The same is true of libraries that limit a child to certain selections according to age, not ability or interest. However, classrooms which focus on instruction in which children have many opportunities to choose and read books on their own and with their classmates under the guidance and support of the teacher are often places where young gifted readers flourish. We call this type of instruction *whole language.*

Teachers who use a whole language model focus on individual differences and create instructional activities that nurture the talents and abilities of all children. A whole language curriculum ties reading and writing with science, social studies, music, math, and art, and stresses the importance of reading for authentic purposes. For gifted children this environment is very important. Joanne Whitmore, a researcher in the area of young children and giftedness, argues that young gifted children who do not participate in learning environments that support their self-concept for learning and intellectual development may learn to become academic underachievers as early as the end of their first school year.

A second area of concern involves the reading level itself. Parents may find that their child is capable of reading much more advanced material than is presented in the regular curriculum. In order to reach a compromise, the offer of acceleration comes forward from the school (i.e., movement to another grade level for reading instruction or independent work). There is nothing inherently wrong with acceleration in reading. In fact, there is research that supports acceleration of able learners. However, the question is really related to the readiness of the child. If the child is socially and emotionally ready to work with older students and if adaptations are made in the required work according to the age of the student, then acceleration to another grade level may be appropriate. If, however, placement in another grade level is simply expedient for the school and not in the best interests of the individual child, then acceleration should be refused. It takes careful consideration of the individual gifted child and agreement on the part of parents and teachers to make this alternative successful. Parents need to ask about the social and emotional climate of the new environment and the adaptations the school is willing to make in order to meet the needs of the gifted child.

Independent reading is another alternative offered to gifted readers. In this case, the children read at their own pace, at their own level, and complete work independently. Again, this option has been successfully used with gifted readers, but only when opportunities for comprehensive discussion and group work have been provided by the teacher. Children do not develop mature reading abilities in isolation. They need attention, discussion, and challenge to develop their intellectual understanding of the material they are reading. In a strong independent reading program teachers will need to select materials thoughtfully that reflect and extend the reading interests, skills, and emotional levels of a gifted student. Parents of gifted readers should try to be diplomatic but not hesitant in discussing their child's reading ability with the classroom teacher. Bringing in the child's favorite selections and asking the teacher's advice on new reading materials may prompt attention to his or her advanced abilities. Professional educators realize that parents have a wealth of information about their children and are willing to listen and investigate parental concerns.

Just as parents ask teachers' advice, teachers should also ask parents and students themselves, through interest inventories or informal interviews, about the reading interests of the gifted readers. Teachers can use this reading information to investigate student abilities and plan appropriate reading activities.

Parents should keep in mind that as they discuss their concerns with professional educators they are asking questions on behalf of all children. The focus on the needs of the gifted child should also highlight the individual needs of all children within the classroom. It is not a matter of "taking time from others" to promote the intellectual development of one child. It is, rather, a matter of providing an education appropriate to the talents and abilities of all children in the classroom. As with the others, gifted children have a right to an educationally appropriate experience provided in a psychologically safe environment.

When parents discuss their concerns about reading in school they should also be prepared to offer help in and out of the classroom. If you are able to spend time in your child's classroom, bring your favorite reading selections to school and read to and with children. Offer to find reading resources for the classroom that are not only appropriate for your child but appropriate for other children as well. Or spend time at the reading and writing center helping children. Many teachers welcome the additional assistance in the classroom. If you don't have time during the day, offer to compile a list of new books/resources available in the community and return it to the classroom. Check with the local library to see what is new in reading and share this information with teachers and children. If the classroom is equipped with a computer network, establish a "reading and writing pen pal" system between your office or home and your child's classroom. These are only a few of the many ways parents and teachers can work cooperatively to reinforce and extend reading and writing activities in the classroom. While it is important that each child receive an appropriate education, it is also important to remember that we all share in the responsibility to make an appropriate education a reality.

Conclusion

Having a gifted child is often a pleasure and sometimes a pain. The pleasure comes in seeing these children grow and develop into healthy, happy, and successful adults. The pleasure comes from their funny sense of humor, their understanding of situations far beyond their years, and their enthusiasm for learning. The pain can come from exactly the same sources, when their sense of humor is not appreciated, when they are sensitive enough to perceive adult behavior but too young to interact with it, or when they lose their love of learning. The task and challenge for parents and educators is to guide their gifted children's growth and development, nurture their love of learning, and protect them until they become old enough and strong enough to protect themselves.

Without doubt, reading is one of the most important gifts we can give children. As Jim Alvino, a noted expert in gifted child education comments, "not only does reading develop and challenge cognitive skills, it opens up worlds of potential interest and involvement" (p. 294). It is up to us, both parents and teachers, to ensure that our children have the opportunities to discover, explore, and delight in these worlds.

References and Other Readings on the Topic

Alvino, J. (1985). *Parents' guide to raising a gifted child.* Boston: Little, Brown.

Baskin, B. and K. Harris (1980). *Books for the gifted child.* New York: Bowker.

Clark, M. (1978). *Young fluent readers.* London: Heinemann Educational Books.

Halsted, J.W. (1988). *Guiding gifted readers.* Columbus, OH: Ohio Psychology Publishing Company.

Lepscky, I. (1982). *Albert Einstein.* Woodbury, NY: Barron's Educational Series, Inc., 3–4.

McGee, L. and D. Richgels (1990). *Literacy's beginnings: Supporting young readers and writers.* Boston: Allyn & Bacon.

Polette, N. (1982). *3 R's for the gifted: Reading, writing and research.* Littleton, CO: Libraries Unlimited, Inc.

Roedell, W., N. Jackson, and H. Robinson (1980). *Young gifted children.* New York: Teachers College Press.

Saunders, J. and P. Espeland (1986). *Bringing out the best: A resource guide for parents of young gifted children.* New York: Free Spirit Publications.

Whitmore, J.R. (1980). *Giftedness, conflict and underachievement.* Boston: Allyn and Bacon.

Whitmore, J.R. (Ed.). (1986). *Intellectual giftedness in young children.* New York: Haworth Press.

Chapter 20

Parent Volunteers: Partners in Literacy

Elizabeth Gibbons Pryor

Years ago, Betsy Pryor directed the volunteer program in a psychiatric hospital, so she has long known the invaluable contribution volunteers can make to any human services organization. As a classroom teacher, she has encouraged and worked with parent volunteers, particularly in the area of literacy. She has found that children learn to read and write remarkably easier and better when they have adult role models around them who also enjoy reading and writing. The greatest personal benefits of parent volunteers have been the support they have provided her as a teacher and the lasting, close friendships that have flourished between her and her parent volunteers.

A re you a parent? Did you ever wonder what teachers think of parent volunteers in the school? Here's what one typical teacher said: "Parent volunteers are such an integral part of my program that it's hard to imagine working without them. With parents, all things are possible. They make my goals a reality. Together, we form a strong foundation . . . of support for all the children we share. Together, we make a difference" (Brountas 1990). Tributes like this are echoing across the country these days as more and more teachers and parents work together as partners in education. How about it? Wouldn't you, too, like to become a school volunteer?

Why Should I Become a School Volunteer?

One of the best reasons to become a school volunteer is because it makes a big difference. Researchers have found that students learn more effectively and successfully when parents are involved in their children's education (Henderson 1988). When parents are school volunteers they have a more positive view of the school, teachers teach better, and student achievement improves. Everybody benefits!

Volunteers get to know their child's teacher better, provide important instructional assistance, and benefit from improved communication with the teacher. You will also discover what your child is studying in school, then enrich and reinforce that learning at home.

Parent volunteers in classrooms can have a tremendous impact on children's reading development.

As a parent volunteer you may also come to know your child better. You are used to your child's behavior and performance at home, either alone or in small groups of children. Seeing your child interact in larger groups of children the same age, you will probably come to understand him or her in a different way. Being involved in the school is also a good way to get to know your child's school friends and, perhaps, their parents.

What Can I Do As a School Volunteer?

There are many things you can do as a school volunteer in the classroom, in the office, or with the Parent-Teacher Association that will help children develop as readers and writers. Here are some things parents do, but there are many other possibilities.

In the classroom you might read and write with students, edit and publish students' writing, or keep the classroom supplied with fresh reading materials. You could read aloud to one student, a small group of students, or the whole class and then discuss the story. You might listen to a child read or echo-read (you read first, then the child reads) with a student. If you work with students who are writing, you might conference with them in order to help them decide what revisions they should make or read and respond in writing to their journals, setting up a written conversation between you and a student. Volunteers in kindergarten or beginning first grade might write down students' dictated stories on large sheets of chart paper or on regular size paper. All of these activities engage children in real reading and writing and lead to real growth in their development as literate persons.

Students would be delighted to have you give "book talks," in which you tell just enough about a book you've read to get them interested in reading it themselves. Children need to have the example of adults who share their passion for reading and for good books.

School volunteers are invaluable when it comes to producing plays and puppet shows. You might bring in materials (or get donations) to make puppets and help supervise their construction. You might make costumes for younger students or help older students make their own costumes for plays. Scenery is another project with which you might help. Your involvement can help the classroom flourish in literacy related activities that the teacher alone may not be able to undertake. You make a difference.

Other parent volunteers are particularly helpful in collecting, organizing, and arranging the hands-on materials for science, cooking with students, and arts and crafts projects. You could also perform various scientific, culinary, or arts/crafts demonstrations, as well as monitor and assist small groups of students engaged in outdoor education activities, learning centers, field trips, and class parties.

You might volunteer as an editor and publisher of children's writing if your child's school has a publishing center. Volunteers there usually work with students to edit their writing for publication, then type the manuscripts and bind them into books for students to illustrate and add to their classroom collection of student-authored books for all to read.

Keeping the classroom library supplied with fresh library books, magazines, and newspapers is another valuable service that you might perform. Books may be selected from the school library or the public library, or they may be solicited from and donated or loaned by other parents. Teachers are always delighted and grateful to have a variety of age appropriate books and magazines added to their classroom libraries.

There are always things that need to be made in an elementary classroom. You might make (or help students make) items such as board games, bulletin boards, learning centers, big books, or audiotapes of stories. You might enjoy working with students to develop jackdaws, which are collections of items related to particular stories, time periods, or historical events that the class may be studying. A jackdaw can include real or facsimile photos, maps, clothes/costumes, artwork, recipes or food, price lists, time lines, news articles, letters/diaries/journals, or songs/music/dance.

Most parent volunteers are also members of the Parent-Teacher Association (or a locally organized group of parents and teachers). You may volunteer to serve as a committee member, chairperson, or officer of such a group. Through the PTA, you can organize and/or support school-wide literacy activities such as plays or pageants, book fairs, young authors' conferences, or read-a-thons. Themed weeks and months like Right to Read Week, Fire Safety Week, Children's Book Week, and Dental Health month are additional occasions for you to become involved in special school-wide activities and demonstrations. PTA fund-raising activities for school needs, of course, always require many parent volunteers.

Is There Anything Else I Should Know?

Yes! Two other questions that parents often ask about volunteering are (1) How much time will it take? and (2) Will I get any training? The time you will spend as a volunteer depends upon two things: The time you are able to give and the time requirements of the volunteer job. It is something that can be negotiated with the school personnel with whom you will work. Training for volunteers is offered in some schools, depending on the assignment. If you volunteer in the classroom, you will probably be trained by the teacher with whom you will work. Although the service you provide is very important, most volunteer jobs do not require extensive training. Many parents become experts in their roles simply through their classroom work with children.

There is something else you should know. Two qualities are essential in a parent volunteer: confidentiality and reliability. As a parent volunteer you may have access to private information about people (both teachers and students) that must remain confidential. Parent volunteers are expected to be discreet. Students and school personnel rely on the dependability of parent volunteers. Students form attachments quickly and will be particularly disappointed if you don't show up. Teachers also rely on volunteers, so they too may feel let down if you aren't there as scheduled.

Finally, there are two other qualities which will endear you as a parent volunteer: initiative and a positive attitude. Once you have become familiar with the classroom routines and organization, most teachers appreciate your taking the initiative to do things such as straightening up the classroom library or writing center, reading aloud to a small group of students, or organizing science materials for science class. The key to initiative is to check first with the teacher about the things you might do when your "assigned duties" are completed. A positive attitude is best expressed by enthusiasm and positive comments to students and the teacher.

I've been hoping you would ask that question! Contact your child's teacher, the school principal, or a member/officer of the school's Parent-Teacher Association. Ask them what opportunities there are for parent volunteers in your child's school.

If no parent volunteer program is available in the classroom or school, discuss the possibilities with your child's teacher or the principal. If the teacher or principal is not aware of how volunteers could be employed, you might suggest some of the ideas discussed here.

One excellent way to break the ice and begin your experience as a volunteer in any classroom is to take in some favorite books to share with the children. If your occupation prevents you from volunteering during the daytime when school is in session, talk with your child's teacher about ways you might help at home in the evening. For example, you might make learning center materials, select books from the public library to augment the classroom library, type edited books for publication, or make blank books for children to write in.

Teachers interested in having parents as volunteers should first consider the classroom needs that volunteers might appropriately meet. Next, teachers should write a brief description of the various volunteer assignments so everyone understands what the volunteers are to do.

Once the teacher recruits the needed parent volunteers, she or he should provide an orientation to the classroom and training for the volunteer. Most teachers prefer to train volunteers before or after school to prevent interruptions during the instructional day. Some teachers prefer to train all volunteers in a single session. Dependability and confidentiality are two aspects of volunteering in the classroom that should be stressed in the training session(s). Teachers should also suggest what volunteers could do if they have extra time or if normal volunteer work is not needed on a particular day. Finally, teachers should provide some recognition or award for parent volunteers. Regular comments of appreciation, thank-you notes, occasional invitations to stay for lunch, small gifts, or certificates are examples of recognition or awards teachers might utilize to thank parent volunteers for their invaluable and thoughtful assistance.

Volunteering in elementary classrooms may not be easy or convenient for many parents. But those who do volunteer know that the time and effort they give will pay dividends manyfold in the lives of children.

How Do I Become a School Volunteer?

Brountas, M. (1990). Partners in teaching. *Teaching K–8, 20* (3), 78–80.

Fredericks, A., and D. Taylor. (1985). *Parent programs in reading: Guidelines for success.* Newark: DE: International Reading Association.

Henderson, A.T. (1988). Parents are a school's best friends. *Phi Delta Kappan, 70,* 148–153.

Nicoll, V., and L. Wilkie (1991). *Literacy at home and school: A guide for parents.* Portsmouth, NH: Heinemann Educational Books.

Rauch, S., and J. Sanacore, (Eds.). (1985). *Handbook for the volunteer tutor* (2nd ed.). Newark, DE: International Reading Association.

References and Other Readings on the Topic

Chapter 21

The Problems and Promises of Dealing with Principals

Fredrick R. Burton

F red Burton is the principal of Granby Elementary School in Worthington, Ohio. He has taught elementary school in Wyoming and Ohio and his Ph.D., from Ohio State University, is in the area of Language, Literature, and Literacy Education.

A s I walked out of what was a very pleasant parent-teacher conference, I realized my palms had been sweating. Why? After all, I was an elementary school principal who had participated in such conferences for over 15 years. And this particular conference was a very positive one. However, there was one difference. During this conference, *I* was the parent and we had been discussing *my* child.

I suspect that I'm not alone in my anxiety when approaching or being approached by school personnel—*particularly when it involves my child.* When parents find it necessary to work with principals regarding their child's literacy development, there are a few things they can expect that offer great possibilities for a positive experience. But first, let's consider some potential problems, interpersonal land mines if you like, that might just serve to get in the way.

The Problems

There are two problems to good principal-parent communication and both of them are grounded in a very common human feeling—fear. Very few people like to talk about this, but everyone knows it. When parents walk into a principal's office to discuss their child's progress in learning, they're a little nervous. Even if the principal is friendly, nonthreatening and welcoming of parent comments regarding the school, they often walk through the door with at least some anxiety. I'm not sure why. It might have something to do historically with their own negative school experiences. People have similar feelings in other settings as well (such as a doctor's office). Either way, it doesn't matter. The anxiety is there and it can get in the way of helpful communication about children's learning.

However, what may be helpful for parents to know is that the principal may also be nervous. The reason for the principal's anxiety is a little clearer to me. Principals at their best are child, teacher, *and* parent advocates. They want to be helpful and supportive of each of these groups. When there is a problem or conflict among these individuals, the principal is immediately thrown into a value conflict—whom to support? Rather than try to analyze this atmosphere of anxiety that is floating around the principal's office, perhaps our best approach may be simply to acknowledge it and refocus on the common ground that both the principal and the parent have—the child's best interest.

Another problem, although much less frequent, is that parents may fear retribution of some sort from their classroom teacher. Parents will sometimes give this to me as a reason for not having discussed a child's progress in reading or the teacher's classroom approach to literacy instruction with the teacher. I am not saying that this retribution could not happen. It might. However, in my years as an educator I have never witnessed or even heard of it actually occurring. Regardless, the parent should be reassured that this type of behavior is completely unprofessional and would not be tolerated. And besides, sooner or later, the parents and the teacher will need to listen to one another and communicate. I wish there were another way that I could suggest that required less courage and skill, but there isn't. A principal should be willing to mediate conflicts when they do arise and everyone should remember once again their common ground—the child.

Although schools are not immune from problems and conflicts that all organizations typically face, there are some ways that parents can work with principals to promote literacy learning as well as some reasonable expectations that parents can have of their school's principal.

Expectation #1: While for the most part the actual teaching and learning of literacy occurs in the classroom, the principal should be articulating, living, and encouraging the values of the school.

For example, when you walk in the building, do you see children's work artfully displayed in the halls, on the walls, in classrooms, in the *principal's* office. You should. No matter what a principal might say, there should be *evidence* that children's literacy efforts are honored, celebrated, and displayed throughout the school. A way that I've found to be particularly powerful is the school Town Meeting. These are bi-weekly meetings in which the entire school meets for 20–30 minutes to celebrate children's literacy learning. For example, a first grade child reads aloud his first story and everyone in the school applauds. A group of fifth graders acts out a play they have written based on a science study. Again, this is followed by recognition and applause. A second grade boy delivers a short speech he has written on why our school cafeteria should not be using styrofoam trays. More clapping. Not only is this second grader's speech honored, but he also has a genuine format for using language to express an idea.

Expectation #2: The principal should take great pride in classrooms with purposeful, joyful noise.

Principals who demand quiet classrooms are really concerned with control and how it might appear that they are shirking their duties as school administrator. Perhaps their central office supervisor expects it. In any case, classrooms that are quiet *all* of the time, are not classrooms that encourage children's literacy learning. Children should be observed *using* language individually, in pairs, in small groups, and during whole class meetings. Rather than just observe the teacher questioning the children, I often advise parents to listen for the kinds of questions *children* are raising in classrooms.

Expectation #3: The principal as a reader and writer is visible to the children and staff.

This year I led a small group book discussion on a children's novel, *Maniac McGee* by Jerry Spinelli. Earlier in the year I had read an article on leading literature discussions and asked a fourth grade teacher to observe and give feedback to *me* as a teacher-learner. My office is also a place for children to come share their reading and writing because they know I'm interested. After they do so, I will occasionally call their parents at home or work to say I have their child in my office (the prankster in me usually pauses for dramatic effect) and then read their writing over the phone. At other times, I go to the children. I sometimes simply sit down in the halls or classrooms and read with children. It's a good model and it serves to keep my sanity intact on particularly stressful days.

The Possibilities

Expectation #4: The principal should provide resources for teachers to teach reading and writing.

This may appear obvious, but it doesn't always happen. Most school districts are not adequately funded; however, I believe we could do a better job of creatively redistributing the financial resources we do have. For example, when it came time to order materials for the following year, I gave teachers who did not use basal readers and workbooks the money normally allocated for these commercially produced materials to purchase children's literature and other materials they needed for their classrooms.

Another important resource is time. Does the principal eat up precious staff meeting time with mundane announcements (that could have been put in writing) or is staff meeting time used for teacher sharing and discussion about issues related to how children learn language. Our own staff has spent the last two years using staff meeting time to understand and implement the use of literacy portfolios, an innovation in instructional assessment, in classrooms in ways that actually make a difference in the lives of the children—who, once again, are the center of schools.

Expectation #5: The principal should have a vision of what constitutes a literate school community.

A vision is like a compass always pointing a school to "true north." You may not always be going in that direction, but a clear vision, like a good compass continually nudges you in that direction. As a principal, I take every opportunity given to me to share orally and in writing that our school is a "community of readers, writers, and learners," a place where children *and* adults learn and reflect on their learning. Staff oftentimes will jokingly tease me about how often I talk about the importance of *reflection* on their roles as teacher-learners, but they know I value it and expect it. I also know that I must back up my words with financial encouragement, time to learn, and moral support when they take risks and make mistakes.

Good schools are improving schools in which children read and write for real purposes. Notice that I didn't say good schools are efficient schools, ones in which there appears to be a high degree of control by the principal. I also didn't mention anything about good schools and nationally norm-referenced standardized test scores. In fact, extremely high test scores in an area like grammar may mean that your school is spending too much time doing lifeless exercises rather than real reading and writing.

As a principal it is my responsibility to have a clear vision of what good schools *can* do to promote literacy learning. *Your* child's principal should have such a vision too, and should communicate that vision to you. Next time, ask your child's principal to share his or her own vision for children's reading and writing in your child's school.

Chapter 22

Reading Instruction in the Intermediate Grades: Preferred Practices

Karen D. Wood
Robert J. Rickelman

K aren Wood, a former middle school teacher and K–12 instructional consultant, is a professor in the Department of Teaching Specialties at the University of North Carolina–Charlotte. She is the author of more than 90 publications in journals such as *The Reading Teacher, Journal of Reading,* and the *Middle School Journal.*

Robert Rickelman is an assistant professor in the Teaching Specialties Department at the University of North Carolina–Charlotte. He teaches courses in elementary reading methods, content area reading, and reading diagnosis. His professional interests include the relationship between technology and literacy and the whole language philosophy of teaching.

I ntermediate level classrooms can and should be lively places in which to learn. The reason for this dynamic atmosphere is that intermediate level teachers must teach a variety of subjects including reading/language arts, social studies, mathematics, science, and health. Another reason is that students in grades four through six are becoming more and more experienced as readers and writers. Consequently, their work is becoming more sophisticated as well.

In preferred classrooms, groups of students might be observed putting together a class newspaper—complete with illustrations, school sports scores, comics, and classified ads, or they might be writing the dialogue for a play they will perform on the American Revolution. At another time of day, they might be taking a walk on a nature trail identifying and describing the local flora and fauna for a book they are compiling.

All of these activities represent preferred methods of teaching and learning. And all of these activities represent the influence of the whole language movement in the intermediate level classroom. In this chapter we describe preferred instructional practices for the intermediate grades. While the list is not exhaustive, it does highlight some important instructional concerns for teachers, parents, and students.

Students Should Be Encouraged to Read for Pleasure on a Daily Basis

If there is one absolute principle in the field of reading instruction, it is the fact that the best way to improve students' reading performance is to have them read daily. Wide reading improves students' reading fluency. It makes sense that the more reading students do, the more they repeatedly encounter the same words and sentence structures, and the more familiar and readable these words and sentences become. Moreover, wide reading improves students' vocabulary knowledge. It expands their background of experiences and helps them visit places they have never been, feel emotions they have never tapped, and explore new ways of thinking, feeling, and living.

Classrooms in which reading for pleasure is valued are classrooms that are decorated with books—books on varied grade levels and topics. In these classrooms students are given time every day to read on their own. In some cases, time is set aside at the beginning, middle, and at the end of the day for students and teachers alike to read books of their own choosing. Yes, the teacher should read too. The teacher reads to serve as a model for students, illustrating that reading can indeed be a pleasure and a reward. In ideal settings, where an entire school has adopted the notion of reading for pleasure, at a predetermined time everyone in the school picks up a book and begins reading. This includes the principal, janitors—even the physical education teacher. Reading programs such as these have names like D.E.A.R. (Drop Everything and Read) or U.S.S.R. (Uninterrupted Sustained Silent Reading). Time can be allotted to allow students to discuss events in their books with partners, groups, or the whole class. An integral part of an exemplary recreational reading program is sharing—getting someone else turned on to reading your selection, too.

Another preferred practice is to require students to keep a pleasure reading book in their desks at all times. In this way, students who finish assignments early are not punished with yet more work, but rather are rewarded with the opportunity to read on their own.

At other times, the teacher may assign a selection to be read and discussed by the entire class. Groups can be formed to discuss the actions of certain characters, suggest alternative endings, or perform a dramatic interpretation of a particular event.

The possibilities are unlimited in the hands of a creative teacher. Yet one thing is certain: Instilling in students the love of reading gives them a treasure they can enjoy for a lifetime.

Intermediate level classrooms, like their primary level counterparts, are not exempt from excessive reliance on workbooks and worksheets. Workbooks are available to accompany most subjects, including reading, science, social studies, and math. These materials, while originally well-intentioned, have frequently become overused and relied upon as a means of keeping students busy.

We feel workbooks and worksheets should be used sparingly, if at all. For example, in one teacher's classroom, students learn to apply the strategies associated with reading in their own reading. Instead of completing an unrelated workbook page on predicting outcomes, students learn to predict the outcome in the story they are reading. The teacher explains what prediction is, demonstrates the process, and then asks students to apply the strategy to the story being read and, later, to other subjects as well. Questions can be posed such as, "What do you think will happen to the colonists after the Boston Tea Party?" or "What will happen to our experiment if we add two grams instead of one?" or "When do we use prediction in our lives?"

The pages in reading workbooks are made up of activities designed to reinforce specific and isolated skills related to reading. Reading instruction should not be presented in a fragmented manner, such as through worksheet activities that focus on single skills. Reading must be related to other subjects and to real life whenever possible.

The Use of Workbooks, Worksheets, and Dittoes Should Be Kept to a Minimum

---

In the traditional, intermediate level classroom reading and writing were taught separately. Reading instruction often took up the vast majority of time, while writing instruction was as often de-emphasized, and sometimes not taught at all. In fact, in some classrooms, handwriting instruction constituted the writing curriculum.

Today, experts agree that these two critical subject areas should be taught together. The generic term "literacy" is often used to describe both reading and writing. In the real world, most people find that reading and writing ability are *both* necessary, at home and in the workplace. The popular whole language philosophy advocates the integration of reading and writing instruction.

Most whole language advocates strongly advise that reading and writing instruction take place every day. Intermediate level teachers sometimes teach students to read by asking them first to write. What begins in the early grades as scribble writing that only the author can decipher eventually turns into more and more coherent writing that can be shared with others. Some teachers include an author's chair as part of their classroom furniture. Sitting in the chair, budding authors can read their stories to classmates, even critically discussing possible directions for an unfinished story to take. After a story is read, classmates are invited to pick up the book

Students Should Have Numerous Opportunities to Write

discussed to read on their own, or in small groups. Thus, an active writing-reading community is established, with students becoming increasingly proficient in both.

Questions and Assignments Should Be Designed to Promote Critical Thinking

Teachers usually ask many questions throughout a typical day. The questions may help give directions ("Does everyone have their pencil?"), correct misbehavior ("Do you want to go to timeout?"), initiate instruction ("Has anyone ever been to the zoo?"), or evaluate learning ("Who can tell me the capital of Florida?"). One of the least common but most important uses of questions is to promote critical thinking. Critical thinking involves the ability to manipulate information in novel ways and includes activities such as distinguishing fact from fiction, understanding another's point of view, and detecting an author's bias—skills that are often introduced and practiced at the intermediate level.

Critical thinking is an area in which students often perform poorly on standardized tests. One reason for this poor showing is that students sometimes receive little or no classroom instruction or practice. A second reason is that publishers who write teacher's manuals have traditionally focused on literal level thinking skills. Literal thinking involves reciting an answer, word for word, that was previously learned or encountered in a text. For example, if a child learned that Alaska is the state with the smallest population, and was later asked which state has the smallest population, she or he would be asked to demonstrate literal thinking skills.

Parents and teachers can promote critical thinking by simply providing more opportunities for students to think and act critically. Asking questions that require students to analyze and judge information rather than just repeat it would be a good initial step. For instance, instead of asking a student, "Who broke Little Bear's bed?" a child could be asked, "Why do you think Goldilocks went into the house? Would you have gone in if you were she?" Through frequent practice, students can become masters of critical thinking, an ability that becomes even more important at the middle and secondary school levels.

Instructional Groups Should Vary in Activity and Size

In traditional classrooms students are seated in straight rows and assigned seats throughout the school day. On a typical day, students listen to the teacher's lecture about a topic and are asked a series of questions directly from the teacher's guidebook. A handful of students raise their hands to answer. The remainder of the class loses interest. Then, the teacher tells the class to begin reading their books and answer the questions at the end of the chapter. During this time, the teacher remains behind the desk grading last week's papers. Students are expected to turn in their work at the end of the period. The problem with this scenario is that no opportunity is given for students to talk about their new learning either with their teacher or their peers. Such is the result of relying on lectures and rigid seating arrangements as the primary means of conveying information.

A preferred practice, and one which is amply supported by research, would be to use a combination of approaches including lecture and small group or paired work, as well as individual study. Let's look in a classroom where this type of activity is happening. The teacher is at the front of the class giving a lively demonstration of a science experiment on the force of gravity. She explains each movement and procedure and continually invites students to guess (predict) what will happen next. The students' attention is focused on the teacher as they eagerly await the outcome. The teacher then reforms the class into preassigned groups of four as students discuss what would happen to the experiment if certain conditions were changed. The teacher circulates among the groups to monitor, answer questions, and assist with problem solving. After a few minutes, the groups share their responses with the class as a whole. Then, the teacher and students read the next three pages from their textbooks. After each page students retell the content in their own words to their partners. After reading, the class discusses the textbook material and relates it to the experiment from the beginning of the period. This teacher is engaging the class in cooperative learning activities. Cooperative learning is gaining increased support and interest worldwide as research finds the students learn more when they work together than when they work alone. Providing opportunities for students to work together has been shown to increase achievement, expand knowledge and understanding, and improve peer relationships.

Various Forms of Media Should Be Used to Communicate Subject Area Content

Teachers have used different media in the classroom since the earliest days of teaching. While laptop slates were at one time an important part of the daily lesson, laptop computers may soon become a common part of everyday teaching and learning.

Today, the use of media in the average classroom setting is rare. While many school districts are equipping their classrooms with computers, other media forms are not as prevalent.

To further complicate the matter, different media are now becoming common in the home. For instance, videotape recorders and camcorders are now found in many homes. Video games no longer have to be played in arcades. George Lucas, creator of the "Star Wars" movies, once commented that it took him three years, with the best professionals in the field, to finish one movie. A classroom teacher is expected to compete with this media six hours a day, every day of the school year. While it might seem an unfair comparison, Lucas's point is well taken. For a relatively small price, children can spend hours mesmerized by a video game in their homes. Yet these same children often are unmotivated in a typical school setting.

One way to solve this problem is to provide teachers with computers and software that challenge and motivate students to want to learn. Yet, teachers are often frustrated because, while the school system might not hesitate to buy five computers for one classroom, they are limited to purchasing one software program a year. Without stimulating software that ties into the classroom curriculum, the best computers in the world have very limited usefulness.

At home, parents can help by limiting the amount of time their children play video games and watch television. It is common to hear students in school remark that they play video games for three or four hours a day! Parents and teachers must work together to get children involved in other profitable activities.

Instruction in All Subject Areas Should Involve Attention to All Communication Processes Whenever Possible

It is easy to assume that the communication processes of reading, writing, listening, speaking and viewing are the sole domain of the language arts classroom. However, in a preferred instructional environment, that is not the case. On the contrary, these processes can and should be incorporated throughout all subject areas. This practice is referred to as integrating the language arts across the curriculum. An important part of a total integrated language arts program is using literature, both fiction and nonfiction, as a way to learn more about a topic under study. Many books are available that relate to all subject areas.

Let's observe a classroom in which the language arts are integrated with a social studies lesson. Teacher A is observed introducing a videotape and a corresponding teacher-developed viewing guide on the "Industrial Revolution" (Listening). Students make notes on the guide (Writing) as they watch the video (Viewing). Afterwards, they form into groups to elaborate and share their responses (Speaking/Listening). Spokespersons then offer each group's reactions to the video and discussion. As a follow-up activity, students choose books, articles, or other selections to read related to the video lesson (Reading).

Contrast this practice with what is taking place in another teacher's classroom. Teacher B tells the class that they will watch a video. No instructions or expectations about student learning outcomes are given. Consequently, when the lights go out, some heads go down on the desks and some complete a homework assignment for another class. At the end of the video, teacher B instructs students to open their books to page 149 and begin reading about the Industrial Revolution, since they will have a test on the content the next day.

Lively, purposeful activities that allow for student input and interaction are the way to motivate students to want to learn. They also provide alternative modes of expression for students who, for example, can better express themselves orally than graphically or can gain information visually through reading and viewing, as opposed to listening.

Spelling Words Should Be Derived from Subject Area Topics, Not from a Single Spelling Book

Spelling ability is linked to reading and writing ability. Students who have difficulty in spelling can become discouraged from writing. Traditionally, spelling has been taught as a separate course. Students are given a list of words on Monday to memorize for a quiz on Friday. These words usually come from graded lists. All students are responsible for learning the same words each week.

The problem with using a prescribed set of common spelling words each week is that students fail to see how these words fit into the rest of the school day. It is not uncommon for students to use rote memorization to learn the spelling of the week's words. That is, they may learn how to spell a word and yet not even know its meaning. Since the reason for learning these words is vague at best, students often forget them soon after the final quiz. There is no real connection between these words and the other learning taking place in the students' lives.

One preferred practice is to allow students to develop their own set of spelling words. This can be done on a weekly basis. The words are those that have a personal meaning for students. They may be related to children's books, to subject area topics being learned, or to interests outside of school. While each student's list is different, some common words can be assigned by the teacher to all students.

For instance, if students are required to learn twenty new spelling words each week, a common expectation for intermediate level students, the teacher might assign ten words to the whole class. If students are studying tornadoes, these might be words associated with that topic. The remaining words might be unique for each student, words that students, for whatever reason, really want to learn about and learn to spell. Some students might want to learn to spell words that they intend to use in their writing, while others might want to learn to spell words related to camping, soccer, or some other area of interest. The key point here is that students are motivated to learn to spell words that have a personal significance for them, not words suggested by a commercial publisher. With the common words, teachers can make sure that students use them in writing and homework assignments.

The current methods of testing reading skills have been in common practice since the 1920s. Usually, children are given one of two types of standardized assessments: achievement and survey tests. These tests focus on students' progress on a restricted range of reading competencies at one particular point in time, in an environment that is often stress filled and artificial.

For example, a reading test commonly has students read short passages and then answer several questions over what they have just finished reading within an artificially imposed time period. The score of either of these tests might be reported as a single and rather uninformative reading level, usually as a grade level score. For example, parents might be told that their child is reading at the 5.2 grade level. Most experts agree that there is considerably more to reading than what is measured by survey and achievement tests.

Another problem with assessments of this type is that students may not do well on tests for a variety of reasons that have little to do with reading ability. Physical and emotional problems can influence test scores, as can anxiety and attitude. At best, the scores represent a student's ability on a very limited array of reading competencies at only one given point in time. There is no way to know how accurate the scores truly are.

Because the traditional methods of assessing reading ability present such problems, newer methods of obtaining more accurate assessments are being developed. One of the more popular assessment techniques is called portfolio assessment and involves compiling information on the reader from a variety of sources. This type of evaluation may take place over an entire school year. The teacher keeps a portfolio representing examples of each student's work obtained at various intervals throughout the year. Each portfolio may include different items. For instance, one person's may include writing samples, audio tapes of the student reading orally, attitude and interest surveys, anecdotal teacher and/or student records, journal entries, or anything else that the teacher or student feels offers a good representation of his or her ability in reading.

Many Sources Should Be Used to Assess Students' Reading Performance

At intervals, and especially at the end of the year, the teacher and individual students look through and reflect on the portfolio, comparing work from the beginning of the year with that from the end of the year, and allowing students to measure their individual strengths, weaknesses, and progress. While portfolio assessments take considerably more time than more traditional assessments, the results give a broader picture of a student's ability and performance over a longer period of time and a more honest reflection of a student's ability and achievement.

A Final Note

We have attempted to give parents a broad snapshot of some preferred instructional practices at the intermediate level. Previous and traditional notions of reading instruction have limited its scope to an hour and a half of story reading and skill and drill activities. However, the practices described here reveal that effective reading instruction occurs throughout the school day.

Chapter 23

Parental Roles in Reading and Writing Evaluation

Jan Turbill
JoBeth Allen

J an Turbill is a senior lecturer in Language and Learning at the University of Wollongong, New South Wales, Australia. Previously, she taught kindergarten through grade two for 12 years and was a language arts consultant for nine years. She is the author of several books about literacy learning.

JoBeth Allen is an associate professor of Language Education at the University of Georgia. Her interests include how teachers and parents promote children's early language and literacy development.

What Is Literacy Evaluation?

For as long as there have been schools, people have been interested in evaluating students' growth as readers and writers. Evaluating literacy development is a very complex task. Literacy itself is not a simple thing; we can't really say that one person is literate and another is not, or even that one person is more literate than another. For most people the word "literacy" means simply the ability to read and write. But to read and write what?—the newspaper, a novel, a computer manual, a letter to an aunt, an application for a job, a chemistry experiment? Many would argue that being truly literate also means being "computer literate," "art literate," "media literate," and so on. In other words, literacy means being able to "read and write" in the many systems we use to communicate in our culture.

If you are reading this chapter, you probably consider yourself literate. Yet there are some things that each of us can read and some things we cannot. Consider the following example:

> Hold heddle rod H to right of warp; fasten right end of twine to left end of heddle rod, loosely, with two half hitches; push end of heddle rod to left across warp, catching twine with left forefinger, between first two even-numbered threads; throw two half hitches over end of rod.

How confident did you feel reading this passage? Would you say you can read it because you can pronounce all the words? Did you understand what you read, enough that you could explain the information to someone else? If you didn't really understand, are you illiterate? Of course not. It means that if you had the background knowledge of the weaver who wrote it, or if you were a weaver yourself, you would be able to gain some meaning from the text. Literacy involves an interaction of the reader, the text, and the reading event or context for reading.

We are more likely to be able to read and write about things that we have an interest in and know something about. It is important to keep this in mind when we are dealing with the reading and writing of children. Most people are not simply literate or illiterate; we are literate in different areas and use literacy for different purposes.

Evaluating literacy development is also complicated by the fact that evaluations often serve different purposes and different audiences. For example, teachers seek evaluation that will help them learn about their students' development and help them as teachers develop the most helpful instruction. The general public may share this goal, but at the same time many want evaluation that gives them information about how their school, teachers, and students measure up. We all want good schools for our children and good literacy instruction. So how can we find out if our schools are doing a good job?

How Is Literacy Usually Evaluated in Schools?

You probably remember taking a weekly spelling test, reading a passage and answering ten questions, writing "What I Did on My Vacation." Many of us remember feeling frustrated and disappointed at the grade given by the teacher. You might remember asking yourself, "Why do I do so well on the spelling test and then can't remember the same word for another assignment? What does 70 percent mean about my understanding of this passage? I thought my vacation story was exciting; why didn't the teacher like it?"

Many teachers are also frustrated with evaluating reading and writing in such narrow ways, relying on tests written by textbook writers. Many teachers evaluate students' literacy development not just by assigning a grade, but by observing and recording the skills and strategies the student really uses as well as those that the student needs to learn. In this way teachers can plan instruction based on the needs of each learner. For instructional planning to be effective, evaluation has to grow out of what teachers are actually teaching and what students are actually learning. If teachers emphasize strategies for figuring out an unfamiliar word in context, they will evaluate that ability by listening to what students do when they reach an unknown word in their reading, not by having them define "context clue."

Teachers are aware of the complexity of literacy learning. Many evaluate not only the products (the reading and writing the student produces) but the processes (the strategies the student uses to achieve this product) because *both* are important in becoming literate. No one test measures both products and processes. Literacy processes are best measured as they occur in everyday use. Therefore, many teachers write descriptions of what learners do during daily reading and writing times. Teachers then analyze their notes and make lists of what students can do, as well as what each student still needs to learn. These lists and notes become teachers' plans for individual, small group, and whole class instruction. Such descriptive records are similar to the information a doctor keeps on each patient. When examined over time, a pattern develops. These patterns provide valuable information for the parent, the student, and the teacher. The main purpose of evaluation, therefore, is to improve teaching and learning.

Parents can be an important part of the evaluation process. If your child's teacher doesn't ask for your help, perhaps you could describe ways in which you could provide information. Some possibilities include:

1. Saving a few good examples of writing that the child does at home, on his or her own (not assignments).

2. Recording the student's home reading habits; how often, under what circumstances, what reading materials, and how long he or she reads.

3. Interviewing children periodically about what they are learning as readers and writers, how they are learning, what they would like to learn next, and how they plan to learn it. There may be particular questions you or the teacher would like asked, such as how a child feels about him or herself as a reader, or about going out of the homeroom for "special" reading classes. You may be able to get your child talking in a personal, informal way that would be difficult for a teacher to achieve in a crowded classroom.

Teachers realize that the most important form of evaluation to the learner is self-evaluation; the interviewing strategy suggested in the last paragraph is one method of helping students reflect on their learning. Students need to become responsible for their own learning, and to do that they must learn to figure out what they do well, what they need to learn, and how they might go about learning it. We don't want students who wait passively to be told how well or poorly they have done something;

real growth occurs when children examine their own abilities and needs, set standards for themselves, and evaluate their progress. Self-evaluation will not occur if students become dependent on teachers to evaluate them.

Another form of evaluation practiced in our schools is state testing or standardized testing. This testing is usually mandated by the state or school district. The same test is given to all learners of a given age or grade. The results are compiled and recorded as a single score or set of scores. This form of testing is scored so that some learners will get high marks, whereas others will score within the low range, while the majority will score in the middle range. These tests fulfill quite different purposes than measures devised by the teacher. The numerical results, usually recorded as a percentile score, can be used to compare one group of learners with another, one year with another, one ethnic group with another, and so on.

Standardized tests rarely provide feedback for either students or teachers on how to improve teaching and learning. It is not possible to tell how an answer was chosen, what thought processes were used, why errors were made. Yet a difference of one or two answers may be used to determine whether a student is "on grade level" or "below grade level," or even, in some districts, whether a child gets promoted to the next grade.

The major issue is what do these textbook and standardized tests really test? Can they give a complete picture of a student's literacy development? Is it possible to measure the skills and strategies needed to become a literate person? Standardized tests measure learners' performance on tasks that they rarely do in real life, such as reading several unconnected passages on a page and answering questions that try to trick them. These tests do not measure how often a student independently picks up a book to read for information or pleasure, what she does when she gets to a word she doesn't know, or how she searches for information in the newspaper. They do not measure how a student decides what to write about, his strategies for revising, or his proofreading technique. In fact, research is showing that it is impossible to develop any single measure of something as complex as the ability to read or write.

Why Do Some Schools Use Inappropriate Evaluation Practices?

There is a relationship between the ways teachers evaluate learners and the ways teachers themselves are evaluated. Pressure is often placed on teachers to have their students perform "better" on standardized tests, better than the national, state, and local norms. School comparisons are often published in local newspapers. When teachers feel this pressure, they often narrow the literacy instruction to the kinds of things measured on the test. They may even come to view their students as literacy learners in these narrow terms.

For example, a fourth grade teacher might describe a child by saying, "Melissa is a 3.2 reader," meaning that 3.2 is the level of the basal reader she has most recently passed. Conversely, a teacher who keeps detailed records of what and how a child actually reads might say, "At the beginning of the year, Melissa was reading the "Frog and Toad" books. She read them nearly every day for a month before she began to try some of the more difficult books like the "Polk Street Gang" series. She started reading some of these with a friend first; by January, she was reading them by herself. It was a struggle, but she was determined to read them independently, and she understood what she was reading even in passages where she didn't know all the words. Some days she still goes back to old favorites for an easy read. Now, she is the "mystery queen" of the class. She is reading the Cam Jansen books and has started a book club of friends who are also reading, talking about, and writing their own mysteries."

Which report tells you, as a parent, more about your child as a reader? Which is more helpful to the learner, or her teacher? When the emphasis is on achieving a particular reading level or standardized score, teachers and students begin to view themselves in those terms. They say things such as, "I'm not a very good writer; I get D's in spelling" or "I'm the best reader in the class because I'm in Level X." Learners compare themselves with their peers, rather than looking at their own growth, and they think of literacy development in terms of tests and levels.

What Are Some Principles of Useful Evaluation?

Being able to read and write are highly valued skills in our society. Knowing what learners can and cannot do is, therefore, an important responsibility of the school. However, it is equally important that evaluation be useful to others involved in students' learning: the student, the teacher, the parents, the administrators, and the politicians. Here are some principles that should guide evaluation in our schools. Evaluation should

- improve learning and teaching by providing timely, detailed information about the student as a literacy learner;

- consider processes as well as products of reading and writing;

- include the learner, with an emphasis on self-evaluation;

- acknowledge the professional knowledge of the teacher and the ability of the teacher to make informed decisions about the student's future development;

- rely on many sources of information, gathered throughout the year;

- reflect the curriculum being taught in the classroom;

- use information collected in real classroom events rather than artificial test situations.

How Can Parents Promote Useful Literacy Evaluation?

There are many activities in today's world that compete for a young person's time. Activities such as watching television and playing video games will become central to children who do not regularly experience the pleasure of losing themselves in a book or writing to a distant friend. The challenge of both school and home is to find ways of showing young people the multiple, meaningful purposes of reading and writing. Evaluation can either help make reading and writing important and valuable parts of children's lives, or it can create resistance and failure. It can support literacy development or merely measure isolated parts of it. Evaluation can reside in the hands of the learners and their teachers who know them as readers and writers or in the hands of test makers who don't. Parents can promote the kinds of evaluation that are truly useful by considering the questions below.

What Questions Might I Ask Myself about My Child's Reading and Writing Development?

What kind of reading and writing does my child do independently outside of school?

How are family read-aloud times changing in terms of what books we read, how my child participates, the depth of discussion about characters, issues, and personal connections to the books?

How do my children see me as a reader and a writer? Do I talk with them about my own literacy?

What can my children tell me about themselves as readers and writers? How has this literacy awareness changed over time?

What do I notice about my child as we read and write together—is he or she tense or relaxed, interested in the content or worried about the words, interested in my comments or anxious that I will make corrections? And what about me—do I enjoy these sessions? Why or why not?

What Questions Might I Ask a Teacher about My Child's Reading and Writing Development?

What can you tell me about my child as a reader and a writer?

Could you show me examples of what my child has read and written recently? What progress do these examples show?

What can my child do successfully as a reader or a writer?

What can I do to help support my child at home?

How do you keep track of my child's reading and writing progress?

Are there ways I can see my child's independent thinking, problem solving, and learning connections within the different subjects?

What Questions Might I Ask the Principal, School Board, or Other Policy Makers?

Does my child take standardized tests? Why? What do they measure?

How relevant are these tests to my child's literacy learning? How accurate are they in reflecting my child's actual reading and writing abilities and involvement? Have teachers had a voice in formulating the tests?

How will my child benefit from these tests? Will the teachers receive the results in time and in a form that will make their instruction more effective for my child?

How else will test results be used?

How much instructional time is spent on standardized tests (including time spent preparing for tests)?

How much of my child's reading and language study time is spent on textbook testing?

How much money is spent on these tests? Would the money be better spent buying more books for my child and other children to read in class?

Parents are a powerful political group. In many places, parents have lobbied for less standardized testing, more appropriate evaluation measures, and limited testing of young children. They have lobbied against the published comparison of test scores that pits school against school. Parents have lobbied for instruction that meets children's needs, not the "needs" of policymakers who want children to look good on standardized tests. Contact your local parent organization and ask what has been done in your area and in other areas of the country. You can play a critical role in the evaluation of your children's reading and writing development. And your influence can have a positive and lasting influence on how your children view themselves as readers and writers.

Other Readings on the Topic

Cochrane, Orin (Ed.) (1992). *Questions and answers about whole language.* Katonah, NY: Richard C. Owen.

> This book is written as a series of very readable letters to teachers and parents who have questions about teaching, learning, and evaluation. Three of the letters are devoted specifically to questions about evaluation.

Oakes, Jeannie, and Martin Lipton (1990). *Making the best of schools: A handbook for parents, teachers, and policymakers.* New Haven, CT: Yale University Press.

> Chapter Six, "Making the Grade: Evaluation, Testing and Grading" is particularly relevant. Parents may be interested in related chapters dealing with tracking (reading groups, "basic" and "advanced" sections of classes) and classes for children with special needs. Chapters 9, 10, and 11 are addressed specifically to parents, detailing ways for parents to support learning at home and get involved with schools.

Graves, Donald (1992). *Portfolio portraits.* Portsmouth, NH: Heinemann.

> Graves' book describes a method of evaluation that is becoming popular with teachers, parents, and students who value ongoing, realistic, important measures of literacy development.

Note: This chapter originated from the International Reading Association's Committee on Literacy Assessment. The authors wish to thank the committee members, especially Peter Johnston, who provided many helpful suggestions through several revisions. We also thank Shirley Allen, president of the Australian Council of State School Organisations, for her valuable suggestions.

Chapter 24

Parents and Schools Assessing Literacy Growth Together

J. Michael Ritty

J. Michael Ritty currently works for the Catholic Diocese of Rochester and deals with issues of families and divorce. Previously, he was on the faculty of the State University of New York at Plattsburgh where he taught courses in reading and language arts education.

T oday's parents and school personnel are much more aware of children's literacy problems than they have been in the past. Schools are more aware of the need to include parents in decisions, and parents are more informed about the importance of reading and writing in today's world and their rights and responsibilities to ensure that their children achieve competence in literacy. It is difficult for parents (as well as children) when children are referred for special help in reading. Questions arise about what parents can do to protect their children and how to help provide the best educational setting for their children. This chapter attempts to address these issues and help everyone work to achieve the best education for the student.

In today's schools, 10 to 20 percent of the population can be termed "at risk" in reading and writing. This population includes those who have short-term as well as long-term needs, gifted students as well as those experiencing difficulty in learning to read. The schools often are required to provide these students with additional and appropriate services.

It can be a stressful time when children are referred for these special services. While parents and teachers seem to have the best interests of students in mind, they may not always agree about the severity of the reading problem or the appropriateness of procedures for helping students in school. Indeed, at times the wishes of the parents can conflict with those of the school.

Children are most often referred initially for help in reading and writing by the classroom teacher. From a classroom teacher's perspective, children who are referred because of reading and writing difficulties do not respond to instruction in the same manner as their peers. They may be referred when results of tests (especially standardized tests) fall below a certain score or when performance in school does not meet expectations. Whatever the reason, the teacher determines that the child is not reading at an appropriate level and a referral is made for an evaluation of strengths and weaknesses.

Parents can also identify difficulties in children's schoolwork and can request a referral for additional assistance. Papers may come home that parents feel are not indicative of the reading and writing abilities that their child displays at home. Also, parents may see their child performing at a level below siblings and wonder if there is some difficulty with the individual child. Parents may see a drop in overall performance that reflects home difficulties, such as a divorce or illness, even though these difficulties may not affect schoolwork drastically enough to be identified by the teacher. Parents often notice behaviors in their children that teachers do not.

While referrals from teachers may, at first, catch parents off guard when they do not see a problem that the teacher does, there are a number of steps that parents can insist on when they are informed of difficulties by the teacher. These include multi-disciplinary assessments of the reading or writing problems, second opinions from experts within or outside of the school, and consideration of other information and remedies such as regarding the home situation. These same procedures should be insisted on when parents are the ones initiating a referral.

Multi-disciplinary Assessments

When everyone is working and communicating appropriately, the job of assessing the child and determining the most appropriate plan of action can be relatively straightforward and simple. However, assessing a child's strengths in reading and writing and determining needs is a complex job at best and parents need to stay informed about the assessment process. When the evaluation is performed by a single, overextended psychologist who has little actual classroom experience, or an overworked reading specialist/diagnostician who has not been in the classroom for a number of years, the identification of the child's needs and the presentation of instructional suggestions can be skewed away from the child's actual classroom needs. Many school psychologists are not trained in the finer points of teaching reading and writing, and, although they may be excellent test administrators, they perhaps do not have a true feel for the needs of a classroom of 25 or more students. Classroom teachers may not agree with the findings in the report given by such persons and possibly are not able to implement the specific suggestions provided in the report in their classroom situations. Even reading specialists who have spent many years in the classroom may have their own biases when trying to assess individually a child's reading abilities and this can lead to the same narrow-sighted assessment and instructional plan.

To reduce the possibility of such difficulties parents should demand a multidisciplinary team approach to any assessment. A team of experts in related fields can help provide a clearer view of the child than an individual in any one field. Assessment must take place over a period of time with specific goals and purposes identified. Different people involved in an assessment will provide a variety of views of the child so that a more complete and comprehensive assessment of the child and his or her learning needs will emerge. Also, and perhaps more importantly, the instructional plan set forth to improve reading and writing will be much better suited to the needs and strengths of the child and the actual classroom placement.

Multidisciplinary assessments are essential if one is to get as true a picture as possible of the individual child. The classroom teacher can provide information about reading and writing behaviors in the classroom setting, but may not be capable of identifying specific reading or writing problems. The reading specialist is able to identify specific areas of strength and weakness in reading and writing, but may not be able to identify the specific language areas that perhaps interfere with these areas. A speech/language specialist can identify language processing areas that interfere with the reading/writing process, but may be unable to identify how these relate to the teaching of reading and writing. A psychologist can identify the overall cognitive processing style and ability and can provide information on learning modalities, but cannot possibly translate this information into instructional activities that the classroom teacher can use in a classroom of 25 or more students. Other specialists in the areas of neurology, allergies, optometry, audiology, etc. may also be of assistance when these areas appear to interfere with learning.

The point to note is that all specialists working together can provide a much more complete picture of the strengths and weaknesses of the child than any single person can provide alone. By working together, the multidisciplinary team can develop a workable instructional plan that will help the child more efficiently and appropriately learn to read and write. Also, at no point should the parents feel excluded from this process. It is essential that they be involved at all times.

Related to a multidisciplinary assessment is the possible need for second opinions. There are times when the results of an assessment do not ring true to the parents or others involved. At this point, second opinions are helpful.

Second Opinions

Parents have a right to second opinions and should insist on them when necessary. Asking for and receiving a second opinion on a reading and writing assessment is a way to avoid confusing and conflicting results and to provide additional information when further support for findings is needed. We are becoming a nation that routinely seeks second opinions in areas as diverse as health care concerns and buying a car. How much more important is the educational well-being of our children?

While many school systems can provide excellent second opinions, it may be wise to look outside of the school system. Often, when there are difficult evaluations, there can be emotional involvement that interferes with a clear understanding of the situation. Parents have a personal interest in the results of an assessment. Schools may put their professional expertise and reputation at stake. If there are conflicts, the emotional overtones of a situation may interfere with the appropriate concerns for the child. Many times a second opinion from persons not connected with the school can provide a judgement on the reading and writing abilities of the child without getting into the emotional aspects of the situation. This provides information that can be used in conjunction with the assessment developed by the school. Most locales have private evaluation services or university clinics that can help with second opinions.

Making Sense of Assessment Reports

Understanding reports of the evaluation process is another important task for parents. Most reports provided by professionals contain, often of necessity, precise terminology and professional jargon that, when used properly, can make a report precise and easier to interpret. Problems arise when parents do not understand these terms or are unclear about the direction being taken with their child. Parent advocates and persons offering second opinions can be helpful in explaining the information contained in these reports. Many communities and school districts have parent advocates whose job is to help parents understand the jargon used by the professionals. The advocate can assist the parent throughout the evaluation process or through the second opinion process. Schools should be able to provide parents with names of parent-child advocate groups in their local area. Parents should never be afraid to ask questions—repeatedly if necessary—in order to be sure that they understand what is happening with their child.

Becoming Aware of Outside Factors

Many times the difficulties that a child exhibits in school are a reflection of what is happening outside of school. Reading, writing, and other schoolwork can suffer if the child is bothered by outside factors. One such situation is the divorce of the child's parents. Identifying school-related difficulties can be almost impossible if parents are not willing or able to provide information to the school about the home situation.

Divorce is very common in today's society. As many as 50 percent of students will be affected by divorce. While this can be a difficult time, it does not have to be as devastating to the child as many experts suggest. If the parents can work together to inform the school of the home situation, then teachers can provide activities and support that take the child's home situation into consideration. Reading and writing activities can be developed to help the child cope more effectively with the situation (see, for example, Ritty, 1991). An assessment of reading difficulties during this time can be greatly enhanced if parents share information about home life that may affect the child's school performance. It is possible that the child is not reading and writing at an appropriate level due to concern and grief over the divorce.

When all persons involved work together there are few problems, but what happens when the schools and parents do not agree about the procedures or results of an assessment? What happens when parents identify a problem which the school does not see and refuses, or is unable, to respond to in the manner expected by the parents?

When Schools and Parents Don't Agree

There are two types of concerns raised by parents: the truly valid difficulties recognized by concerned parents, and the less valid problems that are reported by overprotective parents.

True problems than can cause parents concern about the progress of their children can arise in a number of ways. The school may not recognize or may be unresponsive to the needs of the child, or may not communicate information properly to parents. Often, this unresponsiveness and miscommunication occurs during the initial stages of a child's difficulties in school or as an assessment is undertaken. More responsive communication, a multidisciplinary assessment team, and second opinions can help reduce this difficulty.

There are also concerned parents who worry excessively about their children. They may push them to be more than they can be or to be what they themselves never were. These parents can bother the school repeatedly about virtually every assignment and grade a child receives. They may strain the ability of the school to respond effectively to the needs of all students. These parents need to realize that each child is a unique person who will produce at the level he or she finds most comfortable. Pushing a child or excessive raising of concerns with the school will only cause difficulty when a true problem may arise.

Although most school personnel genuinely try to follow the plans or programs provided by appropriate assessment, some teachers may fail to follow the plans. What happens when the school has an appropriate plan to work with a student, yet fails to follow it? At this point parents must be aware of the child's educational plan and what goes on in the classroom. They must be willing to take whatever steps are necessary to ensure that their child receives appropriate instruction. Here again, parent advocates and meetings with teachers, specialists, and school administrators can be most helpful.

Parents and schools may never completely agree with one another regarding the "best" educational plan for every student. However, by working together, they can come a long way toward meeting the needs of the individual child. They can keep one another informed about the child's progress at home and school, and develop and implement programs that meet every child's needs.

Ritty, J.M. (1991). Single parent families: Tips for parents and educators. *The Reading Teacher, 44,* 604–606.

For Further Reading